Baptizing Business

Baptizing Business

Evangelical Executives and the Sacred Pursuit of Profit

BRADLEY C. SMITH

OXFORD
UNIVERSITY PRESS

OXFORD
UNIVERSITY PRESS

Oxford University Press is a department of the University of Oxford. It furthers
the University's objective of excellence in research, scholarship, and education
by publishing worldwide. Oxford is a registered trade mark of Oxford University
Press in the UK and certain other countries.

Published in the United States of America by Oxford University Press
198 Madison Avenue, New York, NY 10016, United States of America.

Library of Congress Cataloging-in-Publication Data
Names: Smith, Bradley C., author.
Title: Baptizing business : evangelical executives and the sacred pursuit of profit /
Bradley C. Smith.
Description: New York, NY, United States of America : Oxford University Press, 2020. |
Includes bibliographical references and index.
Identifiers: LCCN 2019053068 (print) | LCCN 2019053069 (ebook) |
ISBN 9780190055776 (hbk) | ISBN 9780190055790 (epub)
Subjects: LCSH: Evangelicalism—Economic aspects—United States. |
Business—Religious aspects—Protestant churches. |
Capitalism—Religious aspects—Protestant churches. |
Executives—Religious life—United States. | Business ethics—United States. |
Christian-owned business enterprises—United States.
Classification: LCC BR115.E3 S625 2020 (print) |
LCC BR115.E3 (ebook) | DDC 261.8/50973—dc23
LC record available at https://lccn.loc.gov/2019053068
LC ebook record available at https://lccn.loc.gov/2019053069

1 3 5 7 9 8 6 4 2

Printed by Integrated Books International, United States of America

Contents

Acknowledgments

In this book I discuss contemporary applications of Max Weber's famous "spirit of capitalism," defined as commitment to work in the expectation of profit. For better or worse, such is hardly a relevant impulse for the writing of most books. The inspiration and support of colleagues and friends is, therefore, critical to the writing enterprise. I am fortunate in this regard.

The seeds of this project were sown and a portion of the cost borne by the H. E. Butt Family Foundation. I am grateful in particular to the Foundation's David Rogers, Terry Tigner, and Mark Roberts for their sponsorship, vision, and guidance. Princeton University's Center for the Study of Religion provided financial support and a workspace during a portion of my time at Princeton. Participants in the Center's Religion and Public Life Seminar supplied intellectual stimulation and incisive feedback on various components of this study. Center Manager Anita Kline deserves special mention for her help with all things practical, not least keeping me on track with respect to dates and deadlines.

For their assistance identifying potential informants I thank Laura Sorrell, John Terrill, and Doug Holladay. For similar assistance and also for guidance in conceptualizing this study I thank David Miller and Michael Lindsay, with respect to whose research on evangelical elites this study is but a footnote.

Princeton undergraduates Caroline Rawls and Adam Mastroianni and Rice University undergraduate Mary Grace Hager provided expert research assistance, preparing me for each interview and coding interview transcripts with skill and insight. It has been a delight to see them proceed to notable academic and professional accomplishments. For timely and capable interview transcription I thank Megan Jackson and Katie Conner.

It is an honor to have been advised by such a distinguished group of scholars at Princeton. Bob Wuthnow, Paul DiMaggio, and Martin Ruef deserve thanks and recognition for their wise and generous counsel. As impressive as their encyclopedic knowledge is their willingness to share it. Special thanks to Bob Wuthnow, whose sterling reputation for wisdom and solicitude undersells the actual experience of his mentorship. Thanks also to Bob's clone, who must surely have conspired with Bob to return to me trenchant feedback on my manuscript within twenty-four hours of receipt.

I am grateful to Rice University's Religion and Public Life Program in the university's Social Science Research Institute, and in particular to Program Director Elaine Howard Ecklund, for providing employment and a venue to advance and present my research during its latter stages. I have met no one as committed to the well-being of her mentees as Elaine, and her example remains an inspiration. I am indebted to Jared Peifer, with whom I worked at Rice, for his keen feedback on the entire manuscript. And without the assistance of another Rice colleague, David Johnson, who helped me navigate the publication process, this book might well have been stillborn.

For sanity during the home stretch of this project I thank E.L. and M.M. And I thank Lindsey Heintz for encouragement and a clear calendar during my writing sabbaticals while at Parsley Energy, where I learned more about C-suite exceptionalism and the ultimacy of in-group ties than any interview could convey.

The executives I interviewed are among the more thoughtful and considerate groups of people I have encountered, and I am grateful for their willingness to share their stories. I hope they understand the depth of my appreciation for their time, trust they will find my analysis careful and evenhanded, and wish them continued success and fulfillment.

Finally, love and gratitude to my wife, Katy, and daughters, Natalie and Julia, for whom the writing of this book has meant considerable sacrifice.

Introduction

In Search of the Christian Mafia

"At Harvard they talked a lot about the Mormon Mafia," said Kyle, a junior executive at a well-known consulting company, "but," he asked, "who is in the *Christian* Mafia? Who are the evangelicals at your company that really value their faith and are willing to have that conversation with you about the struggles at work and maybe help you navigate the political situations?"

Having grown up on a farm in the Midwest, Kyle considers it "a total God thing" that he had the dream, much less the means, to attend Harvard Business School. Now in his late thirties and having already excelled at some of the most esteemed technology companies in the United States, Kyle's sights have been recalibrated. Acclimated to success, he is eager to join many of his classmates at the top of the corporate hierarchy—to find his destination job in which he will reach his full potential. Hence the search for the Christian Mafia.[1]

As Kyle explains, these days an MBA from Harvard is not an automatic ticket to a CEO position. "The big thing is who is pounding the table in your name? When it comes time for reviews, who says 'Kyle's my guy and this guy is the greatest thing since sliced bread and if you don't think so you should get the hell out of the room because he's awesome.' Who is that guy? In my experience, if you have a table pounder or several, you're going to be fine with your career promotion track. If you don't, you're like a ship at sea with no rudder. You're probably not going anywhere."

As an evangelical Christian, Kyle feels that in some ways his faith has positioned him against the tide, preventing him from connecting fully with peers and conforming to the social expectations for rising executives. One of more than one hundred evangelicals I interviewed, he tells of celebrating a product launch with coworkers in New York City. "We get to the 'bar' and they are trying to get me to walk in there. It ended up being a strip club, which I had never been in and didn't want to go in. But they were trying to push me in

Baptizing Business. Bradley C. Smith, Oxford University Press (2020). © Oxford University Press.
DOI: 10.1093/oso/9780190055776.001.0001

there. I had to physically grab onto the doorpost and pull myself out of there. You're almost discriminated against because of your faith."

Where is the Christian Mafia? Management scholars Mitroff and Denton, in a widely read book on spirituality in business, claim to have found it, or at least examples of it, rehearsing with horror the alleged tactics employed by imperialistic Christians attempting to "take over their companies for Christ."[2] In elaborating these "religion-based organizations," Mitroff and Denton draw primarily on a book written by evangelical executive William Nix and endorsed by prominent evangelical businessmen and pastors including Adrian Rogers, former president of the Southern Baptist Convention, the largest evangelical denomination in the United States. Indeed, if a Christian Mafia is to be found, evangelicals—a group of theologically conservative Protestants who have been on some accounts "the loudest, most energetic, and most demanding of all Christians in recent decades"[3]—appear to be prime candidates.

Mitroff and Denton are not alone in their apprehension about the aspirations and influence of evangelical Christians. In *Christian America?: What Evangelicals Really Want*, Christian Smith writes, "Today, many journalists, scholars, public leaders, and ordinary Americans are curious and concerned—sometimes frightened—about who evangelicals are and what they want."[4] US Representative Alexandria Ocasio-Cortez, spurred by a wave of legislation restricting abortion in states identified as evangelical bastions, recently voiced such concern, charging the Republican Party with attempting to turn the United States into a "far-right Christian theocracy."[5] According to a Baylor University survey on religious perspectives, conservative Christians are the second most feared religious group in America, trailing only Muslims.[6] And academics, especially, are wary of evangelicals. In a survey of 1,300 college professors, researchers found that 3 percent held "unfavorable feelings" toward Jews, 22 percent toward Muslims, and 53 percent toward evangelical Christians.[7]

What is it about evangelicals that provokes such unease? For one thing, some of the most visible evangelicals in recent years, including cofounder of the Moral Majority Jerry Falwell, chairman of the Christian Broadcasting Network and host of *The 700 Club* Pat Robertson, and founder of Focus on the Family James Dobson, have been the most out of step with mainstream culture, inviting controversy through their public articulation of far-right perspectives on issues like same-sex marriage and climate change.

More generally, evangelicalism is an activist faith tradition, encouraging adherents to change the world by bringing about the kingdom of God on earth—an aspiration that involves, among other things, caring for the poor, proselytizing, and, for some, changing the culture to reflect biblical morality.[8] This last objective, in particular, generates discomfort. Smith summarizes concerns over evangelicals' ambitions with the following question: "Are evangelicals finally intolerant absolutists who really seek to impose their morals and values upon those with whom they differ?"[9] Survey data suggest that more than one-third of Americans would answer in the affirmative, believing that conservative Christians want to limit their freedoms.[10]

Whether intolerant or not, there is evidence that some evangelicals do wish to advance their values. Studies suggest that evangelicals are the most likely religious group to believe that other religious groups hold inferior values.[11] And evangelicals have been especially active in the political realm. As Hunter explains, "through innumerable parachurch ministries, [evangelicals] assert themselves into one political issue after another and into electoral politics as well."[12] Regarding evangelicals' political strategy, Hunter cites parachurch leader James Dobson, who asserts that "the side that wins gains the right to teach what it believes to its children. And if you can do that, you write the curricula, you tell them what to believe and you model what you want them to understand and in one generation, you change the whole culture."[13]

For all the commotion evangelicals have introduced in the political arena—and most analysts suggest that the force of their rhetoric has outpaced their ability to influence policies and elections[14]—they have been less visible in other domains. Is there a critical mass of influential evangelicals who can and would exert influence in the business world—a network of strategically placed and value-aligned conspirators who hope to transform their companies and industries?

Emerging from the Shadows

It took me a few minutes to place him; the face that caught my eye looked vaguely familiar and, I thought, young for a CEO. I'd been attempting to track down a former colleague online but found myself in a staring match with a different gentleman on-screen. A couple more clicks and it clicked. Most Sunday mornings for the couple years preceding my move to New Jersey for graduate school, the gentleman in question had handed me a bulletin and welcomed me to the worship service at a moderately sized, relatively affluent Baptist church in the heart of Houston, Texas. Ever cordial, with a sincere but low-key warmth appropriate to the early hour, we had chatted enough to know each other's first names, but little more, and I knew nothing about his occupation. There was nothing about him that would have disqualified him as an executive; I suppose he just didn't strike me as the hard-charging type, a particularly commanding presence, or one who enjoys the spotlight. "Greeter," after all, is hardly among the more celebrated roles in the church. And yet he is, apparently, commanding enough to lead a multi-billion dollar publicly traded company with thousands of employees around the world—a role for which he is paid millions of dollars a year.

It turns out I wasn't the only one who was surprised to learn of this congregant's professional standing. A former church staff member who knew the man knew nothing of his lofty occupational status. Likewise, a deacon at the church was unaware, recalling that the unpretentious CEO had showed up on a Saturday morning to help a divorcée he had never met move into a new home.

In retrospect, perhaps none of us should have been surprised. Evangelical presence is on the upswing among corporate leaders and in the upper echelon of other professional domains, as well. Largely confined to the disadvantaged ranks of the stratification system and excluded from mainstream culture-making institutions during most of the twentieth century,[15] evangelicals are increasingly recognized among the upper tier of a variety of sectors, including corporate America.[16] Evangelicals are well represented among small-business owners and direct some of the nation's largest companies, as well.[17]

It is not entirely clear how long these evangelical business leaders have been in place. Lindsay contends that over the past couple of decades it has become more acceptable for elites to embrace a visible evangelical identity, paving the way for more overt applications of faith in corporate environments. And not only that—he argues that this flexibility is the product of the strategic efforts of an interconnected group of evangelical elites.[18] Miller agrees that evangelicals have, during this period, been active in the corporate domain—both as individuals and in concert—having spearheaded what he and others call the "faith at work movement," a coalition of management theorists and practitioners who have pushed for expanding the role of faith in business.[19] On this account, over the past couple of decades certain evangelicals have undertaken to bring faith-oriented ways of thinking to bear on economic activities. Consistent with these analyses, one executive I interviewed claimed not to be able to identify a single evangelical on Wall Street in the 1980s but now works with several evangelicals and can quickly call to mind a number of other prominent finance executives who are evangelicals.

While evangelical Christians have made their way to the corporate summit, whether and how more visible evangelical executives take advantage of new possibilities for expressing their faith at work is an open question. Does the CEO who hands out bulletins on Sunday mornings act with the hospitality of a greeter on, say, Thursday afternoons? Might emboldened evangelical business leaders attempt to advance their values in the corporate domain just as evangelicals have attempted in the political arena? And if so, what are the implications for American business and especially for those companies led by evangelical executives?

For Better or Worse?

While some are wary of trends that encourage the interpenetration of faith and business, insisting, as does renowned consultant and author Tom Peters, that companies should be "spirited but not spiritual,"[20] others welcome such integration, seeing in contemporary Christianity and other religious traditions dispositions that could challenge unhealthy characteristics and consequences of modern capitalism. Some, in fact, have come to believe that religious faith represents a wellspring of resources and concern that might help reshape corporate America by re-humanizing business and fortifying its ethical moorings. Recounting the socially responsible initiatives of several well-known firms led by religiously motivated executives, Marc Gunther, senior writer for *Fortune* magazine, insists that faith-driven "compassionate capitalism" is transforming American business.[21] In light of the so-called financialization of corporate America, characterized by intense focus on shareholder value as an overriding corporate objective,[22] some scholars assert that religious institutions in general[23] and Christianity in particular[24] possess ideological resources that might redirect focus from purely economic ends to a variety of higher goods. Nash, in fact, having studied evangelical executives in particular, concludes that their faith commitments can often "keep at bay the more predatory aspects of advanced capitalism" and "stimulate commitment to high ethical standards and humane employee policies."[25] More broadly, Miller asserts that "if the faith at work movement can go beyond personal expressions of piety, virtue, and religious practices, it has the potential to affect and positively alter the larger cultural value system and norms of the economic sphere, both domestically and globally."[26]

Even as some are apprehensive about the potential influence of evangelicals and other business leaders who desire to bring their faith to bear in corporate contexts and others welcome such integration and anticipate favorable effects, still others suggest that religion simply does not matter enough to warrant interest or concern. Despite the fact that the relationship between religion and commerce preoccupied seminal sociological thinkers like Weber, Durkheim, and Marx, there is an inclination among sociologists to downplay the role of religion in social life. Ryan Cragun, for example, insists in response to fellow sociologist Christian Smith's attempt to drum up interest in religion that sociologists would gladly pay more attention to religion if only it actually mattered. Cragun asserts, "Religion has very little effect on health or criminal behavior. If religion plays any significant role in societal development, it's as a small impediment. And religion has, at best, a marginal influence on migration patterns, communication technologies, consumption, and the economy." The one domain in which Cragun allows that religion is important is politics. "Knowing someone's religion," he says, "significantly improves our ability to predict how he/she will vote." Its influence on political perspectives notwithstanding, Cragun concludes, "If religion explains marginal amounts of variation in a variety of areas, I fail to see how we can fault other sociologists for not caring about it."[27]

Against those for whom regression analysis apparently constitutes a reliable indicator of the magnitude of social influence, a variety of studies demonstrate ways religion has influenced economic behavior and institutions. Keister, for example, marshals evidence that religious affiliation and participation exerts significant influence on individual economic outcomes, both directly through the inculcation of economic goals and habits and indirectly through influencing demographic behaviors.[28] Likewise, Hart contends that the character of religious discourse about the market profoundly influences economic behaviors within it.[29] Abend suggests that only by emphasizing business ethics, derived from religious principles, did business schools come to exert meaningful influence on the shape of American business.[30] At a broader level, Guillén suggests that religion has played an often neglected role in the innovation and diffusion of management paradigms, positing that in Spain, the Catholic Church supported the human relations school for its humane treatment of workers, and in Germany, Protestants supported the scientific management movement for its emphasis on individualism and self-reliance.[31] And of course Max Weber, in his classic work *The Protestant Ethic and the Spirit of Capitalism*, contended that a particular branch of ascetic Protestantism helped shape and spread modern capitalism by breaking down the moral disapproval of capitalistic activity and creating and promoting a methodical approach to economic affairs.[32] While Weber expected that, for various reasons, religion was unlikely to exert perennial influence in a market-oriented economy, Berger reminds us that, even today, "Capitalism does not legitimate itself." Instead, "It depends for its legitimation upon traditional values, such as those furnished by religious morality."[33]

On the basis of these analyses, it seems clear that religion *can* matter in economic life—on both individual and collective bases—and, Cragun's objections notwithstanding, attention to the role of religion in business contexts is on the uptick. Surveying the segment of this growing body of literature that employs quantitative methods and focuses on managerial behavior, Longenecker and co-authors suggest that empirical studies of the effects of religion on managerial behavior have thus far shown mixed and inconclusive effects.[34] This does not mean that religion does not matter. It does suggest that religion's effects are difficult to predict and that quantitative analyses alone are insufficient to understand the role of faith in the lives of people like evangelical executives.

In light of certain contemporary economic circumstances and cultural perspectives, it is possible that the attitudes and actions of religiously committed executives might now matter more than usual. Business, on some accounts, has experienced a crisis of legitimacy and identity, with executives bearing the brunt of the blame. The near collapse of the global financial system in 2008 and the consequent Great Recession, the memory of a handful of highly visible and costly corporate scandals, and the perception, at least, of a transition to a more competitive, profit-oriented corporate environment have contributed to growing sentiment that businesses and their leaders are not living up to their responsibility to society. As of 2012, only 38 percent of the public agreed that business corporations generally strike a fair balance between making profits and serving the public interest.[35] In 2013, business executives ranked next to last among ten professional groups in terms of perceived contribution to the well-being of society.[36] And as of 2015, business executives rated eighteenth of twenty-two professional groups in terms of perceived honesty and ethical standards, ahead of only advertising practitioners, members of Congress, car salespeople, and lobbyists.[37] Similarly, according to a 2017 poll, 59 percent of the public believes that corporations make too much profit.[38] Of this perceived excess profit, most believe that too much goes to executives. In fact, according to most Americans, CEOs are vastly overpaid.[39] In sum, business has come to be associated with illegitimate and excess wealth, and business leaders are some of the least respected members of society.

For executives, public sentiment is an important consideration inasmuch as the regulatory environment in which companies operate, while clearly influenced by the ideological slant of the regnant political regime, is also a function of the degree of trust business enjoys. Moreover, there is a growing realization that in today's business environment, a company's reputation is an important strategic asset.[40] There is, therefore, significant incentive for business to enhance its public standing, and some believe such efforts are especially crucial today.

Public opinion analyst Daniel Yankelovich, responding to indications of public dissatisfaction with businesses and their leaders, has argued that "the social contract with business is in a state of flux."[41] And Khurana, documenting the evolution of business schools, suggests that in light of a mounting chorus of criticism against business, "the time seems ripe for reopening the question of what exactly this institution is for, what functions we as a society want it to perform, and how well it is performing them."[42]

Evangelicals seem well suited to engage such issues. Among religious groups, evangelicals are more likely than all but black Protestants to view their work as a mission from God.[43] Evangelical business leaders, in particular, could address questions about the purpose and impact of business by attempting to do business in ways that would enhance its reputation and be more compatible with their own religious convictions. But does religion actually influence the ways evangelical business leaders approach business? They certainly suggest that it does.

Professional Oxygen

We must have been traveling at least twice the speed limit as we zipped through the streets of Laguna Beach in a sports car that must have been twice as expensive as any car I'd traveled in before. On the way to his next appointment, Ryan dropped me off at my rental car, bade me a hasty farewell, and raced away. Time is money, I thought, especially for a venture capitalist. It was not as if our conversation had felt rushed, but looking back it is clear that Ryan was managing the time throughout, and even before, our conversation. His side of the email correspondence through which we had arranged to meet was always, in a word, efficient—greeting, text, and salutation all on the first line; capitalization, punctuation, and articles optional. During our conversation in a hotel lobby, if a topic failed to grasp his interest, Ryan offered no more than a brief comment, immune to follow-up questions designed to prompt elaboration. When his interest was piqued, however, he would pause just for a moment to compose his thoughts before discoursing. Even then, he often disclaimed that, for the sake of time, he would not pursue the matter as far as he might. And it was clear that he could indeed speak at length about a wide range of subjects. Obviously well-read, during our conversation he referenced, among others, Max Weber, Charles Sumner, Francis Bacon, the Apostle Paul, and Peter the Great. Dulled by discussion of the state of corporate America, Ryan perked up when we began to discuss the religious dimension of business. "Scripture informs my professional life in the way that oxygen informs my biological continuation," he asserted.

Ryan is one of more than one hundred evangelical executives I interviewed over the course of two summers. With Ryan and the rest, there is nothing that obviously distinguishes them from other business leaders. They keep the same schedules, occupy the same executive suites, use the same business vernacular, and, for the most part, drive the same cars and live in the same houses. Ryan certainly looks the part of a venture capitalist: tailored suit, fast car, tight schedule. Yet he claims that his faith is so integral to his work that without Scripture, the foundation of his faith, he could not so much as catch his professional breath.

For most people, a jet-setting, sports-car-driving financier is not the type of person who comes to mind when thinking about evangelicals. Indeed, Ryan is in many ways the antithesis of the stereotypical evangelical. With four degrees in four disciplines from four elite universities, Ryan has lived and worked on three continents and currently divides his time between major metropolises in Europe and both coasts of the United States. Yet Ryan shares with fellow evangelicals beliefs, practices, and religious intensity that transcend geographic and socioeconomic characteristics. Before exploring the ways the evangelicals I interviewed differ from rank-and-file evangelicals, it will be helpful to understand what most evangelicals have in common.

Evangelicals

Evangelicals are a group of theologically conservative Protestants who regard the Bible as God's authoritative revelation and the primary source of moral and spiritual guidance, embrace a personal relationship with God following a conversion experience through which they are "born again" and after which they commit to a life of personal holiness, and are obliged to spread the Christian message, sometimes termed the gospel or "good news."[44] This gospel message is centered on the necessity and possibility of salvation, or freedom from the consequences of sin, through the death and resurrection of Jesus Christ.

Relative to other religious groups, including most other Christians, evangelicals are distinguished by the centrality of the Bible, the personal and often spontaneous and idiosyncratic nature of their religious experience, and the intensity of their religious commitment. Evangelicals consistently rank near the top of lists of religious groups in terms of frequency of religious participation and commitment to spiritual practices like Bible reading and prayer.[45]

While researching this book I came across an offering envelope from a Southern Baptist church attended by one of the evangelical executives I interviewed. Southern Baptists are the largest evangelical denomination in the United States, numbering sixteen million members and, as the name suggests, concentrated primarily in the South. The envelope, slightly weathered from its use as a bookmark and probably now a decade old, had spaces for congregants to enter their name, address, and Sunday School class affiliation, as well as areas to indicate any financial contributions to the general budget, a building fund, and a separate capital campaign. The envelope, to be completed and submitted weekly, also contained a series of check boxes as follows: Present, Bible Brought, Bible Read Daily, Lesson Studied, Giving, Worship Attendance, Number of Visits to Prospects, and Number of Visits to Members. The expectations and accountability expressed by this checklist reflect the values and intensity of commitment that characterize evangelical Christians.

Consider the time it would take to check all of the boxes on the offering envelope described above: to attend a Sunday School class and a worship service, read the Bible daily, study a lesson in preparation for the Sunday School class, and visit both prospective and current members of the church could easily amount to ten hours per week, not to mention time dedicated to prayer and midweek activities at church. Then there are the financial expectations. Many evangelical congregations encourage members to contribute both "tithes" and "offerings." Tithing, generally considered a biblically prescribed baseline level of giving, consists of contributing 10 percent of income to God's work, usually focused on supporting the local church. Contributions to building funds, special campaigns, and other religious causes and activities represent offerings, which are given over and above the standard tithe. At least 10 percent of one's money and 10 hours of one's time per week represents a substantial expectation, even if evangelicals contribute far less on average.[46]

One CFO I interviewed, explaining the type of commitment required of evangelicals, observed, "Jesus said, 'Any of you who does not give up everything he has cannot be my disciple' . . . *everything*. None of us are perfect at it, but it's a state of the soul. That's the one thing I would really want you to understand about me. This life of following Jesus—if it doesn't start there, it's leaving from the wrong station."

The intensely personal nature of evangelicals' "relationship with God" is an important dimension of the evangelical approach to faith. Evangelicals talk to God and God talks back. In summarizing how he would describe his faith to a stranger, one of the executives I interviewed said, " 'I want you to meet a guy that you can be friends with for the rest of your life.' And I tell them about my relationship with Christ and tell them how I'm involved with the Father, Son, and Holy Spirit every day. I start my day that way and end my day that way. I've got a buddy twenty-four, seven." This executive describes the evolution of his effort to pray regularly. "I met with a very, very wise Christian counselor who was taking me through a valley experience I was having and we were talking about the apostle Paul and trusting God and praying. He says, 'Do you pray unceasingly?' I go, 'Are you kidding? I don't have time for that.' He said, 'I'm going to teach you how to do it.' And he taught me. He said, 'Write this down: what does God want me to do next?' He said, 'I don't care if you're walking from your car to your office and you're picking up a piece of paper. Which piece of paper should you pick up? Emblazon that on your brain. You go into a meeting, what does God want me to do next? You're about ready to do public speaking, and so on.'" As these comments indicate, evangelicalism as taught to adherents is an intense, personally appropriated, comprehensive, and continuously enacted religious identity that places premiums on both orthodoxy and orthopraxy.

Demographically, self-identified evangelicals differ from the general population inasmuch as they are overwhelmingly white (76 percent), relatively uneducated (just 21 percent of evangelicals are college graduates), and slightly less likely to earn at least $100,000 (14 percent of evangelicals compared to 19 percent of the general population).[47] In the United States, they constitute a considerably larger portion of the total population in the South and the Midwest than the West and especially the Northeast. Notably, 55 percent of evangelicals are women.

Consistent with this intensity of commitment, 79 percent of evangelicals consider religion "very important" in their lives, 79 percent pray daily, and 58 percent attend religious services at least once a week. Evangelicals are on average more inclined toward strict understandings of religious texts and concepts than are adherents of many other religious traditions; 55 percent affirm a literal understanding of the Bible as the Word of God and 41 percent assert that there is only one true way to interpret evangelical teachings.[48] In cases of apparent conflict between religious and scientific understandings, many evangelicals defer to religious interpretations. For example, 57 percent of evangelicals believe human beings did not evolve from less complex life forms, but rather always existed in their present form.

On some accounts evangelicalism is the most politically conservative Christian tradition.[49] Only 13 percent of evangelicals identify as liberal, while 55 percent identify as conservative and 27 percent as moderate.[50] Sixty-four percent of evangelicals favor smaller government and among religious groups, evangelicals are among the most likely to oppose abortion (63 percent believe abortion should be illegal in all or most cases) and homosexuality (64 percent oppose or strongly oppose same-sex marriage).[51] Consistent with their inclination toward conservatism, in the 2016 presidential election, almost two-thirds of white evangelicals voted for Donald Trump.[52]

While evangelicals are a theologically conservative group with a clear leaning toward social conservatism, evangelical perspectives on economic issues are more complex, as research suggests that theological conservatism does not necessarily translate to economic conservatism.[53] Accordingly, evangelicals evidence more diverse perspectives on economic matters, as we will explore in more detail in the next chapter.

Evangelical Executives

The business leaders I interviewed demonstrate characteristic evangelical sensibilities; they talk freely about their relationships with God, cite

Scripture frequently, claim to engage consistently in personal spiritual disciplines like prayer and Bible study, attend church regularly, and believe that faith should inform all aspects of life. Nevertheless, while they share with rank-and-file evangelicals a set of core convictions, informants differ from most evangelicals in important ways. Most obvious, of course, is their professional standing. The evangelicals I interviewed are business leaders, by which I mean they now or in the past occupied a position of significant responsibility in a for-profit enterprise in a US context. The majority of those I interviewed were the top-ranking officer in their firms, and I estimate that nearly all held positions that would be considered among the top 2 percent in terms of rank and responsibility in their companies. They are significantly better educated and, of course, wealthier than most evangelicals, which could influence the nature of their religious convictions and their intensity of religious commitment. Max Weber long ago observed that the content of religious belief is shaped by the material condition of its adherents.[54] Religious groups at the lower end of the socioeconomic spectrum, such as early Christians and a significant proportion of conservative Protestants today, generally construct "theodicies of misfortune" that insist that wealth and other manifestations of privilege are indications of evil. Well-off religious groups, in contrast, typically construct "theodicies of fortune" that maintain that privileges are deserved blessings.[55]

Executives are important subjects of study in that they often have at least some discretion to shape both the competitive strategy and internal dynamics of their firms, and also because they typically serve as the public faces of their organizations. Informants are unique even among aspiring evangelical business leaders in that the majority of them have reached the pinnacle of their professions. This study is, therefore, characterized by "survivor bias"— those who are interviewed are those who have succeeded in business. For the most part we do not hear from those who have, for any number of reasons, failed to realize their desired level of professional success or even left the business world in favor of other pursuits, perhaps as a function of dissonance between professional responsibilities and faith convictions. In addition to those who have reached the top of their professions, I interviewed a handful of aspiring evangelical business leaders who were in the earlier stages of their careers. These upwardly mobile evangelicals who are yet on their way provide a helpful contrast with those who have already arrived.

In order to identify evangelicals, most studies employ one or more of three primary methods: denominational affiliation, self-classification, and/

or adherence to characteristic evangelical beliefs.[56] In this analysis I rely primarily on self-classification and articulated beliefs. On some accounts evangelicals constitute up to 30 percent of the US population, but their prevalence depends on how they are measured. In terms of their cultural location, two divergent portraits of evangelicals have emerged. On the one hand, Hunter describes evangelicals as relatively isolated and peripheral to mainstream society, relatively poor, poorly educated, and marginalized, and characterized by eroding orthodoxy, commitment, and salience as increasing exposure to modernity undermines the plausibility of the evangelical faith, especially for younger evangelicals.[57] Smith and coauthors, on the other hand, depict evangelicalism as a vibrant subculture energized by productive tension with mainstream institutions, with which evangelicals engage but retain symbolic distinction.[58] Pluralism, on this account, strengthens evangelicalism by supplying relevant outgroups with whom evangelicals compare themselves. The divergence in these two accounts is largely driven by measurement differences.[59] The process by which I define and identify evangelicals, discussed in the Appendix, is similar to the approach used by Smith et al., and as such, evangelicals of the variety they and I studied are less common than are those Hunter examined. On this tabulation, the population of evangelicals to which the executives I interviewed belong likely constitute around 10 percent of the US population.

Diverse Informants

An important feature of this study is the diversity that characterizes informants and their professional contexts. In fact, informants constitute the most diverse group of evangelical executives yet studied. The majority of informants held leadership positions in privately owned companies, which differ from publicly traded firms in important respects. They are, for one thing, not subject to the same reporting requirements as publicly traded companies and therefore may not experience the same pressure to deliver quarterly financial results to the satisfaction of Wall Street analysts and institutional investors, potentially enabling a longer-term orientation accompanied by the ability to make economically or socially productive investments that involve significant up-front costs. Private companies may even, with the permission of their capital providers, orient their efforts toward objectives other than that of maximizing economic value. It should be noted that while the majority of informants held relevant positions in private companies, more than half of informants had current or prior experience in public companies and would therefore be familiar with the pressures and dynamics associated with such business contexts.

Informants are relatively evenly distributed across companies of different sizes, as measured by number of employees. Companies of different sizes accommodate or necessitate different organizational structures, number and concentration of capital providers, types of funding, and levels of external scrutiny—all of which can influence the discretion executives enjoy to pursue objectives consistent with their faith convictions.

Different industries experience different levels of competition and regulation, which can influence the culture and objectives of associated companies. Informants' companies belong to a variety of industries and produce different types of goods and services marketed to different types of customers and with more or less obvious connections to the public good.

Because more than three-quarters of evangelicals are white and because women and minorities are underrepresented in the higher ranks of corporate America, achieving some level of racial and gender diversity among informants proved a considerable challenge.[60] As the interview process progressed, I began specifically to solicit connections with women and minorities whom I might interview. Overall, 9 percent of informants are non-white and 17 percent of informants are women. Contributions from these underrepresented groups, along with the variety of corporate contexts informants occupy, give dimension to the chorus of voices we will hear. That said, the reader is encouraged to bear in mind that the majority of informants are white men, who, in contrast to the glass ceilings that have constrained women and minorities, have benefited from the so-called glass escalator effect en route to disproportionate access to the upper echelons of corporate America. We might therefore expect to find it comparatively easy for them to identify God's favor when discussing their careers and the professional contexts in which they have flourished.

Discourse and Interpretation

I chose to conduct interviews, as opposed to administering surveys or other quantitative methodological possibilities, because interviews are especially helpful for accessing information about personal beliefs, values, and identities—all important material for this study—and in light of and guided by the productive application of similar methodologies to religious topics and other cultural dynamics in recent studies.[61] Some scholars, sensitive to the potential disconnect between what people say and what they do, discount the value of discourse for understanding social phenomena.[62] Let the record show, therefore, that there is no guarantee that events actually happened the way informants say they did. But bear in mind that our objective is not biography, but perspective. Even biased recollections and unfulfilled intentions provide evidence of what informants believe to be good, right, appropriate, and defensible.

Interviews are well suited for exploring the ways evangelical executives individually and corporately construct and transmit meaning. Observing that the only evidence Weber provided in support of the existence of a new capitalist spirit among businessmen was citations from Benjamin Franklin's writings, Marshall argues that the type of data necessary to confirm or disprove Weber's thesis would consist of interviews with the entrepreneurs and workers in question.[63] Interviews elicit accounts that elucidate sense-making processes, allowing scholars to describe real people struggling in concrete situations to act as moral agents.[64] As evaluative statements, accounts provide insight into informants' moral repertoires. As public declarations, accounts indicate what informants believe to be socially desirable or acceptable to a particular audience. Accounts are important, therefore, for ascertaining the willingness and ability of executives to deploy a moral language that challenges the instrumental logic of the market. Accounts, moreover, feed and are a product of "disputes" that force people to bring to the surface implicit concepts of value and worth instead of automatically conforming to institutional norms and exogenous pressures.[65] Despite their limitations, therefore, interviews and the accounts they generate provide a rich repository of interpretable meaning that are well suited to the present analysis.

Of course, the usefulness of interviews hinges on interviewing the right subjects. It would hardly be informative to interview executives with trivial faith commitments inasmuch as such commitments would be unlikely to influence these executives' perspectives or behaviors in professional contexts or elsewhere. If we are looking for candidates to comprise a Christian Mafia, or more generally exploring the possibility that faith actually matters in business contexts, we should look for executives with a sufficiently robust faith commitment to catalyze actions borne of religious motivations. Therefore, I purposefully engaged executives with a demonstrated or at least reputed interest in the relationship between faith and work. I sought out business leaders who are not merely exposed to or embedded in the corporation and the church, but deeply invested in them and adept at the strategies of action and vocabularies that are associated with them. The best interviews come from those who, to borrow Weber's metaphor, are "musical" in both the world of business and the world of religion. Accordingly, a number of informants had participated in programs sponsored by organizations designed to prepare Christian business leaders to integrate their faith and their work, indicating an interest in attempting to do so. Indeed, as was the goal, my sense is that I was generally referred to individuals who are considered to be exemplars par excellence of the incorporation of faith at work. As such, informants are likely to have devoted considerable thought to the topics addressed in the interviews, making them less susceptible to conditioning by the interview context and content, itself.

As I hoped, the evangelical executives I interviewed demonstrated considerable passion, emotion, and deliberation when discussing the role of faith in their professional lives. I was in almost every case shown plentiful hospitality, greeted warmly, and wished well. While informants were uniformly enthusiastic about the project, several did express apprehension about how interviews would be used and a few were concerned about confidentiality.[66] Despite a general trend toward increasing receptivity to expressions of faith in corporate contexts, some evangelical business leaders remain reticent to broadcast their faith commitments.

Without question, their faith informs the way evangelical executives like Ryan, for whom the Bible represents a lifeline, and Kyle, who lamented the apparent absence of the Christian Mafia, *talk about* business in general and their work in particular. Their stories are fascinating—full of variety, irony, and unexpected juxtapositions and affinities. Their accounts call into question popular and scholarly descriptions of evangelical executives, a group whose very existence calls into question long-standing and increasingly obsolete stereotypes of evangelicals in general. These accounts suggest that religion matters—in business as elsewhere—albeit in different ways and to different effects than are implied by common narratives regarding the strained relationship between business and religion.

1

Rethinking the Conflict Narrative

While most research on evangelical elites has focused on politics, what little research has been conducted on evangelical business leaders has generally emphasized the type of conflict narrative that Kyle articulated, wherein evangelicals must struggle to carve out a niche in the corporate domain or, as in his strip club anecdote, hold on for dear life as they are swept along toward unchristian contexts and choices. Laura Nash organized an insightful study of evangelical CEOs around seven proposed tensions between their faith convictions and their business responsibilities. Nash starts with "the notion that there are indeed inherent, recurrent tensions between Christianity and business practice in a capitalistic system," contrasting "the musts of business" and "the musts of religion" and describing her research as "a portrait of spiritual struggle—a struggle by individuals to understand and act in the marketplace."[1]

Nash's analysis of evangelical executives fits with a broader body of scholarship that elaborates the conflict between business practices and religious expectations. Researchers at Harvard University concluded that mere exposure to money triggers a "business decision frame" that in turn promotes unethical intentions and behavior.[2] According to these researchers, "a business decision frame entails objectification of social relationships . . . in a cost-benefit calculus in which self-interest is pursued over others' interests."[3] The implication is that business by definition promotes egocentrism and is therefore specifically opposed to the other-regard encouraged by evangelicalism and other religious traditions.

Another study of the effect of corporate contexts on individual perspectives, conducted at the University of Pennsylvania's Wharton School of Business, one of the most influential business schools in the world and training ground for a significant proportion of corporate executives in the United States and beyond, illustrates the profound influence of business mandates on moral reasoning. In this study, groups of executives and business students from eight countries were instructed to play the role of an imaginary pharmaceutical company's board of directors according to a

Baptizing Business. Bradley C. Smith, Oxford University Press (2020). © Oxford University Press.
DOI: 10.1093/oso/9780190055776.001.0001

hypothetical scenario in which one of their company's leading drugs was causing an estimated fourteen to twenty-two "unnecessary" deaths a year and would likely be banned by regulators in the company's home country. More than 80 percent of the corporate "boards" decided to continue marketing the product both domestically and overseas and to take legal, political, and other necessary actions to prevent the authorities from banning it. No group decided to recall the product. In contrast, when asked for their personal assessment of the decision to continue shipping the drug, 97 percent of another set of business students, managers, and faculty members said the decision was "socially irresponsible." Thus, 80 percent of the participants acting in a corporate capacity made a decision that 97 percent of those acting in a personal capacity judged morally unacceptable.[4]

These analyses suggest that corporate roles can powerfully shape behavior, prompting people to act differently in corporate environments than they would elsewhere and intensifying the challenge of integrating one's faith and one's work. Ethnographic research corroborates this evaluation, suggesting that firms often have a morality of their own, observance of which is necessary to climb the corporate ladder, and that "what is right in the corporation is not what is right in a man's home or in his church."[5]

The above-mentioned studies carry forward a long tradition of thought that holds that profit-oriented economic activity tends to promote greed, envy, and trivial satisfactions at the expense of moral and spiritual commitment to more substantive concerns.[6] Drawing on these insights, some scholars distinguish sharply between the religious and economic spheres, suggesting, for example, that the dispassionate calculation esteemed in market relations excludes the more affective evaluations encouraged by religious institutions.[7] Other researchers conclude that financial value, which represents the primary evaluative criterion in the market, conflicts with other evaluative criteria oriented to, among other things, divine grace or other-regard.[8] These contrasts encapsulate the essence of the proposed conflict between Christianity and commercial enterprise. Christians pledge primary allegiance to God, businesses are preoccupied with the pursuit of profit, and Jesus declared that "you cannot serve both God and money."[9]

Weber, too, considered it self-evident that money-making enterprises oppose the Christian ethos, asserting, "Surely it scarcely needs to be proven that the spirit of capitalism's comprehension of the acquisition of money as a 'calling'—as an end in itself that persons were obligated to pursue—stood in opposition to the moral sensitivities of entire epochs in the past."[10]

Focusing on Jesus' teaching, Weber observes that the Gospels and the church forbid the charging of interest, without which the competition for capital that characterizes rational capitalism could hardly take hold. More broadly, Weber insists that the Bible favors economic traditionalism, from Jesus' petition for *daily* bread to the eschatological expectation that Jesus' return was imminent and accumulation of money or possessions therefore senseless.

Responding to these dynamics and the conundrums they ostensibly pose, in recent years evangelical Christian presses have published practical guides for business leaders, offering to help them bridge the "Sunday-Monday gap" and succeed in business "without selling your soul."[11] My conversations with evangelical executives suggest, however, that in their opinions such dangers are overstated.

No Bad Feelings

When I first contacted Nancy, the CEO of a publicly owned restaurant chain, she offered that if I wished to converse with her about matters of faith and work before our scheduled interview, I could call her during her vacation. After all, she emailed, "I can't vacation all day!" A natural and energetic leader, Nancy suggests, "When I try not to be a leader, I just fail miserably." Nancy's propensity for leadership has afforded her opportunities for influence, some of them unsolicited. The week of the interview she had attended a meeting with then First Lady Michelle Obama to discuss ways to combat childhood obesity. "I sell fast food for a living," Nancy deadpanned, "so this is a conflict on a lot of levels." Among those points of conflict is Nancy's political orientation. "I'm not really a big fan of [the Obama] administration," she admitted, "and I'm going to get yelled at because I serve fast food for a living." For these reasons and despite the honor of the invitation, Nancy did not want to attend the meeting. But feeling compelled to view the situation through what she calls her "faith construct," Nancy concluded, "Okay, faith model: I will be respectful to the First Lady of our country. I will stand. I will be polite. I will not exhibit one iota of disdain for the wife of our President, ever. That's faith based—overcoming whatever my humanness is to do that. That's biblical—to respect people and treat all people with dignity."

Alas, this perspective did not make the meeting any more pleasant. "When [Michelle Obama] says, 'Will you serve carrots in your restaurant?' my first mind said, 'Ugh, nobody buys carrots!' But I will go home and think about carrots. Yes, too many children are not eating enough carrots, and I will think about my role in feeding carrots to people. I mean that seriously. That's a 'taking your faith to work thing' and putting it up against the business realities that nobody buys carrots and I'm going to throw away more carrots than I'm going to sell. How do you deal with that? How do you make money and sell carrots? But if I'm a faith person, I've got to think about it."

Nancy may indeed think about it, but our conversation suggests that she is unlikely to make material changes to the menu. In response to criticisms leveled against fast food restaurants, Nancy is quick to encourage moderation and deny responsibility for consumer behavior, even making a theological principle of the right of consumers to manage their diets. "You know, I really believe in that whole concept of free will," she says. "A central faith principle for me, therefore, is personal responsibility. I think we're given a lot of choices in life to do or not to do and it's our responsibility to figure this out. I can drink too much. I can smoke. I can lie, cheat, or steal. I can do any of those things that are bad for me, and relatively speaking, fast food is one of the least of those possibilities. I am not into regulating what I am allowed to eat or drink or smoke." Essentially, by providing food that is, in her estimation, unhealthy only in excess, Nancy provides opportunities for the cultivation of restraint. "I probably come more from the school of moderation," she asserts. "My grandmother lived to be 97. She made a really good custard pie. She didn't eat it three meals a day."

Nancy is eager and able to deflect criticism regarding the health impact of the food served at her restaurants and of her work and business in general. "It starts on the first page [of the Bible] where God said, 'There will be work.' I can't find anything wrong with that when I read that chapter on creation. I think [God] intended for it to be good and fruitful and healthy and purposeful. He made the garden really beautiful, so that might have been our first clue that it was going to be a good thing. Only our human nature has twisted work into something not good. My theology of work is a very positive theology; therefore, I have no bad feelings," Nancy claims.

Nancy's sentiments are typical. Very few of the evangelical business leaders I interviewed perceived meaningful conflict between their professional responsibilities and their faith convictions. "This may sound 'Pollyannaish,'" admitted one executive, "but I don't know that we've got any ethical dilemmas." Another informant echoed this sentiment, stating, "I don't think there's any conflict between the application of Christian ethics and the business environment." More specifically, one executive suggests, "If you think about the things that Christ has asked us to do in the Scriptures, it's consistent with what a business should do anyway. You know, to be honest and straightforward, to not steal, and not kill, certainly [laughter]. So, I think it's all consistent."

When Things Go Wrong

The tendency to deny or downplay conflict between the values and objectives prized by business and those valued by faith does not mean that informants do not experience challenges or are insulated from or immune to criticism associated with their work. "I just had a very difficult time at work, including a double-level demotion for something I didn't do that they wanted to blame on me," reflected Raymond, an investment strategist for a Fortune 500 financial services firm. Once seen as a candidate to lead the powerful Wall Street firm for which he worked, Raymond still occupied an important position but was no longer part of the inner circle of top executives. The pretext for his demotion, he recounts, included accusations of deceptively enhancing the apparent performance of the portfolio for which he was responsible—a charge he denies. While he won't claim that his visible faith commitment had anything to do with his demotion, neither will he rule it out. "When I was on the executive committee there were about a dozen people and there were two of us that weren't Jewish. The other guy was a non-practicing whatever, making me the only Christian. So who knows? I never felt anybody thinking, 'Because you're a Christian we're going to push you aside,' but who knows?" What is clearer to Raymond is that his allegiance to Christ indirectly contributed to his demotion, explaining that his colleagues and the executive team, in particular, "bleed [the company]." "I don't kiss the holy ring every time I'm in New York. I just try to do my job." While Raymond would not characterize his professional life as one fraught with tension, he recalls occasions when his unwillingness to embrace a win-at-all-costs culture resulted in adverse consequences. "When those around me or above me have said, 'You've got to go kick that guy in the teeth,' when I've decided I should tackle the issue a little bit differently, have I gotten yelled and screamed at for some of the stuff I've done? Absolutely. All kinds of four-letter words, physically pushed, it's all happened!"

Phillip, too, explains that his career in business has not all been smooth sailing. The CEO of a privately owned family entertainment company, Phillip states, "If I can help other twenty-five to thirty-five-year-olds avoid making the same mistakes I did, I think that is huge." The mistakes Phillip references consist of allowing his career to overwhelm his life to the point that he developed a drinking problem and imperiled his marriage. A high achiever with an MBA from Harvard, Phillip ascended rapidly up the ranks of the automobile industry through a combination of talent and hard work. "When I was going through the meltdown, I never stopped working except when I slept," he recalled. During the most difficult period, he estimates that he was out of the country 70 to 80 percent of the time, sometimes for two or three weeks in a row. "I hated that experience," Phillip reflects. "I hated the trips. I hated the environment." And it wasn't just the schedule or the workload that was problematic. He explained that in the parts of the world he worked, "bribery is part of the culture. They do not even see it as wrong. You are just kind of expected to pay government officials to get favors, and [companies there] don't see anything wrong with it. American companies try to play by American rules, and a lot of times they get slaughtered in the process. I just hated that issue. It is very much a relational, tit-for-tat deal—pay to play. It was kind of like Chicago politics. I just didn't like it." Moreover, he complained, "As an American businessman, they always try to set you up with prostitutes because they want you to have a good time. It is just an embarrassing, awkward situation when you say no and offend them. I just hated all that."

Phillip's climb up the corporate ladder placed him in moral predicaments and jeopardized his family relationships. Raymond endured painful and personal attacks at work, perhaps prompted by his faith commitments. And yet, despite the fact that their work has occasioned significant hardship and resentment, the overriding theme of their accounts is an intense resolve to characterize business as a worthy vocation.

When I asked Raymond what types of conflict he encounters, if any, between the demands of his work and his faith convictions, his first response was, "Fewer than I might expect." Eventually he conceded that early in his career, when he had less discretion to say "No," his time with his family was limited by the demands of his job. But he insisted that at this point, such constraints are minimal. When questioned about the finance industry's intense focus on profitability—an orientation Nash posits as in tension with the love of God, Raymond was quick to observe, "If every firm maximized its value, the standard of living of each person on this planet would be a little higher." As for his own compensation, he states, "My view is, 'God, to the extent you want me here, I'll earn as much as I can and I'll give it all away.'"

In reflecting on the ways his career adversely impacted his family—another of Nash's proposed tensions[12]—Phillip blames himself, not the nature of business in general, public company incentives in particular, or even the particular circumstances he found so difficult. It was not the hours, the travel, or the obsession with financial results that caused him to neglect those things he now values most, but his own obsession with advancing his career. If only he had cultivated an appropriate perspective and been motivated by the right things, Phillip believes, he could have acted out his faith as he does at his current company, where he does so with the support of the company's owners. When asked what might have helped him avoid the dark place he inhabited at the nadir of his personal and professional journey, he replied, "The Bible. If I would have just followed what it said. I think most people have way too much knowledge and way too little execution. The decisions I made to do what I did were not really biblical. I think all the answers are in the Bible if I would have followed what it said."

Having transitioned to a private company owned by committed evangelicals, Phillip now finds abundant opportunity to apply his faith at work. When asked if he thought the people-focus that characterizes his current employment context would translate to a publicly traded company, such as those for which he previously worked, he replied, "Unequivocally. I feel like they can work because I have seen them work. Actually, I think they maximize the profits of the business, which is what anybody in a publicly owned company needs to do." Evangelical executives like Raymond and Phillip perceive little conflict between Christian values and business values. It is not that business and religion don't mix, as scholars sometimes assert. Indeed, it is not the presence of Christian values in the business world that engender conflict and dysfunction; rather, according to evangelical business leaders, it is their absence.

A Sore Spot

The evangelical business leaders I interviewed professed little angst about the propriety of their profession. Their struggle, instead, was to convince others of this propriety. Nancy's ambition for and exercise of leadership roles have been a source of tension with the faith communities to which she has belonged. Regarding her role as a business executive, Nancy confides, "I've been told by pastors at my own home church that what I'm doing is not biblical, certainly a disservice to my family, and maybe even sin." She characterizes the circumstances of female Christian business leaders as one of inherent conflict and laments, "Frequently you do not receive the support of your minister in your church or your neighbor or your best friend. You have to have really rigorously decided that you are okay, spiritually, with work, because you have to defend it all the time."

And defend it she does. "What's more rich than providing meals to people?" Nancy asks. "It's a very caring kind of work when you think of it that way." "When a restaurant is well run," she boasts, "we provide a real sense of family and community, a place you enjoy going every day; you do something well and good, take care of people, and feed them." When discussing the purpose of business, Nancy waxes theological. "We're part of God's economy," she states, "and in doing our work, which I think is His will, you combine a community that is relational and healthy for humans to live in at the highest order. And at the lowest order we sell meals and make money." For Nancy, business is a venue for ministry—a place where she is able to influence others. "I really believe that we have vocational callings," she explained, "and that ordinary, everyday work—whether you're making sandwiches or making electronic equipment—can be a place where you exert influence on people's lives, or touch people, or influence their spiritual journey. So work to me is an outright mission field, and it will be mine in my life. I will never go to Africa and serve my church. I'm not cut out to do it. But this . . . I'm cut out to do this in a spiritual fashion and touch lives." While Nancy's compulsion to defend the spiritual value of her vacation is heightened by the gender dynamics that characterize evangelicalism—a topic we will explore in more detail—she is typical of the executives I interviewed in wishing to view her work as ministry.

Second-class Citizens

"I didn't grow up in a Christian context," explained Jin, the founder and CEO of a privately held software company. "I became a Christian in high school and basically I was a converted pagan. And like many people who get serious about their faith, in my enthusiasm I wanted to be a missionary or a pastor or something. But some folks were helpful in saying there's a much broader sense of vocation." He confides, "I think part of the challenge for me—and I'd even say a struggle—is that from the evangelical context from which I come, we've had a sort of dualist view of the world in which the spiritual stuff is what's important and the material stuff isn't that important. I think recovering the sense that everything in life can be holy and is intended in fact to be redeemed and sanctified can be challenging."

Jin was not alone in the struggle to find spiritual significance in business. He recalls, "My vice president of sales and marketing—a woman—grew up in a Christian family and we processed some things together. Finally, she said, 'I finally feel like I'm validated as a human being. My sister is a missionary, and I always felt like a second-class citizen.' Actually having someone who understands that what she's doing here is just as vocationally significant in God's kingdom as what her sister is doing was transforming for her. I think oftentimes there's this sort of guilt that we ought to be doing something else instead."

For some evangelical executives, the perception that business is a second-class occupation is difficult to overcome, producing angst and guilt. "I've asked that a lot," shared the CEO of an investment firm. "Should I be in business? Or should I be more about spreading the gospel." Similarly, another executive confided, "I've gone through times in my life where I've been like, 'Gosh, I could be doing something so much greater.' I used to think I need to do something like mission work or youth [ministry]." For this executive, as for others, it is not that business is bad; rather, the nagging question is if business is good enough. For evangelical business leaders, the struggle is less about reconciling faith and business than finding and defending their place in the spiritual hierarchy.

The Evangelical Imperative

"It's not about me," explained the CFO of a publicly traded energy company, echoing the opening line of one of the best-selling books of all time. "Whatever I'm doing, the larger purpose is to change the world, to point the world to God," he said. *The Purpose Driven Life* by Rick Warren, founder and senior pastor of an evangelical megachurch in Lake Forest, California, and one of the best-known evangelical spokespersons and activists in the United States today, serves as a manifesto of sorts for many evangelicals. By the end of 2005, almost one-fifth of American adults and nearly two-thirds of evangelicals claimed to have read the book.[13] A number of the executives I interviewed mentioned and/or quoted from it, and in fact, nine of the evangelical business leaders I interviewed specifically quoted the opening line without prompting.

According to Nancy, the fast food purveyor we recently met, "My favorite line in *The Purpose Driven Life* is in the first paragraph where Rick Warren writes, 'It's not about you.' A lot of people live their whole life and never figure that out. If you believe you were created by God and that he's the big guy and you're the ant, it is completely defining in how you approach work." For the executives I spoke with, appropriate business practices start with an appropriate perspective on business, and fundamental to this perspective is the idea that everything can and should have a purpose that transcends personal satisfaction. In fact, most of the executives I spoke with were quick to deny that they were in business for themselves, asserting instead that their work was in service to others. Nancy reflects, "I've worked for a lot of people when it was just about them, and how many points they racked up, whether it be dollars and cents or boats or planes or awards or golf games—whatever they value personally. I've made a very conscious decision to separate from that model."

In elaborating our purposes in life, the opening chapters of *The Purpose Driven Life* emphasize one key contrast—that between the temporal and the eternal. "The things we see now are here today, gone tomorrow," Warren writes, "but the things we can't see now will last forever."[14] Likewise, Warren quotes celebrated Christian author C. S. Lewis to the effect that, "All that is not eternal is eternally useless."[15] In light of the importance of the eternal relative to the temporal, Warren recommends that "Christians should carry *spiritual* green cards to remind us that our citizenship is in heaven."[16] For evangelicals, in order for something to be of lasting significance, it must contribute to spiritual objectives, which include, according to Warren, worship, service, fellowship with other Christians, conformity to the character of Christ, and evangelism—all of which represent different dimensions of what it means to "glorify God" and all of which are ostensibly foreign to commercial enterprise.

The evangelical imperative is to live with purpose by participating in eternally significant activities. For evangelical business leaders, this means understanding their work, oriented as it is around material processes and outcomes, in spiritual terms. While some studies suggest that many Americans now prefer to seek meaning outside of work, the business leaders I interviewed have not abandoned hope of finding spiritual meaning at work[17]—indeed, in light of the evangelical imperative, for one thing, and the typically all-consuming nature of their jobs, for another, they *cannot* abandon hope of finding spiritual worth in business. Compelled to contribute to eternal objectives but almost fully consumed with professional responsibilities, evangelical business leaders have little choice but to find spiritual meaning in their work—a task that is complicated at times by the perspectives of some of their coreligionists.

Evangelical Perspectives on Business

For many of the evangelical executives I spoke with, the burden to frame business as a worthy vocation is intensified by criticism from within their own religious tradition—criticism that emanates from the religious convictions they presumably share. Perhaps surprisingly, on the whole evangelicals are less committed to economic conservatism than is commonly assumed. Having analyzed quantitative and qualitative data on the economic perspectives of various Christian traditions in America, Hart found no connection between theological conservatism, such as characterizes most evangelicals, and economic conservatism.[18] Likewise, Woodberry and Smith insist that the average white conservative Protestant is more economically liberal than are mainline Protestants.[19] More recently, however, Felson and Kindell specify that the relationship between theological and economic conservatism does hold for better-educated conservative Protestants who are, in their judgment, more ideologically consistent.[20] This analysis supports Iannaccone's conclusion that the economic perspectives embraced by various Christian groups, including evangelicals, are best explained by familiar sociodemographic factors.[21]

Summarizing the differences between evangelical and mainline Christian economic perspectives and, in contrast to most previous analyses, focusing in particular on better-educated Christians, Steensland and Shrank assert that evangelicals present a more positive view of markets than do their mainline counterparts.[22] At the same time, the authors find no evidence that mainstream evangelicals uncritically embrace free market ideologies. Rather, evangelicals emphasize the need for moral, and specifically biblical, constraints on unfettered markets, in contrast to mainline Protestants, who see state intervention as a more promising approach to economic regulation.

Given the diversity of opinion that characterizes evangelical perspectives on business, it is likely that the evangelical executives I interviewed encounter coreligionists who are, at minimum, distrustful of successful businesses and their leaders. Indeed, only 19 percent of evangelicals say their place of worship encourages them to make a profit in business, which is less than respondents from any other Protestant or Catholic tradition.[23] And it is not just that some evangelicals are lukewarm regarding the respectability of business; some evangelicals are vehemently critical of business and the socioeconomic conditions that both enable and derive from free enterprise.[24] Evangelical business leaders face two primary lines of criticism from within their camp. The first centers on business as a corrupt activity within a corrupt economic system. The second is oriented around the perniciousness of wealth.

An Immoral Order

Arising primarily from the academic community and most ardently from what is sometimes called the "evangelical left," some evangelicals assert that business as practiced in capitalist systems is responsible for a great many of the economic, political, cultural, and environmental evils in the modern world. The well-known Christian writer and political activist Jim Wallis, for example, has stated that capitalist "economic institutions act to make profit, accumulate wealth, and exploit the poor, workers, and consumers, while ravaging the environment instead of providing for the equitable distribution of goods and services."[25] The essence of the critique articulated by evangelicals like Wallis is that free enterprise is a fundamentally immoral order in which the few profit at the expense of the many. This group reserves for business leaders particular disdain. As Gay documents, "they hold the American business elite responsible for treating employees 'as one more resource to be cheaply exploited,' for requiring 'near depression-level unemployment,' for foisting largely useless products on consumers, for producing frequent periods of inflation and recession in which only the illusion of affluence is preserved, for neglecting modernization of basic industries, for developing what has been called the 'national security state,' for squandering valuable natural resources, and for the general deterioration of human potential."[26] Moreover, Gay explains, "The [evangelical] left assumes that in the capitalist political economy virtually all social power is concentrated in the hands of a tiny business elite and that the rest of society, including what is ostensibly a democratic polity, is manipulated to the advantage of this elite."[27] Citing a variety of Scripture passages indicating God's special interest in and concern for the poor, critics of this persuasion argue that profit-oriented business is directly opposed to fundamental Christian concerns.[28]

Concerns about the nature and effects of commercial enterprise among the evangelical community are not confined to members of the evangelical left. Though generally less strident, many mainstream evangelical scholars who research and discourse on political economy evidence concerns about business, as well.[29] While acknowledging some positive aspects of capitalism and the businesses that flourish in it, mainstream evangelical scholars lament the inability or unwillingness of businesses to consider the common good and to incorporate spiritual concerns. Especially troubling to these commentators is the assumption, thought to be associated with capital enterprise, that ever-increasing measures of production and consumption constitute the sole or best criterion of human progress. Whereas the left considers the adverse effects of the market economy the deliberate and devious objective of the business elite, the evangelical center is more willing to admit that outcomes associated with a market economy are unintended but nevertheless suboptimal consequences.

Ungodly Wealth

As evangelical business leaders find themselves enjoying a measure of success that is largely unprecedented for evangelicals and a degree of prosperity that has been unknown to the vast majority of the world's population, their wealth and status places them under the critical eye of some of their coreligionists. Due in part to their history of marginalization and a subcultural identity that trades on embattled status,[30] many evangelicals are suspicious of material success and especially the accumulation of wealth, drawing sharp contrast between spiritual objectives and material concerns.[31]

Keister observes that literal Bible interpretation can discourage the accumulation of wealth, and other than historically black Protestants, evangelicals are more likely than any other religious group in America to insist that Scripture should be taken literally—more than twice as likely to endorse a literal interpretation as either Catholics or mainline protestants.[32] Relevant Scripture passages are numerous. In the Synoptic gospels Jesus advises, "Do not store up for yourselves treasures on earth, where moth and rust destroy, and where thieves break in and steal. But store up for yourself treasures in heaven, where neither moth nor rust destroys, and where thieves do not break in and steal; for where your treasure is, there your heart will be also."[33] "The love of money is the root of all kinds of evil," admonishes the author of the first epistle to Timothy.[34] And Jesus warns that "it is easier for a camel to go through the eye of a needle than for someone who is rich to enter the kingdom of God."[35] Jesus's encounter with a rich young ruler is particularly striking. Upon inquiring as to how he might inherit eternal life and after insisting on his fidelity to the Jewish law, the ruler was enjoined by Jesus to "sell everything you have and give to the poor," stating that this was the key to treasure in heaven.[36] While portions of Scripture are more tolerant of riches and more than a few biblical heroes are affluent, the contrast between material and spiritual goods is a prominent theme in the Bible.

Keister also notes that conservative Protestant religious doctrine includes more messages centered on the idea that God favors the poor than do other religious doctrines.[37] And she observes that injunctions to tithe, as are common among evangelical congregations, discourage wealth accumulation, as well. Although he denies any inherent connection between material and spiritual condition, Blomberg, in what is perhaps the most comprehensive treatment of the subject from an evangelical perspective, concludes that "in a remarkable number of instances throughout history, poverty and piety have been found hand in hand, as have wealth and godlessness."[38] For various reasons, then, evangelical beliefs and habits disparage wealth such as executives typically enjoy.

Friendly Fire

While evangelical executives are eager to defend business against animadversion from all quarters, it is intramural criticism that truly rankles. The responses these executives provide to what we might think of as non-religious challenges to the worth and propriety of various business practices and objectives are generally dispassionate and carefully reasoned. On the other hand, narrow conceptions of ministry prompt informants to use emotion-laden terms. That your work is part of your faith calling is no trivial matter to these executives, eliciting arguments that are emotional, subjective, and personal. Evangelical executives are highly sensitive to what one informant identified as "friendly fire." Criticism from members of their own faith communities smarts the most and engenders the most impassioned responses.

"I bristle when people say they have to go to Africa to do ministry," seethed the CEO of a family entertainment company. "I bristle at the idea that full-time church staff are the only ones in ministry." Likewise, the CEO of a technology company ranted, "At the First Presbyterian Church in Oklahoma City, my pastor was from Princeton Seminary. That was the school of choice. A lot of the guys getting out of high school decided that they were going to be a doctor, a lawyer, or a preacher; it wasn't a spiritual decision in a lot of cases. I would have had lots of attention over the next four to eight years as I studied for the Presbyterian ministry. I didn't do that, and they didn't give a rip what happened to me until I came back with enough money to make a significant contribution to the annual fundraiser."

Pastors, in particular, are singled out for particular reproach. Said one executive, "Pastors are seriously ill-equipped to deal with this. Why it is that there has been all this talk about Christians in business and so on, and seminaries are just completely tone deaf to these things? You'd think they'd expect a pastor to take a basic course in economics at least so they can read a balance sheet and income statements, so you can run your own church let alone help people." Another adds, "I think it's a real mistake to think that for me to actually participate in Christ's agenda as a business person, what I need to do is bring my Bible, set it on my desk, start a meeting with prayer and somehow mention Jesus as often as I can. I think this is a huge fallacy in the church, and it's because pastors have very little under-standing of this whole arena."

So disenchanted are some evangelical business leaders with the perspectives articulated by fellow believers that they feel more at home at work than at church. An African American executive at a prominent pub-licly traded food company lambastes "this whole mindset that the man is bad, the corporation is trying to do something to you, you sell your soul to work there, blah, blah, blah." "I was Vice Chairman of a Christian college," he recounts, "and they said, 'Ah, we'll pray for you, brother.' I was like, 'No, don't pray for me. Pray for yourself.'" "I used to tell them all the time, 'You guys make me excited to come back to work.' You know, honestly, you hang out with people at church and people at church meetings . . . some-times I'm glad to run to [my company]. I'm glad to be here rather than hang out with some of the brethren." This executive, like many others, has little patience for those who would question their calling or disparage the spiritual value of their work.

A Sacred Domain

It would be difficult to overstate the burden evangelical executives feel to justify their career choices. For the evangelical executives I interviewed, feeling
good about their occupation is less a perquisite of than a prerequisite for professional success. Indeed, understanding the spiritual value of their work is
central to their identities as evangelicals. Informants can live with disagreement about the types of contributions their businesses should make. What
they cannot tolerate is the idea that the contributions they make are not
somehow spiritual contributions, or at least sanctioned by God. They refuse
to accept that what they are doing is any less important than what anyone else
is doing, insisting that their work is part of their calling—that they, no less
than clergypersons, are ministers.

Evangelical executives experience conflict not because business and religion are inherently opposed, as some have argued, but because they are made
to feel like second-class citizens by members of their own faith communities. How deeply this criticism penetrates is difficult to ascertain, though it
is probably fair to speculate that for at least some informants, assertions regarding the value of their work are driven not entirely by settled convictions,
but also in part by anxiety or even guilt. Even Nancy, the fast food CEO who is
steadfast in her calling to business, wonders, "Am I doing enough? You know,
that kind of massive question of—I'm being a CEO, I'm being an industry
leader, but I'm not doing anything right now in my church." The accounts
informants provide are addressed primarily to critics within their faith tradition and should be read with this audience in mind, but perhaps also serve to
assuage their own consciences. Burdened to fulfill the evangelical imperative
to find eternal significance in their work and sensitive to criticisms leveled
against businesses and their leaders by members of their own faith communities, the evangelical executives I interviewed are keen to defend business—
to themselves and others—as a sacred domain and their work as part of their
commitment to ministry.

Sacralizing the Secular

In sociological parlance, sacredness connotes distinctiveness. To be sacred
is to be exceptional in some way—to stand above or transcend ordinary

daily life. Émile Durkheim, for example, posited a clear distinction between the sacred, as borne of and most clearly manifest in what he called "collective effervescence," or experiences of intense and shared religious experience, and the profane, as represented by everyday experience.[39] For the evangelical executives with whom I spoke, in contrast, to say that something is sacred is not to say that it is distinctive in some way, but in fact just the opposite—to provide evidence that it is like everything else over which God exercises sovereignty. During the course of my research I attended a retreat for Christian business leaders, the theme of which was "Christians in the Marketplace: What Would It Look Like if God Was Running the Show?" Later I will discuss this experience in more detail. For now, I simply observe that, apparently without coordination, both of the instructors who shared teaching responsibilities—one a pastor of a relatively prominent church and the other the dean of the business school at an evangelical university— oriented their introductory remarks around the following quote from the Dutch theologian Abraham Kuyper: "There is not a square inch in the whole domain of our human existence over which Christ, who is Sovereign over all, does not cry, 'Mine!' "[40]

Popular Christian author and speaker Henry Blackaby regularly meets with and advises executives from Fortune 500 companies, including some I interviewed, who are members of a group called the CEO Forum. A couple decades ago Blackaby published a Bible study called *Experiencing God: Knowing and Doing the Will of God* that has proven immensely popular to this day, with several million copies sold, and was referenced by some of the business leaders I interviewed. The study focuses on one key Scripture passage that quotes Jesus as follows: "My Father is always working, and so am I."[41] The core advice of Blackaby's study, derived from this passage, is that faithful living in any context requires finding where God is working and joining God in that work. The implication of this advice, at least as understood by the executives with whom I spoke, is that business is a sacred domain by virtue of God's activity therein. While businesspeople can be holy or not, the underlying status of business as a sacred institution remains constant. It is not informants' responsibility to make business sacred, but rather, recognizing its sacred character, to speak and act in ways that are consistent with God's activity in their careers, firms, and industries.

In order to affirm the sacred nature of business, informants not only asserted that their work qualifies as ministry, they also downplayed the difference between the work they do and the work done by clergypersons, to whom the vocational ministry designation has traditionally been restricted. The founder of a professional services firm recalled, "It bugged my dear friend and senior pastor when I was chair of the board of our church and head of personnel that I wouldn't call them 'staff' and 'lay.' I'd say 'people who are paid for ministry' and 'people who are not.' I see them as no different; some of us are paid for the work we do in ministry and some of us are not." Other evangelical business leaders describe themselves in terms typically reserved for clergypersons, even daring to suggest that they might be more effective at the work of ministry than those who are paid for such. One entrepreneur, for example, whose company, for each product sold, provides a pre-specified number of meals to the hungry or school credits to girls rescued from sexual slavery, shared, "I've been asked to be a pastor a couple of times and every time I'm close to it I have no joy. In fact, a pastor asked me two weeks ago, 'Would you be willing to consider being a pastor?' and I said, 'I *am* a pastor,' and he says, 'Well, what do you mean?' and I said, 'Let me tell you what happened yesterday.'" The previous day, this business owner had apparently been engaged by a customer in an extended conversation about family, parenting, and the difficulties the customer was experiencing with his teenage daughter. Claiming to have such encounters on a weekly basis, he concluded to his pastor friend, "I'm a pastor. I'm in closer than you will ever get because I'm sitting there with my products and I'm safe to these guys now."

Downplaying the distinction between clergy and laity is important to the evangelical business leaders I spoke with, but is just one component of a broader impulse to break down the distinction between the sacred and the secular. "I would like to buy a Borders bookstore and call it a Christian bookstore because to me all of life is under God," stated the CEO of a commercial real estate firm. According to another executive, the distinction between the sacred and the secular is the primary source of the disintegration many people experience between their faith and their work. "The problem is that we think some things are secular and some things are sacred," he said. "It filters down all the way to the idea that playing a guitar for worship is more spiritual than doing a doctoral thesis or doing a spreadsheet or doing an audit. We love to compartmentalize; we find it safer that way," this executive opined.

Naturally, the purported equivalence of the sacred and the secular supports related assertions that business is ministry, and even that business and church are essentially the same. Said a serial entrepreneur who believes that the purpose of business is to "serve others to the glory of God," "That's the problem—people have taken the view that church is different than business and it's not. The church absolutely gets a burr up its saddle when I make this kind of comment. The difference between a profitable business and a non-profitable church is simply tax law. Any church that operates on a deficit for a continuing basis won't be around. There isn't a pastor around who says, 'I'm not worried about the money coming in.' In fact, it's the first question they ask when they go in on a Sunday because they are concerned if the revenue will exceed the operating expense. As long as that happens, they are going to stay in business. If the music goes the other way, they are in big trouble. They are careful to manage the church money and operations so it doesn't go under, and a business is no different. The reality is the church has the same objective as a business."

The CEO of a technology company who teaches seminary courses that encourage students to think about business as ministry, reflects, "When I'm at the Doubletree in Pasadena, I have to get up in the morning and say, 'Am I going to the jet propulsion lab today, or am I going to Fuller [to teach at an evangelical theological school]?' One's a block away; one's a mile away. I work both places. I came to the conclusion that neither is more spiritual than the other. It's just what does God want me to do today?" Citing Scripture to justify his perspective, he continues, "If you look at Galatians 3:23—'Whatever the task, work heartily as serving the Lord, not serving men.' Where Christ has you that day, if you apply that verse and try to follow his guidance that day—figure out what he wants you to do and do it—you can't sort out the secular from the sacred. It's all His."

* * *

Thus far we have observed that evangelical executives demonstrate an intense compulsion to defend and assert the religious worth of business. In this chapter we have considered *why* that might be the case. Next, we will investigate *how* evangelical business leaders justify and defend business, focusing on the two primary critiques elaborated above—that the market represents an immoral order and that the pursuit of profit and wealth is ungodly. We will see that informants combat negative perceptions of business by explicating a God-ordained and God-upheld connection between virtuous behavior and favorable business outcomes, and that informants assert the positive contributions of business through appeal to a flexible source of ostensibly external moral authority—the Bible—that effectively functions as an internal source of moral authority with broad legitimating power. We will also explore *when* evangelical executives assert the spiritual value of business, namely after they have attained a degree of success, status, and wealth that multiplies their discretion and influence and insulates them from most repercussions associated with talking about or acting on their faith. After this we will investigate *where* informants claim to exercise particular forms of influence, showing that there are salient differences between, for example, small and large companies and between public and private companies. We will also explore the distinctive challenges and opportunities encountered by the women I interviewed. Throughout we will find that according to evangelical executives, in cases of apparent conflict between faith and business, it is faith, not business, that must be reconceived.

2

A Place for Saints

"Let me tell you a story about two merchants," offered Gary, the founder of a publicly traded computer products retailer. "They were roadside peddlers of local produce," he began. "They were in this small town. They were poor people. They lived day to day and if they didn't make money that day, they would be thrown in prison because they would have debts. These guys were typical; like everyone else, they would lie, cheat, and steal. They would use inappropriate weights and measures. These two men—and this is a true story," Gary assured. "These two men were caught up by the Spirit of God and began to study his word and they became Christians. They began to say, 'Lord, is there anything about our lives that is not right before you?' The Holy Spirit led them to the issue of honest weights and measures. So they decided that they would focus on being honest men and they would give honest weights to people. This was a tough decision and you can't appreciate it until you understand where they were. They were in the grocer section of town, where everyone is advertising the same product at the same price. All of them are cheating and everybody knows it. These two guys come along and instead of saying a penny for a pound of apples like everybody else, they say a penny point one or a penny point two. The people come in and look at your wares and say, 'I know you're cheating me and now you're gouging me! Cheating and gouging, why would I ever buy from you?' These guys were so worried about how it was going to turn out that they agreed they would check each other's weights and measures. Well, nobody thought about *the God factor*. When God became involved—when He saw what they were doing—He gave them favor among the people and people began to trade with them. All of a sudden they had more business than anybody else in the whole vegetable department. This went on for a period of time and they decided that they would create an organization that had a series of rules from the Bible. They created one-hundred-forty-four rules and a service organization because people came to them and said, 'What are you doing that's different? Why are you so successful and we're failing?' They said, 'Well, we are following God. You have to commit your life to God and you have to follow him and follow these

Baptizing Business. Bradley C. Smith, Oxford University Press (2020). © Oxford University Press.
DOI: 10.1093/oso/9780190055776.001.0001

rules and we will come around and check you on a regular basis.' Well, they created what are called livery companies today. That little town went from a backwater little city—a village, really—to the financial center of the world. It's London. These two men changed everything."

The God Factor

I confess that this episode in commercial history was new to me, and for our purposes its authenticity—doubtful though it may be—is less important than what we can learn from it about how executives like Gary conceive of God and God's role in business. In the story Gary related, God is seen watching the behavior of businesspeople, ready to bless those who transact with integrity, such that differential success can be explained by God's favor or lack thereof. "The Bible is all about prospering," Gary asserts, "but we don't prosper unless we walk with God."

The idea that business is a domain in which virtue pays is a central element in the accounts provided by Gary and others, and a crucial component of their defense of business as a worthy profession. In the previous chapter we saw that for many evangelicals, all of life can be considered sacred inasmuch as it holds spiritual significance and is inhabited and ruled by God. In contrast to the portrait of an immoral order painted by some critics of business, for Gary and others, business is a moral order in which God ensures that justice obtains.

In many ways the story Gary shared about the grocers is autobiographical. Well established in his career before he began taking his faith seriously, Gary explains that he had "received Christ" at a Billy Graham crusade when he was fifteen, but subsequently "forgot all about it." It wasn't until he was thirty, he recalls, that he thought about religion at all. At that time, he and his wife decided to let their son make up his own mind about religion, unencumbered by the dispositions of his parents, for whom "religion was pretty much irrelevant." Having decided to expose their son to different faiths, Gary and his family began their tour at Gary's childhood church. As he tells it, they never left. Gary reminisces, "God got ahold of us and changed our lives."

These days Gary describes himself as "an evangelical fundamentalist charismatic believer." "I believe it all," he gushes. "I believe the entire Bible. I do deliverance. I preach and I speak in tongues. I just believe it all." Like many evangelicals, Gary accords an active role to spiritual forces in our lives.

When he speaks of "doing deliverance," for example, he means casting out demons. During our conversation, moreover, Gary made reference to Satan as "hiding" in certain false assumptions. Speaking in tongues, which Gary also practices, means uttering incomprehensible vocalizations, often as part of personal prayer but sometimes for interpretation by someone gifted to do so. It is, therefore, natural that Gary perceives God actively involved in his career as in other pivotal events.

As an entrepreneur, Gary sees evidence of God's willingness to bless the companies he has established, and he is convinced that the companies he built were more successful than competing companies. Acknowledging that with the exception of their degree of success, his companies might not look any different from the outside, Gary allows that "secular people invested in my company just like Christians did. They didn't see the difference until they came inside the company." "But," he points out, "people knew the difference inside. Within the company, they knew they would be treated fairly in the sense of what is righteous and what's appropriate and what's correct. They knew that they would be viewed as equals, whether they were men, women, homosexuals—the issue was are you the right person for that job? They knew when we did things and it wasn't right for the customer that we would take the time to correct it no matter what it cost. The customers began to understand this and they would turn to us because they knew that they could trust us. It was a sense of trust and a bond. We created what businesspeople call 'goodwill,' and what I would call an appropriate level of behavior before God. It wouldn't necessarily be so obvious; I don't think people have to wear their faith on their sleeve, although I tend to. They just have to operate within the principles of God." Like the early London merchants, the businesses Gary founded were successful, he believes, because they operated according to biblical principles.

Gary's career, however, has been marked not just with lofty successes, but with crushing disappointments, as well. "A number of years ago, I sold this company that I'd built from scratch," he relates. "When we sold the company to another company, the stock was at forty-eight dollars a share. They asked me to please hold on to my shares for at least ninety days because I would be the largest shareholder in the combined company, so I said that I would be very careful and wait. During that period, it came out that the company we sold to had misrepresented the value of their inventory, which gave them a hundred million dollars in earnings over a three-year period. Well, the stock went from forty-eight to four. Literally, I was starting over. I sat there thinking, I'm older in years and I'm going to start over, after twenty years? I was absolutely numb."

Consistent with evangelicals' understanding of a personal relationship with God, Gary turned to God for a direct explanation. "I just couldn't do anything. I was praying. I was asking God for direction. I didn't know what to do. My wife was worried about me and I wasn't hearing from God and one day she went outside and was sitting on the grass and she said, 'Lord, I'm worried about my husband. If he keeps this up, he's going to die. He's really in bad shape.' As she was sitting on the grass, the Lord spoke to her. He said, 'I know Gary's heart. I will fill in the voids. Gary has inquired of me, I know his heart, and I will fill in the voids.' She heard this twice, so she ran upstairs, came in my office and said, 'Gary, I just heard from the Lord! Let me tell you what He said.' What she told me—in my spirit, I agreed with her, I received it, and I was completely changed and everything was back to normal."

Perhaps so, but this episode seems to have made a powerful impression on Gary. Already convinced that faithful living and success in business are correlated, this episode reinforced for him the converse—that unfaithful living, in this case misrepresenting inventory—leads to failure in business. And this was not the only time this principle was made apparent to Gary. "I was involved in starting a company many years ago in telecommunications," Gary related. "As we put the deal together, the CEO said, 'Look, I'm working in another company, and I'm going to copy this business plan off of their copier machine. Then we will distribute them.' I said, 'Please don't do that.' He said, 'What do you mean?' I said, 'We are working on our personal time here. Eventually you want to start this company, but don't start stealing from your company. That's just wrong before God and while you might not be a Christian, I am. I will never support it because of my faith.' The guy just laughed at me. Anyway, he printed this thing at his company's expense and we put forty million dollars into this idea. It was the right market, right place, right time, and it went under. God just wasn't going to bless it."

Summarizing the principles demonstrated by these episodes in his career, Gary explains, "Most people believe that if I were to be in business and be a Christian, I've got a handicap. I've handicapped myself because I can't lie, cheat, and steal like other people do and succeed in business. They just don't understand the nature of God, and they don't understand the nature of people. People don't want to work with folks that lie, steal, and cheat. When they find out that you cheat, they are suspicious and will do anything to avoid you. An example would be the car business. People feel like they are being cheated every time they walk into a showroom. That's just the nature of that industry. To be a Christian, to be a believer, and to follow your faith and the rules God has set is actually a way to make business much more successful—including profitability—than operating by the lie, cheat, and steal approach."

Several of the examples Gary uses to demonstrate the correlation between biblical business practices and favorable business outcomes center on the moral order that characterizes business as an institution, such as when, for example, dishonesty erodes the trusting relationships that lubricate social and economic exchange. In these cases, it takes no special insight to perceive the relationship between ethical or unethical behavior and business results. It is no mystery that people prefer not to do business with those likely to take advantage of them. But other examples require "eyes of faith" to interpret business outcomes as a function of the moral value of associated activities. For example, when his business partner copied his company's business plan for competitive use, Gary says conditions were just right for their new venture, and yet it flopped. In this case, the business should have flourished, but in response to his business partner's transgression, God must have actively intervened to ensure that it did not succeed. Gary's disposition is such that he perceives God actively maintaining the relationship between virtue and profit, always at the ready to show favor to the righteous. "The fact is God is still on the throne," Gary states. "He's in charge of everything, and a corporation's tone should be set by the CEO. And the CEO should be coming from the standpoint of, 'I am going to do what is righteous.' When they do that, companies flourish all the way down the line."

For Gary, God works in two ways to ensure that in business, biblical behavior is rewarded. For one, free enterprise is structured such that, as a rule, virtue pays and vice costs, typically as a function of the relational impact of different types of behavior. And this is not just happenstance, for, according to Gary, "God created capitalism." "God's system is capitalism; it's not socialism," he explains. "That's very clear throughout the entire Bible." But even though God designed capitalism such that doing good generally leads to doing well, there are exceptions, and sometimes, as when actions are not visible to others, God stands ready to show favor or disfavor as necessary. Oftentimes both mechanisms are necessary. For example, once the London grocers had established a reputation for honesty, it makes sense that people would want to trade with them, but God had to inspire customers to begin disproportionately trading with them in the first place.

Made Men

Max Weber long ago recognized that religious affiliation could serve as a competitive advantage of sorts. He writes of attending a baptism ceremony enacted by a Baptist congregation on a cold autumn day in the mountains of North Carolina, during which shivering converts subjected themselves to complete immersion in a near-freezing brook. Weber recounts, "During the immersion of one of the young men, my relative was startled. 'Look at him,' he said. 'I told you so!' When I asked him after the ceremony, 'Why did you anticipate the baptism of that man?' he answered, 'Because he wants to open a bank.' 'Are there so many Baptists around that he can make a living?' 'Not at all, but once being baptized he will get the patronage of the whole region and he will outcompete everybody.'" Still puzzled, upon further questioning Weber came to realize that "admission to the congregation is recognized as an absolute guarantee of the moral qualities of a gentleman, especially of those qualities required in business matters. Baptism secures to the individual the deposits of the whole region and unlimited credit without any competition. He is a 'made man.'" Ultimately, Weber concluded that "in general, *only* those men had success in business who belonged to Methodist or Baptist or other sects or sectlike conventicles," and discovered that "when a sect member moved to a different place, or if he was a traveling salesman, he carried the certificate of his congregation with him, and thereby he found not only easy contact with sect members but, above all, he found credit everywhere."[1]

To assert today that Christian affiliation inspires great confidence in one's business dealings would surely be misleading. One need only review the sordid history of the collapse of Enron to realize that self-professed evangelical Christians, such as was the late Kenneth Lay, hardly enjoy a pristine reputation or record. Nevertheless, it is but a short step from Gary's assertions that biblical business is successful business to the idea that Christianity is a competitive advantage. The CEO of a commercial products company that markets itself as "Christ-centered," in fact, specifically states as much. He told me, "Our valuation firm has reported—and it's an independent firm—that they do believe that the Christ-centered element of our business is a competitive advantage." Having reviewed the report myself, this strikes me as an overstatement. In a section titled, "Adjustments to Earnings," the valuation firm notes, "We considered the Company's contributions to Christian causes, which equal approximately 30 percent of operating income each year. Management believes that Christian giving is a key element in the Company's culture that has contributed to strong employee relations, high morale, and higher worker productivity. Furthermore, management believes that elimination of the contributions would negatively affect culture and productivity. For these reasons, we have determined that the Company's donations are not a discretionary expense." I read this as saying that, now that a pattern and expectation of charitable giving has been established, it would be counterproductive to discontinue it. But this does not necessarily mean that relative to other firms, the company's giving program represents a source of competitive advantage. Nonetheless, it is the interpretation that is important, and the fact that this CEO understands the Christ-centered dimensions of the business to be a source of competitive advantage is telling.

In Weber's account of the ways psychological premiums arising from new interpretations of Christian doctrine accelerated the spread of rational capitalism, Calvinists interpreted success in business as divine favor—as an indication that they were among the elect who were predestined for salvation. Indeed, on Weber's account, even the ability to conduct business in an ethical manner was selectively bestowed by God, and hence counted as evidence of eventual salvation. As such, Weber's Calvinists looked for evidence of God's favor in their own business dealings. Some executives, like Gary, likewise look for a connection between virtue and success in their own careers. As the CEO of an investment firm expresses, "As a Christian, it's made me a better person and worker and a more compassionate leader. I don't think I would be CEO and president today if God hadn't transformed my life and given me a heart for my team and people and the company, and given me a character that my owner/founder trusts enough to give me the keys to his company." Other executives, like the above-mentioned CEO who cited his firm's Christ-centered elements as a source of competitive advantage, take a broader perspective, focusing on the connection between virtue and profit at the company level. For example, the founder of the above-mentioned investment firm does not think his company would have survived the global financial crisis if not for the biblical principles on which he operates his business. Among these principles he lists saving for a rainy day, recalling the biblical episode in which the ancient Israelite hero Joseph stored up grain for the Egyptian people in advance of an anticipated famine. He also cites investing disproportionately during downturns, which he claims is completely counter to typical industry behavior. "These are all biblical principles," he says, "and you don't have to be a Christian to understand them and follow the principle and be blessed."

This business owner and many others made claims regarding the salutary effects of biblical behavior or the adverse effects of unwholesome behavior at the company level. For a few of those I interviewed, the relationship between virtue and economic success applies even more broadly. Gary, for example, pointed out the implications of the business culture that in his mind characterizes the automobile industry. And even more broadly, Gary discerns a connection between a nation's business climate and its economic circumstances. "Here's the negative side of [the principles encapsulated in the story about the grocers in London]," Gary asserts. "Bangladesh. You've got Muhammad Yunus, who is the head of the Grameen Bank. He won the Nobel Peace Prize for his micro-enterprise. The people in that country have had more micro-loans per capita than anywhere else in the world. Well, how is their economy doing?" Gary asked. "It hasn't grown a euro in thirty years. Why? Because they still operate on the same non-faith principles: I screw you; you screw me. Their economy doesn't get any better. But when people begin to walk and operate and exhibit God's truth in an economic environment where it's completely dark, the light is so bright that people are attracted to it. That's how you build a nation." To make clear that the economic problems in Bangladesh do not stem from the fact that the microcredit movement was initiated by someone (Yunus) who is, at least on some accounts, a Muslim, and at any rate not by any account a Christian, Gary adds, "At a country level, Guatemala is 50 percent born-again believers and their economy is in shambles. Why? Because they do not bring their faith into their business life. The fundamental concept in Guatemala is buyer beware; if I screw you, it's your fault. It's just not God, so he's just not going to bless them even though 50 percent of their country is Christian." In Gary's view, biblical behavior is what matters, whether practiced by Christians or non-Christians.

The business leaders I spoke with perceived the relationship between virtue and profit across a range of contexts. Unlike Weber's Calvinists, they do not see the relationship between virtue and profit as restricted to those few whom God favors, but instead as applying to business as a whole. As such, it serves as evidence not that God favors some and disfavors others, but that business is an institution in which moral order prevails.

Complications

Together, informants articulate an expansive application of the principle that God maintains the relationship between virtue and economic outcomes—from individual choices to corporate policies to industry norms to nation-wide economic conditions. This assertion is an important component of their overall attempt to legitimate business as a worthy vocation. For several reasons, however, *demonstrating* the link between virtue and profit proves challenging.

The general character of informants' statements notwithstanding, the extent to which ethical behavior is economically beneficial depends on a number of contextual factors, including, at a broad scale, the quality of a society's educational and legal systems, and more specifically, the visibility, frequency, and degree of consensus regarding the propriety of the behavior in question and the degree and kind of penalties legally enforced for its violation. Moreover, the strength and significance of the links between ethics and economic advantage depend in part on the specific values in question. Cultivating a reputation for compliance with basic moral expectations regarding, for example, fulfilling contracts or avoiding harm to others is likely to result in favorable consequences, or at least in avoiding adverse consequences, whereas acting in accordance with more advanced, demanding, and costly moral objectives such as promoting human dignity or contributing to community improvement is less likely to produce financial advantages.[2]

Evangelical executives rarely make such distinctions. Some did focus on the adverse consequences associated with what Gary called the "lie, cheat, and steal" approach to business. Others, however, claimed not just that avoiding immoral behavior helps avoid adverse consequences, but that engaging in charitable or altruistic behavior pays off, as well. "I think that, interestingly, every good thing a business does will ultimately benefit its profitability," said the managing director of an executive search firm. "The community service that a business does—even if its entire motivation is altruistic—at the end of the day, it's beneficial to the bottom line. The scholarships that it offers, the employee benefits that if offers, the insurance that it offers, all the different things that a company might do, the products that it produces that are designed to aid society—all of those things, if a company does them and does them well, will benefit the bottom line." This executive, like others, suggests that the good things a company does will show up in its financial results. In other words, it will translate to higher profits. Contemporary accounting standards place residual earnings at the bottom line of financial statements, indicating that returns to shareholders are the target toward which firms should orient their activities. Thus, when informants assert that virtuous businesses will be more successful, they apply this concept to conventional success metrics, namely, profits.

In insisting on a connection between virtue and profit, the evangelical executives I interviewed are in many ways echoing a line of thinking that has been championed with enthusiasm by advocates of corporate social responsibility ("CSR") for some time. Stirred to action in part by environmental crises, the wave of corporate scandals in the late 1990s and early 2000s, and a trend toward growing inequality, a host of interest groups and organizations, including non-government organizations ("NGOs") and consumer groups, have arisen to assert claims on corporate resources and to pressure corporations to fulfill their perceived responsibilities to particular constituencies. These groups would add meaning to business by channeling their energy toward various public goods.

While advocates of corporate social responsibility originally appealed to moral principles, almost all contemporary writing on CSR emphasizes its link to corporate profitability. In relatively short order, the underlying rationale for CSR has transitioned from "doing good to do good" to "doing good to do well." As Vogel suggests, "It is impossible to exaggerate the significance of the contemporary claim that there is a business case for corporate responsibility, business ethics, corporate citizenship, environmental stewardship, pollution control, sustainable development, and the like," adding that "while profitability may not be the only reason corporations will or should behave virtuously, it has become the most influential."[3] Whereas around 1970, only one of eight executives surveyed viewed their urban affairs programs as potential sources of profits, more recently, and depending on the survey, between 70 and 90 percent of executives believe that corporate social responsibility creates shareholder value.[4]

As an example of this shift in emphasis, Paine recounts the following: "Not long ago, civil rights leader Jesse Jackson spoke to a group of Wall Street executives about hiring more minorities and African Americans. Rather than appealing to ethical arguments about fairness, rights, or equality of opportunity, Jackson appealed to the executives' financial self-interest. He told them that discrimination was costing them money and that they could not afford to deprive themselves of the talent residing in the non-white population. Jackson's argument would have seemed ludicrous 50 years ago, but in today's economic, legal, and social environment, it rings very true."[5] On the basis of this and related evidence, Paine concludes, "As a result of social and institutional changes, the ethical argument and the economic argument have become much better aligned."[6]

The problem with this approach, whether professed by evangelical executives or otherwise, is that under most circumstances the business case for any but the basic requirements of fair dealing is weak. Allocations to employee benefit plans, environmental remediation, or charitable organizations represent expenses that diminish residual earnings available to shareholders, for which it is difficult for the hypothesized accrual of goodwill, customer, and employee loyalty, etc. to compensate. More virtuous companies internalize social costs that less virtuous companies externalize, putting them at a competitive disadvantage relative to their competitors.

Despite intensive academic attention, scholars have been unable to demonstrate or explain a consistent connection between corporate social and economic performance.[7] Even those studies suggesting a positive causal relationship—often by disaggregating the various behaviors and outcomes encapsulated in generic references to responsible behavior and financial performance—appear to be conditioned on institutional logics that characterize specific academic disciplines.[8] In other words, the purported relationship between virtue and profit is socially constructed.

Not only is there no guarantee that corporate benevolence will pay off, but certain features of the contemporary business environment have made it easier to profit from unethical behavior. For example, innovations in information technology have introduced new opportunities for profitable theft, deception, and invasions of personal privacy.[9] In addition, even conditions in which corporate virtue generates strong trust, such as informants are wont to cite, are inherently unstable inasmuch as high levels of trust create new possibilities for opportunism.

Venture capitalist Peter Thiel, meanwhile, contends that while there is a connection between virtue and profit, the direction of causality is opposite that proposed by informants.[10] Thiel suggests that the competition that characterizes free markets exerts such crushing pressure that corporations simply cannot afford to focus on anything but survival by way of profitability. Citing Google's motto, "Do no evil," Thiel proposes that only true monopolies or quasi-monopolies like Google, to which high profits are essentially assured, can afford to think about anything other than making money. In light of the dynamics that work against a relationship between virtue and profit, the lack of systematic evidence for it, and the possibility that if anything, profit precedes and facilitates virtue, it is one thing for evangelical executives to posit that virtue translates to success and quite another to demonstrate it.

To Measure or Not to Measure?

How do evangelical executives uphold the proposed correlation between virtue and profit when confirming evidence is scarce and counter-evidence plentiful? By declining to quantify the relationship, for one thing. Conspicuously absent from informants' accounts are specific examples in which biblical business practices translated to measurable economic advantage. In fact, informants almost never measured the effect of biblical behavior. They assumed but could not prove that virtue translates to better performance across contexts and levels of analysis. The outcomes they reference typically involve not absolute, but relative assessments—that, for example, a company was more successful than it would have been otherwise. Rarely were these effects expressed in terms of dollars and cents.

In some ways evangelical business leaders can hardly be faulted for neglecting or declining to calculate the effects of biblical business practices. Many of the benevolent objectives companies are called on to fulfill, such as helping others or bettering society, constitute "imperfect duties," which do not create specific obligations to particular individuals. As such, the benefits associated with their necessarily partial satisfaction are often diffuse and may go unrecognized or undervalued. And because the beneficiaries may be unknown, or at least not individually identifiable, the benefactor's largesse cannot be directly reciprocated or clearly tied to favorable consequences generated by beneficiaries or others.[11]

Informants sometimes point out, rightly, that it is difficult to measure the effect of virtue. The CFO of a multinational energy company shared, "We have a foundation through which we provide funds around the world to work on issues with children and education. Those are the two things that we tend to target. I can't demonstrate to our shareholders that there's an absolute dollar return on any of those investments." Likewise, he recalled, "During the moratorium on Gulf of Mexico drilling following the Deepwater Horizon accident, a number of our peer companies let people go. They just said, 'We can't keep you; we have no work.' They fired people. We made the choice to keep our people. Even though there was a cost to our shareholders, we felt like it was the right thing to do to keep their jobs; it wasn't their fault. Ultimately, by holding on to those employees, we could improve our retention. There was, ultimately, a return there. You can't calculate it. It probably would take a long time to see, but in terms of the goodwill of the communities we worked in, we felt like we should do it." Twice this CFO acknowledged, with respect to two different instances of corporate virtue, that it is impossible to measure its effects.

The same CFO, when asked if the social responsibility of business is better characterized by a "do no harm" principle or a more proactive commitment to address social problems, stated, "I think the do no harm principle is just a starting point." After he recounted his company's initiatives to promote women's rights in the Middle East, I asked him how the company would proceed if it turned out there was a trade-off between promoting women's rights and realizing higher returns, perhaps because the women available for hire are less educated than the men available in the area. "I think that we would try to look at it very carefully," the CFO said. "These are small investments we make. If I thought it was going to materially adjust our returns downward, I think I would have to say, 'We have to step away. We have to figure out a different way.' If we can do those things without damaging our returns, we will do it." According to this executive, measuring the impact of the company's charitable programs might threaten their continuance.

Confidence in and commitment to the connection between virtue and corporate results, it appears, thrives on ambiguity and reference to an unspecified long-term time frame. The very prospect of calculation attenuates the commitment to at least some forms of corporate charity. In speaking with this CFO, as long as the initial cost to shareholders could not be quantified and there could be an expectation of deriving some benefit at some point in the future, as in the case of retaining employees following the Deepwater Horizon disaster, the company would proceed to pursue the more socially beneficial action. If, however, the cost of social investments could be quantified, as in the hypothetical trade-offs between promoting women's rights and realized returns, the company would have to step away. Enthusiasm for discretionary social commitments withers as soon as an adverse impact on results can be demonstrated.

Perhaps this explains why informants generally eschew quantification of the effects of virtue. Many remain entirely in the realm of generalities, offering nothing but qualitative assessments of the correlation between the moral quality of corporate actions and business results. A few do attempt to measure, but even these do so selectively. I asked an executive at a restaurant chain if the company would reconsider its policy of remaining closed on Sundays if it turned out that it threatened the viability of the organization. "I've always been asked the question, 'How much does it hurt you to be closed on Sunday?'" he replied. "I've never been asked the question, 'How does it help you?' There's this natural assumption that it hurts us. But let me get a few facts behind it and maybe it'll answer your question," he said just before placing an order at the drive-through of one of his company's restaurants. (That he and other employees regularly eat at their restaurants helps counter criticism regarding the nutritional worth of the food they serve, he believes.)

Turning back to my question, he dug into the promised facts. The widely acknowledged best fast-food restaurant chain in the world, McDonald's, he claims, makes around 2.1 million dollars per restaurant per year, much more than the industry average of approximately eight hundred thousand dollars. Next, he bragged that his company's average freestanding location made three million dollars in the previous year. Based on this difference, he concludes, "Some might say, 'Well, if you're open on Sunday you might do 15 percent more,' but I think that almost anybody at our company would argue just the opposite: if we open on Sunday, we begin to look like everyone else and act like everyone else. I definitely believe that it's your uniqueness and your differences that make the difference. And I also believe that being closed on Sunday creates a little bit of scarcity and scarcity creates demand. We do three million *because* we're closed on Sunday, not in spite of it, is the way we view it."

This executive is one of the few business leaders I interviewed who ventured to attach a financial value to a biblical business practice. At the same time, he acknowledges that Sunday is "arguably the best day to be open because Sunday is the day when most people eat out. So it's a very good day to be open from a purely secular standpoint and a very bad day to be closed from a purely secular standpoint." This is an important qualification inasmuch as it casts doubt on the argument from distinctiveness the executive had just proposed. The facts of the matter, it appears, are subject to interpretation. According to this executive, whether or not being closed on Sunday is an advantage or a disadvantage depends on one's perspective. But even employing a faith-oriented perspective, the nature of the evidence is highly selective. There are many ways to attempt to measure the impact of being closed on Sundays, the most obvious of which is to consider the amount of business that would be expected if the company's restaurants were to be open on Sundays. But instead of assessing the amount of foregone revenue and profit, the executive thinks and speaks in terms of the incremental revenue and profit the firm supposedly earns on the days its restaurants are open. The metric chosen to demonstrate the financial consequence of a specific biblical business practice—revenue per restaurant per annum—is so broad as to be subject to the effects of essentially all of a company's strategic decisions, as well as many other circumstances outside the firm's control. In addition, the selected comparison—to a competitor's annual revenue instead of to the company's potential revenue if open on Sunday—is also expedient, shifting focus away from the six days versus seven days comparison. In the end, to interpret industry-leading revenue per restaurant per year as a function of being closed on Sunday is to impose a perspective on the metric. "I certainly believe that it's a big advantage to be closed on Sunday," this business leader concluded, before acknowledging, "I think most of the world would interpret it the other way."

Such is a typical pattern in the relatively few instances in which informants attempted to provide quantifiable evidence that biblical business practices translate to economic advantage. Evangelical executives often pointed to broadly favorable business results as consequences of biblical practices and sometimes referenced associated upfront costs, but rarely put the two together such that a return on investment could be calculated. This allows them to take the eventual payoff on faith and shields them from the burden of evidence. As the CEO of a pharmaceutical company insists, "You must never knowingly behave unethically in a business environment, even if you believe that it's in the business's best interest in the short term. I'm absolutely confident that the first thing you should ever do is say that behaving ethically trumps other consequences. The consequences of behaving ethically are that you damage the bottom line of your company? So be it. It is still an obligation upon you to behave ethically," he maintains. "I also believe," he continues, "that it will always, in the long term, turn out to be the right business decision." Likewise, according to the executive whose restaurants are closed on Sundays, "A mission-motivated company, in my opinion, will always outperform a money-motivated company in the long run." For these CEOs and others, any costs of virtuous behavior are incurred in the near term, and eventually God will see to it that things turn out better than they would have otherwise. As an African American CEO of an investment firm put it, "You might lose the battle, but you'll win the war."

Casting the hypothesized benefits of individual and corporate virtue off into the future enables executives to forego the commensuration process by which near-term costs are weighed against long-term benefits. In most cases, the "long run" never arrives, and the calculation is never made. With respect to the anticipated payoff for virtuous behavior, evangelical executives can always point to the indefinite future, no matter how much time has elapsed since the action, itself. Ultimately, because their effects transpire in different time horizons, the relative magnitude of the short-term cost and the long-term benefit of virtue is obscured by their remoteness. As such, the unwillingness and, in some cases, inability to match the costs of virtue with associated benefits exempts the purported virtue-profit connection from falsification.

In order to challenge the assumption that charitable behavior inevitably enhances business performance in the long run, I posed to several informants a scenario in which they were asked to choose between two expansion opportunities. While the details varied to fit the informants' particular industries, the outline was that they could choose to expand operations into an underdeveloped area in which both the jobs provided and the products sold were in short supply or into a more affluent area that was already well served by several competitors. As framed, expansion into the underdeveloped area would generate risk-adjusted returns that exceeded the cost of capital but lagged those associated with expansion into the more affluent market.

A few executives refused to play along, insisting that they or the hypothetical executive should pursue both opportunities, even when pressed to choose one or the other and with *ceteris paribus* conditions emphasized. One informant indicated a willingness to consider the opportunity with higher social benefit and lower returns, but only if the return was "comparable" to the other opportunity. As this CEO explained, "I would say that there have to be business reasons for doing it, not just social. If we never expected to get a return out of what we were doing, I don't think we would do it. If we were able to see that we could get a return, even though it may not be what we would get elsewhere, with the prospect that if we do things right we could get a comparable return, we would do that. That's sounding more like an economic decision, but I think what you're trying to do with your question is say, 'What's the price tag that you're willing to put on the social agenda?' There's some, but it's modest. Frankly, if we could make more money here and help those people in some other way then that's maybe a better way to go."

Others insisted that they, personally, might choose the lower-return option, but that fiduciary responsibilities to capital providers require them to choose the higher-return opportunity. "I can't in good conscience, as much as I want to do something good . . .," the president of a commercial real estate firm began before recounting, "There was a situation that happened in our denomination a few years back. Money got redirected by one of the people that was in charge of those dollars at a regional level. The direction they went with it was to help out something that was a very good cause, but they had no right to make those decisions. That person had to be fired immediately and a lot of things had to be unwound because they were working outside their purview. They were allocating dollars inappropriately. Even though it was a good cause they were going after, they had no right to do that. The same would be true when you're a steward over someone's investment dollars. Now, if it's just my own money, then it depends on if I can afford to do the thing that's more social, but absolutely I'd consider it."

True Virtue

The preceding examples demonstrate that the connection between virtue and profit resides most comfortably in the realm of abstract generalization, not the concrete world of calculation. Declining to connect specific virtuous business practices with specific business outcomes enables informants to insist that, at least in the long run, ethical behavior enhances business performance in almost every case. Thorough and accurate measurement of the costs and benefits of virtue in business might threaten to expose as false the belief that virtue inevitably pays off, or at least cast out its benefits to a time horizon that might make the deferral unpalatable to some stakeholders with a shorter investment time frame. But there is another, perhaps more important, rationale for the standard practice of declining to measure the effects of biblical business practices, namely, that calculating the effects of doing the right thing calls into question the motivation for doing so. Calculativeness, Pierre Bourdieu insisted, is the opposite of disinterestedness.[12] To fixate on the anticipated benefits for oneself of an action intended for the benefit of another is to pair the action and the reciprocation as an exchange, he explains, whereas to perform the same act in a way that is beneficial to another without regard for any benefit that may accrue to oneself is to bestow a gift. The factor that most clearly delineates the realm of disinterestedness from the realm of calculativeness, Bourdieu asserts, is the time lag between action and consequence. The farther from view the benefit of an action is, the more readily the actor experiences herself as disinterested.

Recall the oft-cited opening line of Rick Warren's *The Purpose Driven Life*, "It's not about me." In the gospel passage called the Sermon on the Mount, Jesus is reported to have instructed his followers to "love your enemies, do good to them, and lend to them without expecting to get anything back."[13] The fact that any costs evangelical executives incur on account of biblical business practices are incurred in the short term while the benefits associated with biblical business practices accrue in the long term enables informants to experience themselves as acting disinterestedly while simultaneously upholding the connection between virtue and profit that supports their broader claims regarding the nature of business. To decline to calculate is to contemplate specific business practices not as investments, but as sacrifices by which evangelical business leaders fulfill their religious duties.

The business leaders I interviewed may be mistaken in their assessment of the long-term relationship between virtue and profit, but they are not so naïve as to ignore the short-term effects of more or less ethical behavior. As the CEO of a pharmaceutical company stated bluntly, "In the short term, there are surely benefits to unethical behavior." Consider the costs anticipated by a commercial real estate executive and his firm's lawyers when pangs of conscience prompted him to be more forthcoming in his negotiation strategy. "I felt like I was lying to people," he explained, "because I had to make them believe that what I was arguing for was something that I really wanted, when in many cases, it was not. It was just to make them think I wanted it, so that when I gave up part of it or all of it in exchange for what I really wanted, it seemed like a fair trade, when in fact it was all just a game. Everybody played that game. But I decided I didn't want to do that anymore, and that I wanted to bring my ethics and my faith, I guess, to my business. I wanted to just say what I wanted and nothing else. I actually thought that whoever I was negotiating with always had a fair economic interest, and that if they reasonably did what they were supposed to do, that we should make sure that they got what they bargained for. I told that to my lawyers and they said they wouldn't represent me, actually. They told me that there were only two people in that company that could bankrupt it; one was the chairman, and the other was me. We were the only ones dealing with big enough pieces, and if I wanted to do that, I had to go to the board of directors and get their permission. So, I did. I asked them. And to their credit, they said, 'Okay.' I made the switch and it turned out to be the right thing to do. People responded very well to it. I found that it was really a better way to do business. I ended up with no altercations and no lawsuits. I didn't have to sue people to get them to do what I wanted, and they didn't have to sue me. Even though we were inevitably in tough situations, everybody was able to come to a just result."

For this business leader, even though negotiating with integrity apparently could have bankrupted the company, it turned out to bring unanticipated business benefits. It is essential for him and others to maintain that they do not act ethically in anticipation of enhanced business prospects. Indeed, informants consistently and emphatically denied engaging in biblical business practices for the sake of the favorable outcomes they would produce, characterizing such consequences as byproducts of, not incentives for, right behavior. "I was recently interviewed by a periodical about the diversity of our firm," said the head of an insurance business. "Our firm is extremely diverse, and I have intentionally pursued diversity. We have every ethnicity, every faith—just every kind of diversity you can imagine here—and it's a major part of our strategy. The periodical continued to drill down on why we were seeking diversity. How were we going to create revenue because of our diversity? Now I'm a thinker, and I know demographics, and I know data on this point, but I think I frustrated this magazine by stating, 'I am seeking diversity because it's the right thing to do, and it's a calling, and I'm doing it not for additional revenue or capturing a market that is increasing.' It was the most interesting interview because they really did not believe me, I don't think, that that's why we did that."

Some informants even suggested that inappropriate motives actually threaten the favorable outcomes that are ordinarily associated with upright behavior. "I think that all great goals are best achieved indirectly," explained the managing partner of an executive search firm. "I think that if profitability is the singular goal, then I think it can be elusive, but I think if excellence, and service, and customer service, and all of those things become the primary goal, then I believe that profitability is more likely to follow." The conviction that biblical behavior leads to economic benefits if and only if it is pursued for its own sake poses a dilemma for the business leaders with whom I spoke. On the one hand, it would be nice to give evidence of the relationship between virtue and profit, crucial as the relationship is for demonstrating God's involvement in and endorsement of capital enterprise. And indeed, a business can hardly operate without measurement. On the other hand, to measure the effect of an action that is assumed to be advantageous is to call into question the motivation for doing it.

Think back to Phillip, whose travails in the automobile industry left his family on shaky footing. Eventually, Phillip left the automobile industry to join a family entertainment company financed by evangelical Christians. Phillip recalls, "When I was in the car business I would go to a board meeting and every question you got was always about the numbers—only about what your margins were, what your growth was. Now," he contrasts, "at a board meeting I get just as many questions about people scores—our guest scores, our employee scores, reinforcing all the time that our own people and customers have to come first." Phillip believes that the willingness to measure and compensate according to adherence to its stated values is a hallmark of a worthy company. "We put our money where our mouth is," Phillip boasts, explaining that employees who score highest on two dimensions—those corresponding with what he calls 'to-do goals' and 'to-be goals'—receive the largest raises and increase their likelihood of promotion. This system of measurement was one of Phillip's primary emphases upon joining the company. The owners of the firm, he told me, have three objectives: 1) profit, 2) be "a great place to work for great people," and 3) maintain and demonstrate "Christ at the heart." Of the third objective, Phillip prodded, "Hey, I'm a Christian, and I don't know what you mean. If you don't measure people, you can't say whether you're doing a good job or not. How am I supposed to measure this?"

When it comes to evaluating conformity with company values, which he has designed to correspond with biblical principles, Phillip is an enthusiastic proponent of careful measurement. But when it comes to connecting specific business practices with financial outcomes, he demurs. While Phillip is proud of his company's commitment to environmental responsibility, he speaks of deliberately downplaying it in order not to compromise the authenticity of the effort. "Some of our buildings are actually wrapped around trees. We've always done it because that's what we were taught to do and we believe it's the right thing. We really don't try to measure the financial success. We don't have a metric. We also don't market it. You try to market it too much and it doesn't look authentic," Phillip said. Phillip's company diligently measures adherence to biblical values, but declines to measure the consequences of such adherence, believing that to do so would compromise their authenticity.

The result of this selective measurement is that Phillip and other evangelical executives are able to make what we might consider costless sacrifices. Phillip is able to claim, on the one hand, to do the right thing irrespective of the cost, as in preserving trees. He is also able to claim that virtue translates to a healthier company. Putting employees and customers first, Phillip believes, is the key to the company's success. "I do not buy the argument that the focus on people isn't profitable." "For a guest service company like ours," he explains, "the level of enthusiasm that the guests experience can never raise any higher than the enthusiasm of your own employees. If you don't spend a lot of time and energy and resources making them passionate, happy, and excited, there is no way they are going to turn around and do it for your guests. If you add all those things up, those are exactly the right things to do for the long-term health of the business. It works financially. We have outperformed our competitors. We have great returns. It definitely works."

A Place for Saints

Max Weber claimed that some professional domains are more or less accommodating to people of Christian religious convictions.[14] Politics, for example, is no realm for saints inasmuch as it requires a willingness to employ questionable means in service of admirable ends. On Weber's account, traditional ethical systems, such as the so-called gospel ethic encapsulated in the Sermon on the Mount, brook no compromise and as such are too idealistic to be of much value in political contexts. While they express how the world should be, they fail to accommodate the way the world actually is. The political task is, on Weber's understanding, inherently at odds with the gospel ethic inasmuch as political action is, by definition, the use of force. For Weber, the decisive means for politics is violence, and as such, it is incompatible with Jesus' instruction to turn the other cheek, which Weber takes as a prescription for pacifism. In light of this incompatibility, Weber insists that "it is in the nature of officials of high moral standing to be poor politicians."[15]

At the heart of the tension experienced by politicians committed to a Christian moral perspective, according to Weber, is the conflict between two opposing ethical frameworks he calls the ethic of ultimate ends and the ethic of responsibility. An ethic of ultimate ends makes intent the most important factor in evaluating a particular course of action. Proponents of this orientation adhere to absolute and inflexible moral principles, and having done so, accord responsibility for the outcome of his actions to God, secondary actors, or other material or spiritual circumstances. In contrast to the ethic of ultimate ends, under an ethic of responsibility, the ends of an action justify the means implemented to accomplish them, even when such means are incompatible with sound moral principles.

Christians make poor politicians, Weber believed, because they adhere to an ethic of ultimate ends. "The Christian does rightly and leaves the results with the Lord," Weber says, and indeed this is exactly the division of labor implied by informants' articulation of the connection between virtue and profit.[16] Evangelical executives are responsible for acting disinterestedly, believing but, they claim, not motivated by the fact that God will bring about a just result—one in which virtue is rewarded and vice punished. Herein lies the great value of the asserted connection between virtue and profit for the evangelical business leaders with whom I spoke. Weber assumes that the ethic of ultimate ends and the ethic of responsibility are ultimately in tension because, he insists, "No ethics in the world can dodge the fact that in numerous instances the attainment of 'good' ends is bound to the fact that one must be willing to pay the price of using morally dubious means or at least dangerous ones."[17] But the purported connection between virtue and profit defuses this tension by maintaining that the key to the attainment of good ends is the employment of good means. By emphasizing the connection between virtue and profit, evangelical executives reconcile the ethic of responsibility and the ethic of ultimate ends.

Reconciling means and ends in business allows evangelical business leaders to rebut criticisms regarding the supposed immoral nature of business, to which they are clearly sensitive. As we have seen, one of the primary criticisms that evangelical business leaders face from coreligionists is the charge that business is a morally dirty domain in which profits are generated at the expense of others. Even if, say, increasing living standards is a worthwhile aspiration and a probable outcome of free enterprise, critics allege that it comes at too high a cost. The supposed connection between biblical behavior and business success inoculates the evangelical business leaders I spoke with against this criticism. It allows them to maintain that, in contrast to a domain like politics, business is a domain that rewards righteous behavior. Said the former head of a prestigious global consultancy, "I sometimes find public officials, on a general basis, to be, frankly, less forthright and express more personal concern than they do about the general public. But I rarely find that in business because in business it doesn't pay. In business we don't do things that don't pay. But the fact of the matter is that unless my clients trust me, unless my customers trust me, unless my employees trust me, they're not going to want me around. And I sure can't have any hope of having a successful operation. So it all depends on the series of constituents that is held together by the glue of integrity."

Alexis de Tocqueville wrote of the ancients that they talked continually about the beauties of virtue while studying its utility only in secret.[18] Today what was once a source of shame is carried out in full view. Whereas Adam Smith's case for the morality of an economic system that is driven by the pursuit of private interest was based on its social consequences, today social contributions are justified by their contributions to private interests. The virtue-profit connection does nothing to challenge the fundamental orientation of corporate capitalism toward maximizing shareholder value. In fact, in some ways the virtue-profit connection is corporate America's new legitimating myth, enabling the facile reconciliation of social and economic commitments, and evangelical executives are one of its carriers. Moreover, the connection between virtue and success rests on a functional explanation that is inherently conservative; the myth that virtue necessarily pays enables executives to say that those companies, including their own, that generate healthy financial returns must, in fact, be virtuous. In so doing, it downplays the need for reform.

* * *

In this chapter we have seen that in order to assert that God has sanctioned and is at work in business, evangelical executives emphasize that business is a moral order in which virtue is rewarded and vice punished. Like other advocates of the connection between virtue and success, informants point to relationships such as that between a favorable reputation and customer acquisition and retention, and between principled leadership and employee morale—the likes of which are presumed to translate to healthier financial outcomes. To these utilitarian arguments evangelical business leaders add theological arguments, namely that God both established the framework in which virtuous behavior is beneficial and actively intervenes to ensure that biblical behavior is rewarded. While the connection between virtue and success is often grounded in natural relationships, layering on evangelical perspectives on God's providential control over all things transforms the connection into a non-falsifiable spiritual principle that holds even in the absence of corroborating evidence.

The idea that God ordained and is involved in business is a common and critical claim for rebutting the types of accusations we saw in the previous chapter. Indeed, Gary, himself, is sensitive to such criticisms. "People believe that the Bible does not support business," Gary complains, "and they are completely wrong." "The church is completely out of touch with this," he grumbles. "For the most part they believe that God has nothing to do with business. It's dirty. It's filthy. So they don't really want to be involved." For Gary, in contrast, God is everywhere involved in business, and far from being a dirty place where the wicked prosper, business is a God-ordained institution where moral order prevails. In presenting business as a moral order,

executives like Gary acknowledge what is now a sociological commonplace—
that all social institutions are embedded in and governed by moral orders
that are, in turn, manifestations of underlying narratives and traditions. In
this case, the narrative centers on a just and active God who designed private
enterprise such that virtue is generally rewarded, and who intervenes when
such is not the case. Even when virtue appears to be costly, evangelical business leaders interpret such costs as lessons from God that, presumably, will
pay dividends in the long run. As such, they are able to maintain that business is a domain where the good flourish and the blameworthy struggle—a
place, in other words, for saints.

3

Affirmative Religion

Emphasizing the proposed connection between virtue and profit helps evangelical executives ward off certain criticisms of business, to which they are clearly sensitive, but elaboration of the biblical principles that constitute virtue is necessary to assert the positive value of business and establish that by pursuing a career in business, informants are satisfying the evangelical imperative to contribute to eternally significant objectives.

The Bible is especially important to evangelicals, almost two-thirds of whom claim to read Scripture at least once a week—a considerably higher percentage than the 25 percent of Catholics and 30 percent of mainline Protestants who report the same.[1] I was frustrated upon waiting for one of my interviews to begin, wondering why, even though the appointment time had come and gone, I was being given an extended tour of the office. As it turns out, the insurance company CEO I was scheduled to meet had apparently become so caught up in his "quiet time," a designation many evangelicals use for their daily time of prayer, that he lost track of the time. "I'm running a few minutes late because I sat on my porch this morning in an extended quiet time with a trickling little waterfall and just really got into Scripture," he explained.

For evangelical business leaders, the Bible represents the primary explanatory and justificatory resource—the way they make sense of their circumstances and defend their decisions—as well as a repository of motifs and endorsements that are useful for articulating the spiritual contributions of business. The CEO of an energy company, reflecting on his dialogue with a Christian counselor, remarked, "We started studying the Bible. I would ask questions and then she would say, 'Well, let's look at what Scripture says.' So I started looking at how much wisdom there was and how much truth there was in what she was showing me. There was basically an answer to everything if you knew where to look for it." For this executive and many others, the Bible has all the answers. As the CFO of another energy company expressed, "The Bible is the very best resource that I go to. I actually go to very, very few

Baptizing Business. Bradley C. Smith, Oxford University Press (2020). © Oxford University Press.
DOI: 10.1093/oso/9780190055776.001.0001

external resources. I am not a reader of the latest pithy book from a secular or spiritual author."

According to the founder and president of a large, privately held commercial real estate firm, his understanding of the fundamental themes of the Bible informs his approach to managing his company. "I work to glorify God and care for people," he claims. "If you just sort of start at Genesis and read all the way through the Bible, the two things that sort of overwhelm me are how much God loves us and, number two, he doesn't want you to get any glory." This perspective dictates to whom this executive devotes the majority of his care and concern. "It goes back to glorify God and care for people," he explains. "Who are those people? People are anybody that God puts you in touch with and obviously, if you're sitting in the cubicle next to somebody, it's as important for you to minister to them as anybody. My customer is not the most important thing to me. The people that work in my office are the most important thing to me." His business is of spiritual value, this executive believes on the basis of his reading of Scripture, because he takes care of his employees, which includes paying for Bible teachers to teach at the office and, he claims, paying people well so that they have opportunities to give more away.

Ironically, in turning to the Bible to assert the positive value of business, evangelical executives draw on the very same resource that their critics use to denigrate business. But the way evangelicals are encouraged to read and interpret Scripture and the ambiguity and broad applicability of some important biblical motifs enable evangelical business leaders to marshal support for that which others believe it condemns.

Interpretive License

We have noted that a number of evangelical executives cited Rick Warren's book, *The Purpose Driven Life*. A relatively short book by word count, with just over 300 large-print pages, the treatise contains nearly one thousand quotations from Scripture. Warren's emphasis on Scripture is apparent early on, as he suggests near the outset, "If you really want to improve your life, memorizing Scripture may be the most important habit you can begin."[2] To that end, he markets a Purpose-Driven Life Scripture Keeper Plus in which to organize Scripture memorization cards. Throughout the book, rarely is a principle espoused without a supporting quotation from the Bible. If Warren wants to make a point, he quotes Scripture. What he does not do is explain Scripture. With three Bible quotes per page on average, there simply is no room for any sort of in-depth analysis of the text. Warren plucks snippets from all over the Bible and lets them stand on their own, assumed to be straightforwardly understood and applied.

As an important resource for evangelicals in general and for many of the executives I interviewed, *The Purpose Driven Life* represents an example of how to approach and use the Bible. In isolating verses from their context, it goes against sound hermeneutical principles, according to which passages must be understood in the context of their immediate pericope and broader literary units. The book implicitly endorses the doctrine of "the perspicuity of Scripture," denoting that all of sound mind are able to understand and apply the Bible without help—a doctrine that encourages evangelicals to trust their own interpretation of Scripture.[3] This, the executives I spoke with are eager to do. "I think the Bible is too limited by commentaries," says Gary, the charismatic entrepreneur we met in the last chapter. Likewise, the customer-focused real estate mogul introduced above, discourses, "I think we probably underestimate God's ability and his spirit in us to convey most things. And I think a lot of us spend too much of their life seeking out somebody that's going to give them the right answer. I'm not even sure they would know the right answer if it hit them in the head. I think we talk about it too much. A little time by yourself praying and in the Word, it's amazing—you read something fifty times and all of a sudden God's spirit makes you see something that you never saw before. It hits you right where you need it. I just think we tend to read too many books about the Bible, too many books about what God says, too many books about what you ought to do, and not nearly enough time reading what God said. Not my interpretations about what he says; not books about what he says—I think God can be pretty doggone clear through our spirit about what he wants to say."

If *The Purpose Driven Life* encourages evangelical executives and their coreligionists to make liberal use of Scripture, trusting their own interpretations along the way, another resource—this one endorsed by individuals and organizations that desire to equip evangelical executives to apply their faith at work—grants permission for executives to apply almost anything in the Bible to their professional lives. The Theology of Work Project is "an independent, international organization dedicated to researching, writing, and distributing materials with a biblical perspective on non-church workplaces."[4] The initiative has generated support from people like the executives I interviewed for this study and the ministry organizations that desire to support them. While the project focuses on "work" in general, the contributing team consists largely of businesspersons and theologians, and as such there is a clear emphasis on for-profit enterprises. A subheading in a document titled "A General Introduction to a Theology of Work" poses the question, "How do you do a theology of work?" According to this document, "The simple answer is, you study the Bible." The document goes on to explain, "What we have done is to go through the Bible book by book and surface what we might not have seen about work had we not been looking for it." From every chapter of every book in the Bible, contributors to the Theology of Work Project discern principles that in their judgment apply to contemporary business. From passages in Leviticus on skin diseases and mold infections to prophetic expectations in Daniel that God will overthrow pagan kingdoms and replace them with his own kingdom to the Apostle Paul's instructions regarding slaves and masters, contributors find connections to contemporary business realities. The executive editor of the Theology of Work Project observes, "Often the most interesting resources come from the most unexpected places. Who would have thought that the Song of Songs would have so much to say about workplace relationships and employee satisfaction?" he asks, "or that the best example of a manager in the Bible is the Valiant Woman in the Book of Proverbs?" He adds, "I was surprised that Paul's discussion about yoking oxen in 2 Corinthians would have so much practical guidance for workplace relationships in business today."

There is good reason this editor is surprised. I scoured several commentaries on these three passages and did not find a single reference to business. The key to finding lessons regarding work in such passages, it seems, is to go in looking for them. But this is exactly the type of hermeneutical lens with which the evangelical business leaders I interviewed are apparently equipped, ready and willing to describe business in biblical terms and with the use of biblical metaphors. From the Bible evangelical business leaders find guidance on why business is important in the first place and appropriate for them in particular. And for the executives I interviewed, the lessons of Scripture are context-independent. They have been sanctioned to apply biblical metaphors and lessons—including those with no apparent connection to business—to their occupational contexts. This permission assures that evangelical executives are able to find and use principles and endorsements that fit their particular circumstances and dispositions.

Breadth of Meaning

When the aforementioned real estate executive reads the Bible from beginning to end, he concludes that the overriding emphasis of Scripture is to glorify God and care for others. Another real estate executive tells of studying Scripture at the beginning of his career when, he recounts, the markets were down 50 percent and he had some time on his hands. "I had a good friend who was a new Christian and I said, 'Why don't we read the Bible and find out what it has to say about money and possessions?' I told him, 'Why don't we split it up? You take the Old Testament. I'll take the New Testament.' He didn't know the difference. I think the big thing we came away with is: What's our part, and what's God's part? Our part is to be stewards. God's part is He controls everything. He prospers one and puts down another. So in general, you do the right things and God will prosper you. Those principles became sort of guideposts for me, for all of my business career." These principles, reminiscent of the virtue-profit connection we explored last chapter and which, this executive claims, gave shape to all of his business dealings, bear little resemblance to the themes the other real estate executive emphasized. Both read the same Bible, but they come away with different lessons.

While some informants, like these real estate executives, attempt to distill Scripture into an overriding motif, others pick a theme verse or passage that for them represents the key to understanding their professional lives. The chairman of an industrial products company related that he had grand plans for a sweeping study of Scripture during an extended vacation. "I was going to reread the New Testament real slow along with all the notes and everything. I had this big plan," he recalled. "Anyway, I didn't do it. I realized that I had blown the opportunity. Here I said I was going to do it and I didn't." Despite the missed opportunity, his disappointment quickly evaporated, he relates, because he soon came across a verse that saved him the trouble of reading the New Testament in the first place. "It was funny; I don't know how many times I read [1 Timothy 1:5], then I came across it and the first five words really got me. I couldn't believe it. It says, 'The goal of our instruction is . . . ' I didn't read past that. Wow! That's as important as anything in the Bible! It says, '. . . love from a pure heart, a sincere faith, and a clear conscience.' I thought, 'Wow, that's a tough one.' So be pure, sincere, and clean of heart. God's really put that on my mind that that's what love really is. What I got out of all that was—love is the New Testament." A generic lesson, for sure, but one that has shaped, he believes, the way he has run his company and inspired him to the point that he includes on the company website pages titled "What's Love Got to Do With It?" and "God's Love," and even designed and aired a television commercial that depicts the need for more of God's love. This one verse, this executive contends, transformed his approach to and understanding of business. Connecting the dots, he says, "You're supposed to love other people all day, every day. I see business as every bit of a ministry as everything else. In relationship with your coworkers—in my case distributors—and then their employees and our dealer accounts and their families."

Like this executive, the owner and CEO of a furniture company homed in on one particular passage that has provided inspiration for him in his career. "I adopted Psalms 37:4 as my life verse in my early twenties," he told me. "It says, 'Delight yourself in the Lord and He will give you the desires of your heart.' As I pursued those desires, while continuing or maintaining my delight in the Lord, He is the one who gave me these ideas and drives and passions, so I felt free to pursue those." For this CEO, the fact that he enjoys business makes it a calling, as confirmed by one particular Bible verse. Similarly, a well-known CEO of a technology company recalls how he came to view business as ministry. "After I joined my first company, I became a Christian, and then really felt called to the ministry. It was sort of like, 'What are you doing, God?' It seems rather bizarre considering work and school and everything was going extremely well. Then, Colossians 3:23 really sort of came into my life and it was clear that God was calling me to workplace ministry. I felt very much a workplace minister ever since that." Later, he explained, "A Christian business leader would be one who is living by Colossians 3:23—'working hardily as for the Lord and not for men.' You're treating Christ as CEO and your current role as a temporal one."

Several informants note that the Bible has more to say on economic matters than on most other subjects, but few seem to appreciate that the Bible assumes a personal economy in which market participants know those with whom they transact. In most cases today, of course, the economic context is much different. Thus, there will be, at minimum, substantial challenges in deriving from the Bible principles that translate directly to current professional contexts. Evangelicals are not without strategies for doing so. Blomberg, author of a thoughtful and comprehensive study of biblical material on poverty and wealth, recommends running each Old Testament passage through a grid of its 'fulfillment' in Christ to see how its application is altered in the New Testament age, acknowledging that "one must often relate situation-specific mandates to broader, more timeless, categories."[5]

Blomberg observes, "the closer the situation in any given portion of our contemporary world corresponds to the features—in this case the socio-economic features—of the world behind any given biblical instruction, the more straightforwardly one can transfer the principles of those texts to our modern age. The less the correspondence, the higher one has to move up the 'ladder of abstraction' to look for broader principles that may transcend the uniqueness of specific situations."

Well-reasoned as this interpretive approach may be, it is of little concrete help to evangelical executives navigating the currents of contemporary economic life. If anything, moving up the ladder of abstraction permits diverse interpretations and applications. And given their disinclination to consult specialists, along with the absence of conciliar authority in the Protestant tradition, evangelical business leaders unsurprisingly evidence what Smith has described as the "pervasive interpretive pluralism" that frustrates evangelical attempts to define the core tenets of their faith but permits evangelical executives to understand even the most generic principles and injunctions as applying to business in particular.[6] Armed with confidence in their ability to interpret and apply the Bible, and emboldened to comb through Scripture for passages that confirm their perspectives and speak to their circumstances, the Bible represents for the evangelical executives I interviewed a treasure trove of legitimating scripts.

An Ample Resource

For many contemporary readers, the Bible is an outdated complex of inflexible moral proscriptions that serve to constrain behavior. This view accords with some scholarly perspectives that see religion primarily as a regulatory example of culture. Friedland and Alford, for example, posit that "Contemporary Christian religions seek to convert all issues into expressions of absolute moral principles accepted voluntarily on faith and grounded in a particular cosmogony."[7] These moral principles, moreover, conform to an institutional logic that is in tension with the logics of action that characterize other social domains, including the economy. For Friedland and Alford, religion is an essentially competitive institution that attempts to subsume all other domains, including the market, under its particular rubric of meaning.

Weber, too, as we have seen, understood religion as essentially in conflict with economic life. For him, at the heart of the Christian ethic are the unyielding injunctions spoken by Jesus in the Sermon on the Mount, during which Jesus is reported to have overruled the ancient code of justice called the "lex talionis," or law of retaliation. "You have heard that it was said, 'Eye for eye, and tooth for tooth.' But I tell you, do not resist an evil person. If anyone slaps you on the right cheek, turn to them the other cheek also. And if anyone wants to sue you and take your shirt, hand over your coat as well. If anyone forces you to go one mile, go with them two miles," Jesus said.[8] On this account, Christian character requires going well beyond the basic requirements of fairness. It requires supererogatory acts to the point of significant personal sacrifice.

This helps explain why Weber perceives such tension between "religions of salvation," including Christianity, and "worldly" institutions. Weber perceives conflict between the manner of thought and action enjoined by "brotherly" religion and those that characterize essentially every other domain of social life, including the economic, political, aesthetic, erotic, and intellectual spheres.[9] For Weber, Christianity puts one on the outside looking in, constantly at odds with worldly standards. And as noted earlier, Weber gives pride of place to the economic sphere as the domain in which tension with religion has been most obvious. Whereas the executives I spoke with use the Bible to validate their perceived callings to business, Weber's reading of the Bible led him to conclude that the only way to reconcile business and Christianity would be to violate the character of one or both.

In contrast to scholarly and popular perspectives that paint religion as a restrictive phenomenon, one of the most consistent themes put forth by sociologists of religion in recent years is the trend toward more flexible and personal interpretations and applications of religion. With the publication of *Habits of the Heart* in 1985, Robert Bellah and colleagues set off alarm bells regarding the apparent trend toward individualism as increasingly characteristic of American life, a theme picked up more recently by Putnam, among others.[10] In the sociology of religion, Wuthnow and Roof have elaborated the concept of spiritual seeking, and Roof has championed the idea of individualistic spirituality as paradigmatic of American religion.[11] More recently, Madsen contends that there is such a thing as "American religion" and that it is characterized, above all, by individualism.[12] Religion, on this account, has become a buffet of sorts, from which various beliefs and practices can be selected or passed over as tastes and circumstances dictate.

While this account, on the whole, may be overstated, there are some indications that evangelicalism has been affected by the trend toward individualism. For example, studies suggest an erosion of consensus among evangelicals on theological matters and moral and political issues, as well.[13] But in many ways evangelicalism has always been an individualistic religious tradition, encouraging spiritual improvisation such as personally interpreting Scripture or praying without liturgical language.[14] The doctrine of "the priesthood of the believer," denoting that all Christians have direct, unmediated access to God, encourages evangelicals to pray to and hear from God directly.[15] For evangelicals, faith is intensely personal, and the faithful are expected to personally appropriate and creatively apply their faith in all areas of their lives.

The business leaders I interviewed certainly demonstrated abundant idiosyncrasy in interpreting their callings and responsibilities in business. Nancy, for example, the fast food proprietor who experienced criticism for her career choices, states, "My biblical understanding is that your calling is between you and God. It's quite possible that you don't know my calling, and it's entirely possible that you might not understand my calling. I am not the judge of your calling, and I can't think of you as the judge of my calling."

When asked to express the purpose of business, Phillip, the executive who left the auto business for the family entertainment business, specifically distinguished between *the* purpose of business and *his* purpose in business. The purpose of business, according to Phillip, is to "create income, create jobs, and create a service that people feel a worthiness to pay for." At the same time, he explains, "My purpose at work is to show that God is at work in my life." This sense of personal calling gives evangelical executives considerable latitude to emphasize different contributions made by business to different groups of people.

Omni-valuation

In order to demonstrate the breadth of rationales employed by evangelical executives in asserting the sacred character of business and to contrast this approach with the idea that religion represents a distinctive, consistent, and competitive logic of action that is incompatible with a market orientation, I draw on Boltanski and Thevenot's taxonomy of competing evaluative principles.[16] Boltanski and Thevenot undertake to explain how people resolve circumstances in which they are challenged to justify their actions or intentions, as they are in the interviews I conducted. For these researchers, social life is best analyzed as a series of discrete situations in which individual actors negotiate agreements as to the course of action that is most likely to enhance the form of the common good that best fits the situation. During the course of such negotiations, individuals draw on six fundamental and mutually incompatible "orders of worth," each epitomized by a distinctive evaluative principle, form of evidence, characteristic relationship, and human qualification.

- In the *market world*, worth is expressed by price or wealth, as accrued through impersonal and dispassionate exchange.
- In the *inspired world*, worth is not earned, but conferred by grace and independent of recognition by others. Worthy persons in this world are spontaneous and creative, and produce objects of intrinsic value that resist traditional pricing and valuation.
- In the *domestic world*, worth hinges on one's position in hierarchically arranged personal relationships, as often characterize family dynamics. Worthy beings embrace their role, be it authoritative or subservient, and faithfully discharge their responsibilities to those to whom they are personally connected.
- In the *civic world*, worth inheres in collectivities, while individuals are devalued as such. The worthy eschew self-interest and personal attachments in favor of communal goods, inciting others to collective action.
- In the *world of opinion*, people and things are deemed worthy by virtue of the quantity of attention they command, irrespective of their merit or affiliation.
- In the *industrial world*, worth is based on productivity, as generated by professional competence and measured by statistics that capture dispensations of time and energy.

According to Boltanski and Thevenot, these six orders of worth, though not necessarily exhaustive, "are sufficient to describe justifications performed in the majority of ordinary situations."[17] While their research, based on textual analysis, does not indisputably demonstrate such comprehensiveness, the analysis that follows does not depend on it. I use Boltanski and Thevenot's systematization as a heuristic device, looking for at least rough correspondence with their proposed categories. The point is not to validate their typology, but to demonstrate that evangelical executives use a variety of apparently incompatible evaluative principles to motivate and justify their vocational choices.

Although logically each of the six principles of worth is incompatible with all of the others, some pairs are nonetheless more antagonistic than others. The industrial world, wherein efficiency is valued, can be straightforwardly, though not inevitably, shown to be in service of the market principle of worth, and it is thus no surprise that the industrial principle also holds some sway in commercial contexts. The other principles of worth are considerably less compatible with the market world of worth. Consider the following corporate activities: donating products and services to the less fortunate (civic); producing custom, one-off products that express the artistic creativity of the producers (inspired); indulging nepotistic hiring practices (domestic); and advertising indiscriminately across market segments (opinion). Each of these would, under most circumstances, pose a challenge to the market-oriented order of worth. Yet, as the following examples demonstrate, to designate what really matters in business, evangelical executives draw not just on the market principle that has been shown to dominate corporate affairs,[18] but also on those principles of worth that stand in contrast to this orienting principle. These various justifications are in turn supported by appeal to Scripture-informed concepts that are consonant with the particular principle of worth invoked.

The Market World of Worth

"I spoke at a theological school one time," recalled the former head of a prominent consulting firm, and I said, "My calling is to create wealth!" And somebody said, "What a terrible idea!" And I said, "Otherwise we wouldn't be meeting in this lovely building today. We would be meeting in a tent, if we were able to afford a tent." I said, "How do you think you're in this building? How do you think the Chair that teaches you was created? Because somebody created wealth." And I said, "What we do is by creating wealth, we raise the whole standard of living of humankind."

The market world of worth is oriented to wealth, both individual and corporate, and is measured in such terms. And as we have seen, the evangelical perspective on wealth is complicated. Wealth accumulation is sometimes regarded as unbecoming or immoral in conservative Protestant religious instruction, depressing the incentive to pursue lucrative careers and engage in disciplined investment strategies and contributing to relative asset poverty among conservative Protestants.[19] Generally speaking, the evangelical executives I spoke with, like the consulting executive quoted above, exhibited few such qualms. Nancy, for example, in defending the profit-orientation of business, stated, "I believe somebody has to create wealth. So the idea that God might have made some enterprise to create wealth makes sense to me." Another executive located wealth creation among God's fundamental purposes. "God has called us to create wealth," he said. "That's sort of the creation mandate. He's created us as workers, or in his image as entrepreneurs."

The spiritual justification for wealth creation emboldened a few informants to measure their own worth by their wealth. "I had established two lifetime goals that had to do with money, two that had to do with family, and two that had to do with personal things," recalled a former media company executive. "The first that had to do with money was to make a fixed net worth in my lifetime. It was a big number." More than one executive expressed the intent to, as one put it, "earn as much as I can and give it all away."

While some of the executives I interviewed assessed their own worth by their wealth, others evaluated the worth of their firms by the wealth they created for others. "Increasing shareholder value is what God wants us to do," insisted a former CEO who owns and operates a firm that advises current CEOs. "The Parable of the Talents is a perfect example," he said. "Someone gives you a dollar—he wants you to do something with it. He wants you to at least return that dollar with a little extra change. So to me, it's wonderful." The Parable of the Talents, attributed to Jesus in two of the canonical Gospels, tells of a master who, before departing for travel, entrusted his property to three servants, allocating to each an amount commensurate with his ability. Upon his return, the master rewarded two servants who had doubled the value of the property with which they were entrusted, but severely reproved the third servant, who had buried his "talent" so as to preclude its loss. It is most unlikely that this parable has anything to do with business. As commentators observe, the parable is one of several in the gospels that urge an appropriate response to the spiritual message Jesus preached.[20] Nevertheless, from this account, among others, some evangelical executives derive the concept of stewardship, according to which Christians are encouraged to view their resources and abilities as belonging to God and to be used in God's service. Combined with the sentiment, attributed to King David in the Psalms, that "the earth is the Lord's and everything in it, the world, and all who live in it,"[21] some evangelical executives equate stewardship of God's resources with maximization of shareholder returns. As one CEO puts it, "Work is managing God's resources His way. That description of work has been really compelling for me. Thinking about the idea that all the resources that I have at my disposal as a leader—in my worldview those are God's resources. Thinking about being a steward of those resources and then managing them in a way that would be God-honoring is pretty powerful for me."

That the capital entrusted to evangelical executives actually belongs to God would likely be a surprise to many shareholders, and perhaps even a source of alarm. According to the founder of an investment firm, "You might learn at Harvard Business School that we exist at the pleasure of our shareholders and for their benefit. To a certain degree, and in a legal sense, that's true. But the spiritual aspect of this is you can just throw all that away and cut to the chase. And the cutting to the chase is that this company exists at the pleasure of God and he can wipe it out any moment he wants to. When I gave my life to God, I became a manager. I'm a steward now. I'm squat. So that completely reframes what I'm doing and how I think about it."

Whether on this basis shareholders have any reason to be concerned is far from clear, as this company founder boasted that adherence to biblical principles had actually enhanced investor returns in both good times and bad. Most informants interpret the biblical stewardship mandate not as challenging, but rather supporting traditional understandings of the purpose of business. According to an energy company CFO, "In the end, this business is about profit. It's making money. It's a stewardship; we at the leadership of the business have a stewardship to take the assets that our stakeholders provide to us and give them the best return that we can for their investment. I think that's biblical." For this executive, increasing profits constitutes biblical business. In support of this perspective, he, too, cites the Parable of the Talents. "I think the Parable of the Talents probably is the passage that's most key. In my view, everything is owned by God. This business is God's. Even though we may not acknowledge it, day in and day out it doesn't exist without God's providence. One of those tasks I'm given as CFO is to manage the resources of this organization the very best I can and generate the very best return that I can. It ain't about me; it's about those others whom I serve. I see it holistically, I guess, and I feel the Parable of the Talents supports that."

As these remarks suggest, the concept of stewardship supports the market world of worth and generally blunts any inclination to engage in anything that might diminish shareholder returns. Still discussing the implications of an orientation to stewardship, the same CFO recalls, "In the Gulf Wars this company supported the military. One of the contracts that the company had was the support of the ground forces on the ground in Iraq. There were a lot of people who were antiwar, saying it's wrong, it's ethically not right for you to do this, and you are earning a profit on the war effort and war profiteering. It was a 2 percent profit on the work we did; it was very inconsequential. My view is: wait a second, I have this obligation to our shareholders. They are investing the resources to do this. The government has asked us to support the troops. I don't think that our moral obligation extended to say we're not going to do that because we are antiwar."

The Inspired World of Worth

In the inspired world, worth is not earned, but conferred by grace and independent of recognition by others. Worthy persons in this world are spontaneous and creative and produce objects of intrinsic value that resist traditional pricing and valuation.

For several informants, the creative dimension of the inspired world of worth was particularly important. For some, in fact, creation is a fundamental metaphor for work. As one venture capitalist stated, "A good theology of work starts with a fundamental understanding of the creation mandate and our invitation to participate in creation and how that rolls through every moment of our lives that we have here on earth. It's just a whole different mindset that you have in terms of approaching life as a co-creator.' " "Venture capital is a marvelous profession in terms of creativity," he explained, "of the creation of value, the creation of workplaces, of new technologies that make the world better—that make people's lives better. If our mandate is to bring order to the universe, to bring order out of entropy and to bring it all under the crown of the Lord, then any work that we do that brings about that order—that brings about the creation of value including eternal value—is a useful pursuit in and of itself." Put simply by a junior executive at a software company, "I believe our God is a creative God and a God of creation, and that business is an outlet for creativity."

Sometimes informants applied their appreciation for the creative dimension of business to their personal sense of motivation and worth. One entrepreneur, commenting on the nature of success, confided, "I mean, what's success? Monetary success, fame, status? I don't think that ever interested me as much as maybe other people. Money's probably a secondary driver for me. I think it's just the idea of creating something new. I think that intrigues me more, whether it's starting up a company or nonprofits. I think that has always sort of driven me." Another technology company CEO described the experience of writing his first computer program as "an 'aha moment' where I felt like it was almost like creating something *ex nihilo*—out of nothing. It was a sense of feeling like this is what I was created to do." While the Latin phrase *ex nihilo* does not appear in Scripture, it is often used by evangelicals to designate the fact that God is the only creator of the universe and that he alone is eternal.[22] For this CEO, the fact that writing a computer program is in some sense participating in "God-like" activity supports the spiritual value of his work.

The Civic World of Worth

The civic principle of worth is outwardly oriented, awarding value to the broader collectivity and emphasizing solidarity with those not necessarily associated with one's own interests or those of one's immediate group or company. Emphasis in the civic world is on responsibilities to unidentified, impersonal others.

Here again, informants provided theological justification for this orientation and also concrete examples of its implementation. "I think this Hebrew notion, *shalom*, or the common good—part of our job as business people is to be concerned not only narrowly about our specific activity—of course that's what we're focused on, but somehow it contributes to a larger purpose and part of that purpose is for that larger community that we're a part of," explained one CEO. "I think every company perhaps needs to find its own identity and place in the common community and society." For this executive, contributing to *shalom* means looking for ways to cooperate instead of compete, even when such cooperation might impair financial performance. "One of the things that I've been wrestling with in our business context," he said, "is that we exist in an ecosystem with various software vendors who compete with us, and the obvious strategy is to say, 'We're going to beat them. We're going to be the best at this. We're going to beat them at their game.' That's sort of the traditional model of competition. But I think at least for me, I've been challenged recently to ask, 'Are there ways to cooperate?' We actually had some conversations with another company and basically said, 'The need is so great in the world. I mean, we could compete directly but maybe there is a way to cooperate technologically rather than duplicate each other's work and waste scarce resources on something that we could be better off cooperating on.'" Acknowledging the discrepancy between this type of relationship and the standard market approach, the CEO explained, "I think the hard part of trying to think larger and perhaps more Christianly is that the common good might lead you some place that self-interest might not."

A number of evangelical business leaders cited human flourishing as a key objective of their firms. Sometimes, this was focused internally on employee well-being; other times it was oriented toward the community. "At this company we are trying to promote human flourishing through our product," explained a serial entrepreneur. "We don't believe sickness and disease are a part of God's best for people and they derail people from accomplishing their vocation as well as the larger purposes for life."

While this executive highlighted a deliberate effort to enhance the lives of those to whom he and his employees have no direct connection, others emphasize the incidental diffusion of benefit as profit trickles down to multiple outsiders. "By producing a profit you have provided all kinds of goods and services to many people," explained the founder of a business advisory firm. "You've helped society by virtue of doing that. You provided a job for [someone] in your factory and [that person] can go get a haircut. You provided for a beautician and a waitress. Isn't that kind of wonderful?"

The Domestic World of Worth

If informants at times emphasized impartiality and impersonal relations such as characterize the civic world of worth, they generally placed even greater emphasis on the domestic world of worth, which is attuned to particular individuals as distinct centers of value. In the domestic world, personal relationships matter. Informants consistently highlighted the personal nature of their attempts to incorporate their faith at work, citing concrete examples of their and their companies' impact on particular individuals.

Informants regularly emphasized family responsibilities. The managing director of a financial products company confided, "Our definition of success is extremely different in that we have a huge desire to have people maintain balance, and so by and large, our people can work fifty hours a week. We clearly state that if you go outside the fifty hours that we recommend you work, then you sort of discount your successfulness in that week. We measure marriages, and families, and children's growth, and physical fitness, and spiritual growth, and mental development, and community involvement." This executive takes time to meet with employees' spouses to discuss his desire for them to experience a balanced life and healthy relationships. Another executive enacted significant family-friendly policies at a major consulting firm, allowing consultants, for whom the consulting lifestyle can take a severe toll on their home life, to work nine months a year or four days a week for reduced compensation. Another executive recalled hearing an employee recount the way his work life had positively influenced his home life. As the executive tells it, he and a group of team members had taken a prospective hire out for dinner when one of his colleagues said to the prospective employee, "I've got to tell you—these values, they don't just work at work; they work at home! A couple of months ago I went home to my wife and I said, 'Honey, we're trying to honor each other more at work, and I realize I could probably do a better job of honoring you at home, and I'm going to work on that.' I've got to tell you, it has changed my relationship with my wife." According to the executive who observed this conversation, "I sat there at that table, and I started weeping that night, because it was one of the first times that God so clearly opened up my eyes to the fact that how we choose to live and act as leaders makes a difference in the lives around us, and not just their lives, but the lives of the people that they touch, too."

Sometimes informants apply family-oriented metaphors to their firms, as when the former head of a global consulting firm referred to employees as his "children." The owner of a contracting company with about forty employees, having specifically described his firm as a family, became emotional when recalling the contributions of a former employee. "My chief engineer walked in one day in this room and said, 'Well, I've got ALS, Lou Gehrig's disease.' I said, 'What are you going to do?' He said, 'Well, I don't want to travel or anything. I just love working on this stuff.' So I said, 'Well, what if we try to make your strengths productive and your weaknesses irrelevant.' So he worked for another three years. He passed away this last year. But at the end he was getting up at three o'clock in the morning to come to work by 8, and up to 11 getting into bed at night. We hired his wife as his personal assistant so she could be with him during the day when he was totally paralyzed and confined to his wheelchair, and he worked up until the month of his death. That's the kind of family . . . I mean, that tells more about us than lots of things that I could say or are in the brochure."

The Opinion World of Worth

The world of opinion, or fame, is difficult to reconcile with the oft-cited sentiment that "It's not about me." Nevertheless, informants sometimes appealed to reputation-oriented principles of worth, generally for instrumental purposes but sometimes as explicit claims to worth on account of recognition.

A number of informants referred to business in general, or to their standing in business and the associated reputation, as a platform through which to accomplish meaningful objectives. Drawing on the Sermon on the Mount, during which Jesus said, "Let your light shine before others, that they may see your good deeds and glorify your Father in heaven," the managing partner of an executive search firm stated, "I think that there is an element of business that clearly is meant to be a platform from which we can let our light shine."[23] The marketing director of a food service company concurs: "I believe that business, like any organization, is a platform to reach people; it's just about what platform you're going to reach. My pastor believes that business gives you the platform to reach people that church will never reach, because church in and of itself is a barrier for some people."

On this logic, it makes sense to draw attention to yourself or your company in order to broaden your platform, and in fact several informants were strategic in this regard. "I started working on a fifty-year plan when I was in Vietnam in 1970," explained the founder of a commercial real estate firm. The fifty-year plan basically had three phases to it. The first phase was twenty-five years of education and military, and whatever else I needed to do, which I had just completed. So then I was looking at fifty years beyond that, and I divided that into two phases. The second phase was twenty-five years to build a business and the third phase was twenty-five years to give back to the community. I've always thought of my life in terms of those three phases: preparation, platform, and patron. I started the business with the idea that I was doing it in part to create a platform to make a difference." Another company founder, this time in the retail real estate business, despite not necessarily wanting the attention, ultimately chose to use his last name for the company moniker, realizing that "the name which I originally thought was neat, then wished had been replaced, has now become a platform and an attribute which allows me to reach and impact people that I would not otherwise be able to reach." One former CEO, proud of his current initiatives in the community, acknowledged, "If you want to do something like I've done, you've got years of hard work to build up where you have a platform that you can begin to do any of the kinds of things I've tried to do." Other retirees lamented the loss of status, recognition, and influence associated with their professional standing.

While most were more subtle, a few of those I interviewed boasted of their reputations. "I am considered an icon in this business," said one, "a big frog in a small puddle." After recounting several of his professional accomplishments, another declared, "If you think I'm bragging, I am. You probably Googled me, and I was elected by my peers, my competition, as the [top recruiter in the United States]. I'm proud of what I did, and I'm proud of the people that I've gotten to know." The same executive boasted, "I could talk to anybody. I could get anybody. Consequently, I have a Rolodex that you would kill for, that anybody would kill for. Name it, and I've known them." Another executive, describing his personal network, offered, "I think I could sit down and name, without stopping, five thousand people."

The Industrial World of Worth

In the industrial world, worth is oriented to productivity, and the focus is on the work process itself. Several executives specifically affirmed the idea that work itself is God-ordained. The retired CEO of a prominent real estate firm related, "One thing I was astonished at, that I should've known reading the Bible, was that there was work in the garden of Eden. There was work before the Fall. Work is no curse. It may have gotten harder. Conditions may have gotten tougher. But there was work before the Fall. I think it's in the Book of John where Jesus said—it haunted me when I read it—He said, 'My father is working, and I am working also.' So, I think there's a nobility to work. Work is good. You may not like what you're doing right now. It doesn't matter whether you like it or not. You may find your passion later in your life, but go get the skill set. Go do some good where you are. Learn a craft. Learn a profession. Help build up." These comments, posed as advice to aspiring executives, are consistent with the industrial world of worth. Essentially, this executive encourages up-and-comers to be skillful and productive. Nancy, the restaurant chain CEO we met earlier, believes that people will work in heaven despite the presumed absence of scarcity. "I'm kind of excited about the fact that there's a role and a responsibility in heaven," she stated.

The idea that work has intrinsic value encourages some evangelical executives to couch their personal worth in terms of their productive capacity. Several decried retirement as unspiritual and contrary to God's purposes. Nancy, for one, insists, "Retirement's not in the Bible. It's not there. Nobody retires in the Bible. So it's a question of how you're going to apply the gifts you've been given for as long as you get to apply them in this world." Similarly, another executive asserted, "I don't believe in retirement. You will not find it in Scripture. I think it's extraordinarily boring. I had a period after selling a business and for about two years I had nothing to do. I was just about ready to be killed or kill somebody. I will put it this way: I want to burn out rather than rust out in the end. So if it's not this company then it's going to be something involved in the business world and it's going to be something similar—building a for-profit business with a very clear purpose of solving and helping solve social issues."

An Easily Satisfied Criterion

Stewardship, creation, *shalom*, light—evangelical executives draw on these and other biblical concepts and metaphors when expounding the spiritual value of business. In so doing, they utilize each of the various orders of worth Boltanski and Thevenot propose as characteristic of social life. According to Boltanski and Thevenot, the various worlds of worth are incompatible. In particular, the tension between the market world of worth—oriented as it is toward self-centered material interests—and those principles of worth that accommodate more transcendent and other-regarding concerns, is profound. But informants' accounts suggest that the dispositions and cultural tools evangelical executives bring to their professional roles enable what I call "omni-valuation"—the use of multiple principles of worth in defending the sacred value of their occupational roles and the business decisions they make therein. Rather than imposing a consistent set of principles, as some theorists insist,[24] evangelical Christianity endorses a host of competing evaluative standards. While other institutions vie for primacy and influence by infiltrating other domains with their characteristic principles of worth, religion in this case expands its scope by sacralizing multiple forms of worth. It trades, in effect, distinctiveness and coherence for relevance.

Crucially, the executives with whom I spoke do not attempt to be all things to all people. Fast food may be unhealthy, but restaurants provide community and character development. Wall Street may not mitigate global warming, but it does raise living standards. One executive emphasizes the products and services a company produces; another emphasizes the way products and services are produced or the economic value they generate. On the basis of their reflections, it appears that in order for evangelical executives to consider business sacred, all that is required is that *some* aspect of business contributes to *some* spiritual objective for *some* group of people.

Practically, this affords evangelical business leaders abundant flexibility to uphold the spiritual value of business in a variety of contexts, supported by all manner of rhetorical devices and forms of evidence. Without such flexibility, we might wonder whether informants could embrace their professional roles with such vigor and enthusiasm, for the scripts that work for a principal in a small venture capital firm, for example, might prove less helpful for the head of an international consulting firm, who is accountable to a broader set of partners. As it is, evangelical executives in all types of companies can find and provide evidence of the spiritual value of their work.

In the previous chapter we explored the evidence evangelical business leaders provide that God is present and active in business, namely that he ensures that moral order is upheld. We also saw that proponents of corporate social responsibility, among others, have in various ways attempted to expand the responsibilities of businesses. Indeed, corporations today are pressed from every side. Fickle investors, obsessed with quarterly earnings reports and desensitized by the irrational exuberance of the internet boom, have come to expect perpetual growth and share-price appreciation. Policy makers, following the near collapse of the global financial system in 2008 and the consequent Great Recession, push for tighter regulation of financial markets and reduced managerial discretion. Activists, citing events like the explosion of the Deepwater Horizon, add mounting social demands to the financial obligations corporations already face. Even within corporations themselves, employees increasingly expect from their work not just financial security, but emotional integration and existential fulfillment. If in the past managers could keep their heads down and focus on maximizing shareholder value, today they must attend to a range of diverse interests.

From a practical standpoint, balancing competing interests represents a considerable challenge for executives today. But for the evangelical executives I interviewed, the interests of various stakeholders also present an array of possible contributions on which to base the spiritual value of business. As the previous examples show, they are equipped with an equally expansive set of religious scripts and motifs that portray the satisfaction of such interests as religious responsibilities. Trends in the character of American religion, along with durable features of evangelicalism in particular, make it relatively easy to find some spiritual purpose to which business contributes. And the competing demands of multiple stakeholders, far from being a moral dilemma, is a moral "out" for any circumstance. Whatever order of worth is utilized, someone always benefits.

The particular group that is understood to benefit depends on professional context and personal disposition, sense of calling, and proximity to particular constituents, which facilitates personal interaction and anecdotes. Ultimately, as related in interviews, articulated callings hinge largely on what types of stories evangelical executives can tell. Considering the variety of spiritual purposes conveyed, it is clear that a full buffet of legitimating narratives is available.

Disruptive Possibilities

Later we will explore evangelical executives' aspirations for impacting their companies and the business world more generally. For the moment I wish to observe that informants' propensity for omni-valuation yields possibilities for incidental influence in the business world, irrespective of informants' intentions.

Some scholars have argued that when it comes to transforming institutions, intentional efforts are less likely to engender change than the typically inadvertent intermixture of apparently discrepant categories and modes of evaluation. Stark, for example, has argued that the juxtaposition of multiple worlds of worth is key to institutional change.[25] Expressing similar ideas using a framework that emphasizes institutionally defined logics of action instead of the more transposable principles of worth, Friedland and Alford contend that episodes of institutional contradiction, prompted by the manipulation and reinterpretation of symbols and practices, are the means through which the institutional structure of society is transformed.[26] Along these lines, Espeland and Stevens assert that it is at the "borderlands between institutions" that claims about incommensurables are most likely to arise, generating the potential for new social categories and arrangements.[27] If these theorists are on the right track, evangelical executives may in fact be well positioned to catalyze change, even unwittingly.

Thinking back to Weber's thesis in *The Protestant Ethic*, when ascetic Protestants attempted to account for their divine standing by measuring their wealth, they committed a domain-violation, just as we saw informants do when, as omni-valuers, they employ discrepant forms of worth in justifying their professional pursuits and behavior. What was new about the phenomenon Weber identified, and what gave rise to new patterns of behavior and ultimately, new institutional arrangements, was the juxtaposition of elements from multiple worlds of worth. Individuals, whose worth hinged on the acceptance of divine grace, measured such worth by accrued wealth, thereby combining the evaluative principle of the inspired world with the evidence of worth associated with the market world. This juxtaposition inspired new strategies of action and, by virtue of the church's moral authority, afforded them the legitimacy that facilitated their widespread adoption.

Weber's analysis suggests that religion is capable of bringing together multiple worlds of worth and providing space for new combinations of apparently discordant elements from multiple value regimes. If so, rather than narrowing the scope of responsibility, as other institutions and principles of worth often do, religion expands it. Friedland and Alford rightly observe that religion is a totalizing institution, acknowledging that religious traditions seek to offer explanations of reality "within which all human activity takes place," thereby seeking influence in every social sphere.[28] It accomplishes this, I have suggested, at the cost of coherence and through the process of omni-valuation, whereby various principles of worth are given spiritual sanction. While omni-valuation compromises the coherence of systems of religious doctrine, this is not necessarily any impediment to its influence. Recall that, as Weber explains, the logical response to the doctrine of predestination is resignation to one's fate, the very opposite of what he observed in his analysis of religious history. Thus, religious beliefs prompted the psychological impulses that gave rise to the Protestant ethic and the spirit of capitalism, but neither were logical consequences of Calvinist doctrine. In fact, any contribution ascetic Protestantism made to the establishment of rational capitalism should be considered an unintended consequence.

Contemporary executives, meanwhile, consistently have occasion to arbitrate between competing principles of worth. Top executives are, moreover, regularly expected to provide public justifications for their decisions, and in making such justifications public, the justifications become available for repackaging and reuse by other individuals and coalitions in their organizations and the network of organizations in which they are situated. Thus, executives can contribute to institutional innovation in two ways: first, by combining elements from multiple worlds of worth; second, by publicly invoking and therefore legitimating various principles of worth, making them available to others for competition and recombination.

Against Boltanski and Thevenot, who attribute to agents by virtue of their common historical heritage a sort of omni-competence, wherein everyone is able to deploy any of the principles of worth in any context, Swidler helpfully explains that we must be facile with culture before we can use it.[29] Not everyone is adept with the concepts and terminology necessary to switch back and forth between various worlds of worth. As I suggested earlier, however, informants are, to borrow Weber's metaphor, "musical" in both the world of business and the world of religion, and are perceived as experts in both domains. As such, their capacity for innovation is significantly enhanced inasmuch as they are bricoleurs who creatively import and export symbols and practices from one institutional order to another.[30]

I argued earlier that the dispositions and cultural tools evangelical executives bring to their professional roles as a result of their faith commitments enable omni-valuation—the use of multiple worlds of worth in making and justifying business decisions. Now I add that this process holds the potential to catalyze institutional innovation. I suggest that evangelical Christianity in particular, as practiced by executives attempting to integrate their faith and their work, confounds tests of worth by attributing spiritual value to a variety of apparently discrepant temporal pursuits and objects. As such, it holds open possibilities for what Stark calls "creative friction" between different orders of worth, disrupting received categories and potentially introducing novel recombinations of ideas, practices, and resources.[31]

To be clear, I am not arguing that wherever there is an evangelical executive, there will be novel business practices. More modestly, I assert that the tendency toward omni-valuation among evangelical executives can produce unconventional attitudes and actions. From seeing customers as children of God, competitors as neighbors, employees as children, CEOs as servants, or organizational fields as mission fields, to measuring success in business by lives touched, adherence to values, or families strengthened, to attempting global change one person at a time, informants sometimes introduce unorthodox values, symbols, and metaphors in the business world, and these intrusions can give rise to unconventional business practices. Even so, given organizations' resistance to change, most new business practices are unlikely to take hold, and those that do are unlikely to be widely implemented.[32] But the greater the opportunity for innovation, as facilitated by omni-valuation, the greater the likelihood that new business practices will be generated, selected, and retained. Institutional innovation, like other aspects of social life, is probabilistic and evolutionary. Most mismatches are sterile, but some may prove fecund. For example, one CEO, referring to an employee-generated policy permitting employees to maintain full pay and benefits while they volunteer full-time at local nonprofits, said, "I'm happy to report that the idea that came out of our operations group was plagiarized by at least two local companies that I am aware of. One of them is a much larger, privately held organization."

Whether or not evangelical executives wish to challenge the fundamental orientation of the marketplace, religion has the potential to prompt institutional change in the business world, but its influence is not necessarily straightforward or intentional. Indeed, inasmuch as they are recombined and redistributed, the justifications of business that evangelical executives articulate could prove more fertile material for disruption than any explicit criticism they register.

* * *

It is ironic that Max Weber, who declined to define religion, attempted to distill Christianity to its doctrinal essence. What makes the Protestant Ethic thesis so provocative is the idea that the psychological incentives produced by a system of belief contributed to the spread of an economic system to which it is in principle opposed. But there is another possible interpretation of the purported relationship between Calvinism and rational capitalism— one that perhaps makes Weber's thesis less compelling even if it helps explain the dispositions of contemporary evangelical business leaders, namely that new theological expressions were devised to accommodate and legitimate changing commercial structures and interests. Indeed, evangelicalism is characterized by just such flexibility—flexibility that enables evangelical executives to place much more emphasis on those aspects of business they appreciate than on those they lament.

The comedian Cathy Ladman humorously expresses the common perception of religion as an apparatus of judgment, joking that "all religions are the same: religion is basically guilt, with different holidays."[33] Evangelicalism certainly fits the stereotype. Evangelicals are typically known for what they oppose, and not without justification.[34] For one thing, evangelicals are the most likely religious group to believe that other religious groups hold inferior values.[35] Evangelicals are also more likely than other religious groups to perceive God as authoritarian—a disposition that bears a strong correlation with disapproval of various behaviors and choices, including abortion and extramarital sex.[36] In business contexts in particular, evangelicals show heightened ethical sensitivity and greater reluctance to approve of morally questionable practices than other religious groups.[37] A scan of the headlines suggests that it does not take much to get evangelicals riled up. At the time of writing, for example, Baptists in the Carolinas are astir over the possible legalization of sports gambling, of all things.[38] Yet despite the evangelical propensity for disapprobation, the evangelical executives I interviewed are remarkably capable of affirming things, and specifically seek to avoid the impression that they stand in judgment of other people and practices. Given the apparent flexibility felt by evangelical executives to affirm the spiritual worth of business, we should steer clear of the misrepresentation of religion as an essentially regulative phenomenon, understanding that even as it forbids, religion also affirms.

4

Success to Significance

Equipped with a sacred text that represents a bountiful repository of legitimating scripts and illustrations, the evangelical executives with whom I spoke are stalwart defenders of business as a constructive and worthwhile enterprise that contributes to physical and spiritual well-being. At this point it is important to remember that the business leaders I interviewed are not representative of the broader population of evangelicals in business. Rather, they are those who, by dint of some combination of skill, drive, connection, luck, and circumstance, made their way to the top of the corporate hierarchy. In most cases we are hearing from informants at or near the apex of their career arcs, when their previous efforts have borne fruit and the perquisites of executive leadership are in full bloom. Inevitably, their perspectives on business are shaped by their accomplishments and the paths by which they arrived at their current positions. Indeed, as we shall see, many informants describe a profound and sometimes dramatic reorientation of perspective as they approach or reach their career summits.

Take Beverly, for example, a former division head and highest-ranking woman at one of the largest financial institutions in the world. "When I took over we were losing thirty million dollars a year," she recalled. "In three-and-a-half years with the management team we completely turned it around and were making one hundred twenty million dollars in profit. So the company was headed on a great path. My management team and I were celebrating at the Yale Club in New York and I was walking back to my apartment and literally when I was walking back I had this very strong emotional moment where I got back to my apartment and I was on my knees and I was like, 'You know, Lord, I know my life is out of balance and I realize now that there's got be more to life than this. My work is my life. I love it but I don't have any friends and I never see my family. I just had what was my greatest moment in my career and I'm disappointed. It's a big letdown.' It really was one of those things that I thought, 'Okay, I can't keep doing this. I have got to find a way to change things.' So the next day I got on a plane and flew to Florida and in the airport I picked up the book *Halftime*, and the thing that really resonated

Baptizing Business. Bradley C. Smith, Oxford University Press (2020). © Oxford University Press.
DOI: 10.1093/oso/9780190055776.001.0001

with me was, well, if you think of life as a football game that you play in two halves, you have the opportunity to be more strategic about how you play the second half. So when I got back to New York I got on a plane, took the red eye to London, and quit my job the next day."

Like many of those I interviewed, Beverly had long felt compelled to participate in ministry in some sense. "There was always a little nagging," she says. "Should I be doing something else? Should I really be a missionary or a pastor? And it always frustrated me." Like the executives in the previous chapter, Beverly looks for guidance from the Bible, which she sees as affirming business. "[The Apostle] Paul was a tentmaker, right? He had a business. He had a trade—a skill that allowed him to carry out his purpose and his mission," Beverly observes. Naturally, in the midst of her mid-career crisis, Beverly turned to Scripture and, after what she describes as the most intense period of Bible study she had ever undertaken, concluded, "You know what? God has given me the skills, the contacts, and the opportunities that I have had for a reason, and it would actually be a bad thing for me to walk away from all of those things and not use them somehow."

This is exactly the conclusion that Bob Buford, a fantastically successful cable television empire builder, endorses in *Halftime*, which, aside from the Bible and *The Purpose Driven Life*, is the resource cited most frequently by informants.[1] Part autobiography, part instruction manual, *Halftime* recounts Buford's transition from media mogul to social entrepreneur and philanthropist. It is a handbook for transitioning, as Buford phrases it, from success to significance.

Halftime urges successful businesspersons to channel their accumulated skills, connections, and wealth into ministry-oriented enterprises, and this is exactly what Beverly did. While she refers to leaving her former company as "retirement," Beverly subsequently founded and now runs what she calls an "impact investment company" that aims to "produce scalable solutions to help solve poverty." Still nowhere close to standard retirement age, Beverly now spends 60 to 70 hours per week providing opportunities for investors to "do well by doing good." Desiring that her new company be known as a "God-fearing business" but having chosen not to identify specifically as a faith-based company, the firm originally included among its stated beliefs the assertion that "faith in God gives meaning and purpose to life." The statement indicates for Beverly the "very strong Judeo-Christian values that drive who we are and what we do and how we treat people." It also generated a lot of discussion, she says, "not all of it good," and was at some point removed from the company's published materials. Whether explicitly faith-oriented or not, owning and controlling her new firm represents for Beverly a chance to enact her faith more meaningfully than she had during her "first half."

Mobility Reconsidered

Scholars and theologians have long posited an inverse relationship between wealth and religiosity, indicating that executives, most of whom are members of the so-called 1 percent, variously defined as the Americans with the highest income or most wealth, are likely to be less religious than the rest of the population. Sociologists, in fact, have usually depicted upward mobility as a secularizing force, and Berger has suggested more specifically that "the capacity of evangelicals to resist the forces of secularization stands in an inverse relation to their success in achieving education and social mobility."[2] Likewise Weber, in his analysis of the Calvinists who fanned the flames of rational capitalism, declared, "We find the most sincere followers of the Puritan spirit very frequently among those in the middle class who operated small businesses, among farmers and the *beati possidentes* [those in possession of salvation]—all of whom must be understood as having been at the beginning of an upwardly mobile journey. Yet we find that many in these groups were prepared quite frequently to betray the old ideals."[3] Weber observed, moreover, that "Puritan ideals of life failed to meet the challenge whenever the test—the 'temptations' of wealth (which were well known even to the Puritans themselves)—became too great."[4]

Contemporary survey data support the proposed relationship between wealth and religiosity. Americans who earn $100,000 or more per year are less than half as likely as other Americans to strongly agree and more than twice as likely as other Americans to strongly disagree with the statement, "God has a plan for me."[5] Likewise, high earners are considerably less likely than low earners to view their work as a mission from God or pursue excellence in work because of their faith.[6] These data support the account of religion as something that compensates for those things adherents lack, and that can safely be set aside once such things have been secured. For Beverly, however, and for many other informants as well, far from dampening religious enthusiasm, success actually catalyzes a deeper commitment to faithful living. For these, fame and fortune do not quench the appetite for spiritual things, but rather activate or intensify such longings.

A Tale of Two Halves

Beverly recognizes that the sacrifices associated with the pursuit of success caused her to miss out on some things of significance. While she is proud of her accomplishments, she acknowledges that they came at a price. It is this cost-benefit equation that Bob Buford explores in *Halftime*.

Buford's story is a compelling one; few have experienced the heights of success or depths of tragedy he has tasted. Buford's father died when he was in fifth grade, his mother perished in a hotel fire when he was thirty-one, and his only son, a young man of adventurous spirit and burgeoning business success, drowned in the Rio Grande in his twenties. Like many of the executives I interviewed, Buford, an evangelical executive himself, describes "a titanic, internal tug-of-war between leading a life of success in business and leading a life of service in ministry," claiming to have experienced a moment of "vocational transformation" in his teens that emboldened him to pursue business success with clean conscience and full enthusiasm.[7] "I somehow knew instantly that preaching, baptizing, marrying, and burying were out, and making money as a TV executive was in," he recalls.[8]

And make money he did. Buford's television network grew at an average rate of 25 percent per annum for three decades. He describes setting a goal to attain a certain net worth in his lifetime, comparing the target to a four-minute mile—that ambitious time achieved by only the most elite runners in the world. With this money, he planned to invest God's Kingdom and live on the interest. The interest, apparently, is more than enough to live comfortably. "Let me be honest about this," Buford writes. "I still have a penthouse in the city, a country home at the East Texas farm, and a new Lexus. I do not believe it is in keeping with my 'calling' to assume a diametrically different lifestyle from the one I have enjoyed throughout my life. Many people avoid taking the risk for a better second half because they mistakenly think it necessitates a drastic change. But I believe God gave me a gift to create wealth and enjoy its benefits."[9] When making the transition to his second half, Buford relates, "I was financially set for life and could afford some false starts."[10]

For Buford, the connection between success and significance is natural and the single-mindedness required to forge the success that leads to significance inescapable. "The first half of life," he says, "has to do with achieving and gaining, learning and earning."[11] This may not, he admits, leave much room for applying one's faith. "I think of the first half as a season in which to develop faith and learn more about the unique way the Bible approaches life.

The second half, when the pressure lets up, seems to be more the time when most people round second base and begin to *do* something about the faith they have developed," writes Buford, applying a sports metaphor inspired by his friend, Rick Warren, author of the abovementioned *Purpose Driven Life*.[12]

For those who, like many of the executives I interviewed, are inclined to participate in ministry and even torn between a calling to vocational ministry and a calling to business, having focused for an extended season on personal success to the point of marginalizing broader significance may prompt unease. This, Buford insists, must be set aside. "*Make peace*," he counsels. "Too many people approach the second half of their lives with regrets over the first half. ('I should have spent more time with my family.' 'I should have developed better relationships.' 'I should have . . .') One of the first things you need to do in halftime is make peace with your first-half set of issues. The key is to keep these things in perspective and accept them as an inevitable part of growth."[13] *Halftime* encourages evangelicals to pursue success, assuring them that the reward is worth the cost because the reward can be translated to significance.

Again, it is important to understand that the majority of the executives I spoke with—most of whom claim that their faith is essential to their work, perceive a connection between virtue and profit, and deploy Scripture in support of their assertion that business is a worthy spiritual vocation—are on the significance side of "halftime." I mean by this not simply that they are in the latter stages of their careers, but that their objectives and emphases have shifted over the course of their careers such that they now place more emphasis on and have more discretion to contribute to religious objectives inside and outside their companies than they did earlier in their careers. For many, the transition was intentional, for some abrupt, for others nearly imperceptible, and for a few quite dramatic. The former head of human resources at a Fortune 50 company, describing her decision to start her own company focused on producing "long-term, sustainable, positive change," recalls, "I actually had a real epiphany experience one Saturday morning where I woke up and heard a voice say, 'Time is running out' and then kind of blurred off. I drank my coffee and was getting ready to run my errands and noticed that one of my clocks had stopped, so I went to get batteries to replace it. As I went into another room, that clock had stopped. Basically, four battery-operated clocks at my house had stopped. So I got on my knees and said, 'I don't know what you are going to do with me, God, but I'm going to go [start this company].'"

Many others can identify a specific inflection point at which they began to think more seriously about contributing to religious objectives. Consider Robert, a homebuilder who points to a series of mid-career transitions that prompted a more serious faith. "One time in my mid-thirties I almost lost the entire company," Robert reflects, "and I kind of said, 'God, give me one more boom and I won't screw the next one up.' One of my greatest regrets during that time was that I had millions of dollars in my hands and no good came out of it. I was driving a BMW and bought a big house, but nothing of any substance had really happened with it. So I kind of had a realization that I wasn't really in it for the money. After I had made a lot then lost it and came back again—I had kind of been rich and poor and rich again—I realized that that really wasn't the driver of happiness, fulfillment, etc. So that's when I really started down the nonprofit track."

These days Robert allocates half of his time and income to charitable endeavors, the majority of which, he says, are Christian-focused. Like Beverly above, Robert attempts to apply his business experience in new ways. Across the organizations he supports, Robert draws on his own experience to build what he calls "competencies" in nonprofits, which include things like board recruitment and strategic planning. He says, "What I found is that the business acumen that helped the company grow can be used in the nonprofit sector as well. There are different boards and donors, etc., but a lot of the same business strategies will work." Having focused initially on local organizations, Robert and a couple of close friends who are Christians and business owners now spend a good portion of their second halves traveling around the world making "challenge grants" to nonprofit organizations.

Pursuing Success

Like many of the business leaders I interviewed, both Beverly and Robert admit that prior to making a conscious decision to reorient themselves to broader initiatives, they were less committed to acting on their faith, and in some ways out of balance when it came to their priorities. While Robert regrets that he did not put his newfound wealth to better use, Beverly believes she could have been more intentional about and visible with her faith. In fact, after spending a few years running a company that operates in accordance with her value system, Beverly now thinks that maybe she did not need to walk away from her former job after all. She reflects, "Only in the last couple of years I realized, 'Wow, actually now I feel like I could go back and do what I was doing,'" albeit apparently in more fulfilling fashion.

It is of course difficult to know if executives like Beverly and Robert would really do anything different if they were able to relive the past in light of their current convictions. When pressed on what she would do differently at her former job, Beverly responds, "This is probably the best example—my time with the Lord was always this thing that when I got too busy took the back seat. Now, it's the thing that overrides anything else." After detailing the value of her early morning devotionals, she realizes, "It's probably had more of an effect on me internally in how I manage stress than how I behave because I look back and go, 'You know what, I have pretty much always behaved a certain way in terms of how I treat people, how I make decisions, my sense of fairness, my sense right and wrong. Those things haven't changed. In fact, this is a perfect example; this is something that would have changed—I haven't always been present. What's interesting is most people would never know that, right? But I think I missed opportunities to be a true greatness to people because I wasn't always present—because I was always planning. I was always thinking ahead fifteen steps. So I would say that's probably the biggest thing that would change." Clearly, Beverly is not contemplating a wholesale reorientation or new approach to business, and she admits that from the outside nothing would really change at all. What seems to have happened is that, with some distance and in light of her newfound significance, she has become more comfortable with her previous circumstances and would now be better equipped to handle the associated stress. Now that she is immersed in her second half of significance, Beverly has, it seems, made peace with the difficulties associated with her first-half pursuit of success.

Like Beverly, many of those I interviewed experienced the rigors of climbing the corporate ladder. Most recall working sixty or more hours a week early in their careers, with some working up to ninety hours a week and a few claiming to have worked essentially all of their waking hours. "Success in the first place was just survival," explained the former CEO of a construction company. "I figured that you just get up every morning and you work as hard as you can." This CEO and many others traveled a lot and were frequently away from their families. Like Beverly, many acknowledge the difficulty of maintaining the quality of their relationships. Despite these difficulties, most articulate few or no regrets regarding the commitment required to reach their career goals, even if that commitment meant sacrificing relationships and objectives that are highly valued by evangelicals. For these executives, the cost of success is the price of significance. In fact, the cost to climb the corporate ladder represents for many informants a necessary and noble sacrifice, or at least a natural progression. Nancy, the restaurateur, contends, "It's absolutely predictable that people have a change of perspective in their mid-forties to early fifties, and it has everything to do with them waking up one day and saying, 'Oh my God, I'm not going to live forever.' Then you go, 'I'd better think about the significance of what I've been doing.'" "I don't have any regrets that I was kind of clueless in my twenties," Nancy insists. "We're all clueless in our twenties. Then we're really busy in our thirties, particularly if you decide to mix family in the equation. Then your first kind of opportunity to reflect is in your late forties. So that's what we do." For not focusing sooner on significance, Nancy and others make little or no apology. Some, in fact, specifically planned to defer significance until accumulating the requisite success. Recall, for example, the CEO who intentionally leveraged his business to build a platform to become a patron.

Unsurprisingly, those who plan for the transition from success to significance seem comfortable with the way their careers have unfolded, including the relative neglect of important things during the first half of their careers. The real estate CEO who thought of his life in three phases said of the second phase in which he strove to build up a platform through business success, "I think it costs you family time. I think it costs you personal time. My answer to [whether building up the company cost me something] is yes, but that was expected, because I don't think you can do Kingdom work—I don't think you can do something that's valuable without it costing you something. The question is, 'Was the cost worth it?' I think our family would say sometimes no, and sometimes we'd say yes. It has been a balancing act and it has not always been perfect. But in the end, I think you have to assume that it's going to cost you something in life. I think one of my concerns about people today is the first thing they say is, 'I don't want to pay that price.' I don't think we have an option on that. I think we have to pay the price of sacrifice in order to hold our society together and be a part of helping people flourish."

Whether contemplated as a precursor to significance or not, the pursuit of success seems to have preoccupied most of the evangelicals I spoke with until they fulfilled their professional aspirations. It is significant and typical that when Phillip, the CEO who left the automobile industry and its associated pressures, transitioned from what he called "to-do goals" to "to-be goals," he had already accomplished his to-do goals.

While some evangelical executives, like Phillip, identified times of disappointment or hardship as catalysts for increased emphasis on significance, such is not a prerequisite. What is a prerequisite, however, as the "success to significance" slogan implies, is success. Even if the transition from success to significance is associated with a personal crisis of some kind, it occurs much more frequently at a professional crest than a professional valley. For Beverly, for example, it was the emptiness she felt at the pinnacle of her career that prompted a search for deeper significance. Even those who long for significance early on cannot skip over the requisite success. Robert, for example, who now allocates half of his time and money to charity, claims to have contemplated being "fifty/fifty partners with God" since attending a mayor's prayer breakfast when he was twenty-one years old, but it was more than two decades before he put his plan into action. "After I reached some success in business and I was in my early forties," he recounts, "I decided it was time to start that process."

The evangelical business leaders I spoke with did not, in general, transition away from the dogged pursuit of success unless and until they achieved their own version of Buford's four-minute mile—a threshold of success that conferred professional and social standing and wealth of an order well beyond what most will ever realize. After attaining complete financial security, some evangelical executives became willing to entertain actions, positions, and strategies that would result in lower profits or personal compensation. For example, in the context of how he hopes his company will change the world, the founder of an online service provider stated flatly, "I don't care how much money we make. I mean, I've already got enough money." Others, however, would need to make still more to cross the threshold from a focus on success to a focus on significance. A senior real estate executive who renovates churches and orphanages on the side, when asked about his hopes for the future, stated that he'd like to do such renovations full-time. On why he chooses not to do so now, he replied, "Unfortunately, I've made a lot of money over a lot of years and built up a lifestyle that's expensive. To maintain my lifestyle costs more than one should reasonably expect from a charity. I haven't been able to convince my wife to downsize. She's gotten used to the princess package. It sounds like I'm blaming her, and I'm not. I love her a lot. But the reality is that every time we talk about it, she gets this haunted look in her eye like, 'Oh my God, he's finally going to do it!' So, I don't."

Most informants are, by virtue of their accomplishments, not just wealthy but well connected and well known. As a high-ranking officer at a publicly traded investment firm put it, "Sure, I live in a very high-flying set of folks, lots and lots of money and lots and lots of beautiful people and lots and lots of chance to be in the best places in the world." Some informants are on television regularly and many enjoy significant name recognition in their areas of business and beyond. Wealth of this magnitude and social standing of this order are generally reserved for the most prominent executives, and indeed those informants who were still professionally ascendant often aspired to the most influential corporate roles. For example, I spoke to several fabulously successful executives who still hoped to become CEOs someday. As one expressed, "I've been General Counsel. I've been CFO. I've been COO. And to be CEO and really kind of be 'the guy' is my next goal." Such aspirations typically dominated informants' agendas until achieved.

Defending Success

Even as they lament—but accept—the costs associated with success, the evangelicals I spoke with embraced and were prepared to defend the associated benefits, insisting that the resources and connections they accumulate are essential to the significance they desire. Few made any attempt to hide or apologize for their wealth or standing in their companies and communities, insisting that they are not preoccupied with such things and that they put them to good use.

Godly Wealth

Earlier we saw that one of the primary criticisms faced by evangelical business leaders is that the accumulation of wealth is immoral and likely hazardous to spiritual health. While the executives I spoke with did not call attention to their wealth, neither did they feel the need to hide or apologize for it. While describing how he takes wealthy associates on tours of impoverished portions of his city, an executive I met at his home remarked of his own residence, "As you can see, I don't sacrifice much." Indeed, I met several informants in their homes, which were invariably impressive structures in impeccable neighborhoods.

Although most informants evidenced little discomfort regarding their accumulated wealth, when questioned about their resources, most did wish to make clear that they put their resources to good use. The aforementioned executive, explaining his purchase of a private jet, noted, "I figured that having that jet got me home one more night a week, and that's really worth it. It costs a lot to fly in a private jet, but one night a week—I had five kids, so I figured, 'Hey, that's a good investment.'" The point of this observation, and many others like it, is that informants use their wealth to benefit others. The CFO of an energy company relates, "We have nice things and drive nice cars. My wife always drives a lot nicer car than I do because I like to buy her things. I love giving gifts to my wife. As an example, and as an executive, if you are using those nicer things for the benefit of others, it's not bad. Our home is an example. Other people have a security system; I've got one installed—never turn it on. I bet twenty-five people have a key to our house and they use it all the time. Every Tuesday night for the last five years we've had young married couples come to our house and my wife and I both teach Bible study and they have fellowship and we mentor those young couples in our home. If we had a smaller home, we could not do it. Some of those young couples have lived with us because they needed a place to live for a while. Some of them lived with us before they got married, so we keep bedrooms available for people to stay in. There was a couple who my wife met. She was working in development at [a university] and she got married and had a baby who had a hole in her heart. They were struggling, so we let them live with us while her baby had heart surgery and we provided their living expenses for almost a month. I have to treat this with loose hands—it's not mine—and allow others to enjoy it. We have a house out in the hill country and we regularly just let people go use it. 'Take a break; it's free; go do it; use this.' I feel like that's what we ought to do."

Some of the business leaders I spoke with do make a point to suggest that they sacrifice in some way in terms of consumption, albeit almost always relative to their wealthy peers. According to a real estate executive, "There's lots of things that we could do, but no, I don't need a private plane. I don't wear a Rolex. We were comparing watches this weekend at this wedding and I'm wearing a hundred-and-fifty-dollar watch and the guy across from me is wearing a twenty-thousand-dollar-watch. My wife drives a Prius and I drive a Lexus; my partners drive Mercedes. We sold this half-billion-dollar port-folio in 2005, and some of the junior partners and our president all went out and bought new Mercedes. My wife bought a $28,000 Prius. Just because you can, doesn't mean you should." Another executive, this one the CEO of a transportation company, acknowledged, "I have a nice home and a nice car and there are people in my town here that don't have enough. I'm not going to act like I don't know what's going on." Regarding his approach to handling his resources, he explains, "My family has recently finished a five-year working plan to challenge ourselves to be realistic about our giving and to make ourselves uncomfortable and to make sure that we prayerfully approach the things that we support and feel connected to those things so that we are helping in more than just a financial way." When asked in what ways his family has made themselves uncomfortable, he responds, "Well, I look at the holistic view of our family's situation and I try to think about—where would we not be able to do something we might like to do versus giving that money to someone who might need it more? Let's take it to a point of some sacrifice. How would you say that? That I don't replace my car every two years; I replace my car every three or four years. I don't buy my kids a brand-new car; I buy them a used car. I don't know exactly where you should draw the line on what's a real sacrifice or not."

Many pick up on Buford's theme of using wealth for influence. Said the retired president of a lumber company, "To condemn or put down people living in good surroundings and having some amount of material goods—I think that's very individualistic. I don't know where that simple lifestyle is, frankly. It could be, for some guy, sitting on a box in his living room and driving a twenty-year-old car and feeling really good about himself. He's living simply. He may not be having any influence, but he's living simply."

For several, the most important realm of influence for wealthy Christians like themselves is among the wealthy. According to Beverly, the financier we met at the beginning of the chapter, "I really do believe that people relate to other people who are like them and who enjoy the things they enjoy or can see the world the way they see the world. So luxury goods—for example, let's say a yacht. Non-believers are going to buy them anyway, being probably more driven by ego and other things to consume luxury goods, right? In order to reach those people other believers are going to have to play in that realm." Regarding his older-model Volvo, the cofounder of a beverage company acknowledges, "People could criticize my lifestyle, too." They could say, 'Why do you have a Volvo? Why don't you drive a Honda?' Because, quite frankly, I like my Volvo. They're safe. They meet what I call the 'minimum expectation.' Quite frankly, I couldn't pull up in a Honda in front of some of the buildings and go to some of the homes of some of the people that [I hope to work with] without making a statement that I don't want to make. Because I don't want to make a statement either way. I pull up in a Volvo, nobody even notices. I pull up in front of some of my friends and their Jettas are leaking, they don't notice it's a Volvo, because I'm not trying to make a statement.

I pull up with all of my friends and it's all Mercedes and Lexus and a few Bentleys, and nobody notices my Volvo. That's the whole point. I don't want my car to make a statement."

While the Bible contains a number of passages that commend the poor and disparage the rich, informants were adept at explaining such passages and redirecting to references that are more supportive of wealth. A real estate executive, commenting on Jesus' statement that "it is easier for a camel to go through the eye of a needle than for someone who is rich to enter the kingdom of God," retorted, "I think everybody always misuses that verse. Read a little further and it says, 'Who then can be saved?' and then 'With God all things are possible.' " Then the executive goes on the offensive. "If you read Job, he says God is walking around talking to the devil and he says, 'Look at Job, he's great, isn't he? Man, I love that guy; he just loves me.' Isn't that what God's doing? Is Job rich or poor? [Rich.] What about Abraham? [Rich.] That doesn't mean he loves all rich people, but he loves some that are rich. What does he say about David? [A man after his own heart.] Absolutely. And David was certainly wealthy. I think God loves rich people just as much as He loves poor people."

After declaring that the fundamental purpose of business is to meet basic material needs, Beverly turned to Scripture when asked about the value of luxury goods. "If you go back to the Bible, God didn't destroy cities because gold was bad or jewels were bad or any of that. There are examples where it says the people were worshipping the gold and the jewels and whatever, so God destroyed the city. It just means anything that people put before God, that's an idol that they worship. If somebody just idol-worships their mail and cannot do anything during the day until their mail comes and that completely dictates their personality, that's their idol, right? Well, then should we not make mailboxes?"

The CEO of a transportation company, deferring to others better versed in biblical interpretation, shared, "I've asked a lot of people that are more knowledgeable biblically than I am and the guidance I've been given is that God doesn't hate rich people. He doesn't look for us to surrender the things that we have. He's asking us to participate with him." One of the stories that comes to mind," he adds, "is the story of Mary pouring perfume on Jesus's feet. [One of the disciples said], 'We could have sold that and given the money to the poor.' [Jesus] is quick to correct and say, 'That's not always the answer.' I think for my family, our approach has been more about—where's our heart?"

In summary, informants are comfortable with their wealth, believing it to be spiritually neutral at worst and consistently pointing to the various worthy pursuits to which it can contribute. A retired commercial banking executive captured the prevailing sentiment, stating, "We need people who have wealth and who are generous. I hope more Christians get richer, who also live out their faith."

Exponential Influence

I noted earlier that few of the evangelical executives I interviewed transitioned from success to significance until they reached the pinnacle of their professions. In support of their lofty aspirations, some informants cited the difficulty of influencing firms and communities from anywhere but the top and emphasized the disproportionate influence that senior executives, and especially CEOs, have in comparison with other employees. The former head of human resources whose transition from success to significance was catalyzed by simultaneous clock stoppages explained, "Anyone can influence the culture, but things really change when the guys at the top change, which is part of why I started my firm. That's why I work [with people] at the top, because the amount of change—if they are willing to change—is tremendous."

The founder of an online service provider confided that raising venture financing initiated a process in which the evangelical Christian presence in his company was progressively eliminated. Consequently, he is now attempting to repurchase the firm he started. Having sought counsel from another of the evangelical executives I spoke with on what he might do or have done differently, he was told, "You need to make sure that you have a CEO who is a strong Christian person, and you need to have a board that's solidly Christian. You need to have ownership of your company in the hands of Christian people." For some informants, this is the only way to maintain a Christian ethos in a firm, which is for some a key to significance. Think back to Gary, the entrepreneur who told the story of the merchants in London, whose commitment to honest exchange caused them to prosper relative to their peers. When Gary was running a company, he claimed it had great success because it operated according to Christian principles. But when he didn't have complete control—as when his business partner misappropriated intellectual property, things didn't work out as well. And when he sold the company, everything fell apart.

The business leaders I spoke with regularly observed that their professional standing had opened up avenues for influence outside their companies. For example, the abovementioned executive who would spend all his time renovating churches and orphanages were it not for the associated lifestyle sacrifices also points out, in defense of his decision not to leave his current role, that the web of connections he relies on to finance charitable renovations is kept current by his professional associations. Robert, the homebuilder we met earlier in this chapter, reflecting on the thought process that went into a self-named company, confides, "For the first five years, I thought it was cool to see your name up on billboards and all of that. As I had kids and realized that they were laboring under the assumption of quote, unquote, a 'famous dad,' I found that people had certain expectations of me, which I might not be able to live up to. I looked hard at changing the name to Craftsman Homes, or some other name, because I really didn't want the nomenclature. Now, I realize that it's become an attribute which allows me to have access and a platform that I wouldn't have otherwise. When I was asked to come and speak to the mayor's prayer breakfast in front of two thousand people, I wouldn't have been asked to do that if I was just the president of Craftsman Homes." Summarizing the disposition to retain one's professional platform, a real estate executive explained, "I decided to keep one foot in corporate America because that's how your phone call gets returned. I stayed on as chairman because people will return your phone call faster if you're [name], chairman of [company], than if you're [name], social justice do-gooder."

Leveraging Success

Whether or not they explicitly acknowledge the success-to-significance paradigm and regardless of the nature and timing of their transition from success to significance, those evangelical executives who reach their professional and financial objectives are not content simply to continue building a larger fortune or indulging new hobbies, substantially all devoting significant time and resources toward objectives they consider significant.

For many evangelical executives, the transition from success to significance involves a transition to a new work context in which they have more discretion to contribute to spiritual objectives in or through their companies. We have seen that this was the case for Phillip, who left the ultra-competitive automobile industry for a more influential role in a more accommodating family entertainment company, and for Beverly, who left a financial powerhouse to start an impact investing company. Many others did likewise. These leveraged the skills, experience, and resources accumulated in the first half of their careers to advance what they considered to be objectives of significance in new professional contexts. Others, including primarily those who had reached the very top of their organizations, chose to remain in those organizations, applying their faith more deliberately in those organizations and/or focusing their attempts at significance in their communities.

Many of the evangelical executives I interviewed are heavily involved in community-oriented and charitable projects. For example, the abovementioned executive who mingles with beautiful people in beautiful places relates an incredible array of impactful activities. He recently purchased a piece of property on which he is developing a retreat center that will serve as an artists' colony for Christians in the creative arts. With a filmmaker friend he is making a movie version of an acclaimed novel by a Catholic writer. He serves as a director of several organizations, including a national Christian ministry organization and a state-level organization that supports families of service members. On the political front, at the time of our conversation he was underwriting, in association with prominent think tanks, a policy piece on federalism and healthcare reform, and also working closely with a politician to, as he describes it, "make him the next president of the United States." He is perhaps most proud of the foundation he established to encourage families, including and initially, his own, to serve together. Now a national nonprofit organization, the organization connects and provides wholesome resources for families around the world. As he explains, "If a family plants small seeds—whether it's effort, compassion, or just time—the results might grow to benefit many." This executive exercises profound influence across the cultural, service, and political landscapes. He, like many informants, has parlayed success in the business world into significance beyond it.

While this executive surely has his hands in more initiatives than most, his concern to make a broader impact is typical. Almost all informants donate to various causes—some, but not all, explicitly faith-based—and the great majority give of their time as well. Most also serve on the boards of nonprofit organizations, some in very high-profile roles. While I did not ask informants to disclose the percentage of their income that they give away, two informants volunteered that they give away half of their income. And several have established foundations oriented toward community initiatives, academia, or ministry activities.

As these examples suggest, informants are committed to leveraging their influence and resources for the benefit of their communities and favored causes, and just as Buford suggests in *Halftime*, are quick to point out that the connections, resources, and opportunities derived from their success in business have opened up substantial opportunities for significance. For the most part, the significance informants now experience is a function of their platform and/or their wealth, both of which they claim to put to good use and without which they believe that their ability to pursue objectives of spiritual significance would be greatly diminished. All this makes it easier to justify their fame and fortune and the institutional contexts in which they have been secured.

An Elite Phenomenon

Because success is a prerequisite for the types of significance pursued by many of the business leaders I spoke with, the halftime transition is an elite phenomenon, available exclusively to those who have realized sufficient agency to set their own agenda and, at least to some extent, call their own shots. This agency is a function of having reached a degree of success that allows them to select into and out of almost any corporate environment they choose. Most informants have achieved professional success to the point that they have realized the majority of their career goals and are financially secure enough to expand their gaze to contemplate new priorities and forms of influence, inside and outside their organizations or in new organizations. To younger readers, Buford says, "If you are in your twenties, don't put this book where you won't be able to find it later."[14] Aspiring business leaders are counseled first to focus on reaching their own "four-minute mile," thereby acquiring the skills, connections, and resources that can eventually be translated to significance.

Not So Fast

It would be difficult to overstate the difference between the perspectives articulated by the evangelicals I spoke with who are still climbing the corporate ladder and those who have "arrived." Whereas those in the second half view their success as validation of their calling, early-career evangelical executives, in contrast, are far less convinced of the virtue-profit connection and doubtful of its relevance to their career trajectories. Kyle, the aspiring CEO we met at the outset, suggests, "Life isn't fair, because you think the good person will win out in the end. On this earth that just doesn't happen a lot. In business, you see people being promoted to pretty senior positions, especially in investment banks when people were really good traders but they're just total 'a-holes.' They just invoke their wrath on a lot of people that work for them. Everybody knows that they aren't good to work for but they keep getting promoted. It's like a minefield within a company. I see that with some of my classmates at Harvard Business School. Some of them are running six-billion-dollar businesses right now and they are a little bit more shady on the ethics. Definitely not people of faith. It's easy to do the whole comparison thing and go, 'Well, if I really have God's favor, then why am I not getting the benefit and why am I not CEO of every company right now?' The reality is that in a broken, fallen world full of sin, it just doesn't work that way."

Just as do those who endorse the virtue-profit connection, Kyle appeals to the Bible when arguing against it. "When you read Paul's letters about some of the challenges that he went through, and you read in Hebrews about people who are examples of faith and they didn't even end up getting a lot of what they had prayed about, in the end, you're just like, 'Man. . . .' Even Job's story where he was a man that had lost everything he had; the end thing is that Jesus is not Santa Claus and just because you pray about something doesn't mean He shows up on Sunday or on Christmas day and gives you whatever you want. It's more complex than that and it doesn't always happen, and sometimes that's for our own character development. I think that's the hardest part about it. It's not the wealth and prosperity gospel that a lot of people are hearing today; it's a lot of challenges and a lot of seven years in the desert when you make the choice to be a man or woman of God. It's not all rosy and, to me, that's the hardest part about it. If you make more compromised choices, in a lot of ways, it would be easier." As Kyle's remarks show, the breadth of content in the Bible is sufficient to make sense of both success and lack of the same.

Part of the frustration voiced by some of the younger executives I interviewed has to do with the difficulty of enacting their faith at work. Some, in fact, have been chastened by the recalcitrance of large organizations. As a program manager in a software company describes, "Initially, I was very frustrated thinking I'm here to see the entire company transformed and a huge revival and I would host prayer meetings every week. Then I realized that a lot of the reason I'm here is for God to discipline me and for God to break me free of a lot of fear." This aspiring executive's perspective on her purpose at work quickly shifted from an external orientation in which she would transform the corporate culture to a much more modest, internal orientation in which she was the one to be transformed.

Of the difficulty associated with living out his faith at the same technology company, a junior executive says, "It's brought a cost in terms of my career and in terms of acceptance from people around here." On the nature of these costs, he explains, "It's hard to say because no one is going to tell me, 'We're not promoting you because you're a right-wing Christian.' No one's going to say that. So I don't know whether it's psychological or it's actual, but it seems like it's actual. I let people know where I stand, in a rather public way, by starting a Bible study. Lots of people do extracurricular things at this company. There's all sorts of activities other people can do and no one criticizes the yoga people or any of the other groups that I'm aware of. But I've noticed that people kind of scowl at the whole idea of a Christian Bible study. I've noticed a difference in the way people interact with me after they know that I'm a Christian. I don't think that I'm imagining these things. I just think people around here are generally pretty hostile to Christianity, and that's just kind of how it is with a lot of people. You just deal with it—try and be gentle."

For the ascendant executives I interviewed, success is anything but assured, and the price of success possibly not worth the cost. Like some other ascending business leaders, Audra is not convinced of the connection between virtue and profit or success. On her career trajectory to date, she confides, "I know that I've been tremendously blessed, but I don't know if that's because of my faith." Acknowledging that were she not born into a family that provided her with abundant opportunities, she realizes that her life could have been much different. "Every time something wonderful happens to me, I do say, 'That was divine. That was God putting me at the right place at the right time.' But does that mean that people who have hardships, who have had tragedies in their lives—does that mean that God put them in the wrong place at the wrong time? That's something that I struggle with."

Audra also struggles with the way her company does business. Ostensibly her job is perfect for her, and she acknowledges that it's the type of executive position for which others would cut off their arm. But it doesn't feel right anymore. The company's stated mission hasn't changed—like others of its kind, it provides mainstream financial services to the underbanked—and she continues to believe that this is vital work. It is a perfect fit with the most salient

aspects of her identity—as a person of faith and an immigrant, it is important to Audra to do work that improves the lives of the underprivileged. She
thought this would be the ideal place to do good by doing well. But now she's
not so sure. In fact, she's come to believe that the company's social mission
can be better addressed by nonprofit organizations in concert with government resources.

With an MBA from Harvard, Audra has long understood that the corporate world can be coldly calculating, but she had hoped there were exceptions.
She suspects, though, that the competitive environment has forced her company to make decisions that aren't always in the best interest of the consumer,
and she's not sure she can live with that. Her faith in business has waned,
and she longs to move on. But she also longs for significance, and of a magnitude that requires substantial success. "I feel that money will give me the
freedom to do the things that I want to do, because from a very young age
I thought I would do things that would really make an impact on people's
lives." Audra did not envision spending her career in business. "For me it was
always through the social and nonprofit sector," she says. "I have given so
much of my time to the community, to young girls, to people in Africa, and
that is what props me up. It's what makes me feel full and edified. And I feel
that that's where I want to find a career—in that kind of work. But I feel like
I can't until I've made money. And so that's how I think about business."

While she professes, "My faith makes it easier to walk away," it seems in
some ways that the opposite is the case. "Oh, what I would give to be able to
do work that takes me to parts of Africa," Audra yearns. "I'm particularly interested in women's issues, women's health issues, educating women; I would
do that in a heartbeat. And I've just sort of resigned myself to the fact that
I will continue to do those things on my personal time, but I need to stay
focused on finding a job that will allow me to make money so that I can ultimately do the things that I want to do. Right now I think those things are
mutually exclusive." For Audra, success and significance are connected in the
long run but mutually exclusive at present.

Examples like this suggest that not only is success a prerequisite for significance, but that in many cases, temporarily suppressing the desire for significance is a prerequisite for success. Buford, in *Halftime*, acknowledges, "Few
people are able to connect their work to their beliefs in the first half. The second
half gives everyone a greater opportunity to do that."[15] The difficulty younger
informants cite with respect to applying their faith at work suggests that many
of those who now feel significant freedom to do so were able to bracket their

faith during the early stages of their careers. Some freely admit as much. "I wanted my faith to be more in harmony with everything I did as I grew older in my career," stated a commercial banking executive. He confessed, "The first decade of my career I think I could have coped with or not worried so much about big disconnects with what I believe from a faith perspective and the values I held from a faith standpoint and what my company was asking me to do. I think I would have tolerated a lot there because I was pretty highly motivated to have a good career." During the first half of his career, this retired business leader acknowledged, "I willingly behaved in ways that made my faith invisible. It wasn't because others forced me to; it's just what I decided it would be convenient to do." But consistent with the success to significance paradigm, he continued, "In the last half of my career, I would have had a very difficult time trying to execute a mission or a vision that wasn't complemented by my faith. I do not think I could have done that. I think I would have found a different place to work." As we have seen, many do just that. Others, like Audra, do not yet have the credentials or connections to select into more accommodating professional environments. Time will tell if she can make peace with business long enough to attain the type of significance she desires.

The preceding examples suggest that aspiring evangelical executives who attempt simultaneously to pursue success and significance face an uphill battle. A mid-career technology executive who now runs a small media company but previously held important roles in large publicly traded technology companies has learned from experience that "we're not going to influence those dominant companies anytime soon." "I think there is this mystique around, 'Oh, I'm a Christian and I work for Sony and I'm going to transform Sony.' I think that is ludicrous. The single most important quality to have when working in a larger enterprise is ensuring your boss likes you. If your boss doesn't like you, you're not going to have the influence you'd like to have. The long-term ability to impact a publicly traded company that isn't necessarily aligned with Kingdom-oriented values . . . I've just not seen it. As someone who's worked with large entities, I've seen that the things that I've been able to accomplish that have been permanent have almost always been economic. The things that I try to put in place that are cultural, social, and focused on people were basically removed as soon as I left." The ability to accept this reality, it appears, may be one key to achieving the type of professional success that is in turn essential to spiritual significance in and through business.

* * *

Paul Schervish has described how wealth can open up possibilities for the wealthy to contemplate new forms of altruism by transcending institutional boundaries, and indeed this seems to be the case for many successful evangelical executives, as their resources, status, influence, and connections across spheres facilitate an array of magnanimous initiatives.[16] Some executives attempt to incorporate their faith in their current business context. Others select into another business context that is more flexible or focus their efforts on social sector initiatives. Regardless of the manifestation and venue, for evangelical business leaders, wealth often catalyzes renewed dedication to faithful living.

Evangelical executives are deeply committed to exercising positive influence at their companies and beyond. But the executives who do so are those—and only those—who have acquired sufficient discretion and resources to exercise influence without compromising their professional standing or altering their lifestyle. The deferral of significance is certainly not specific to evangelical executives. The former Microsoft CEO and onetime world's richest person, Bill Gates, for example, whose public perception morphed from that of evil monopolist to magnanimous philanthropist as he pledged to give away half of his considerable wealth, sustained significant criticism for not distributing his wealth sooner.[17] But while their journey from success to significance is not unique, evangelical executives' explicit acknowledgment and endorsement of this pattern is significant inasmuch as the ability to point to activities of significance that are facilitated by success in business strengthens the case that business is a worthy spiritual calling. Moreover, it is much easier to uphold the connection between virtue and success when that success has translated to tangible significance. For evangelical executives, therefore, even though success must precede significance, the pursuit of spiritual significance legitimates the pursuit of business success. In their articulation of business as a worthy occupation, the positive influence that business eventually facilitates constitutes one more arrow in the quiver.

5

Islands of Influence

As discussed at the outset, some authors and scholars believe that religious business leaders might help reshape American business. While some welcome this prospect, others fear that evangelical Christian business leaders will attempt to "take over their companies for Christ."[1] After all, evangelicals, like some other Christian groups, evidence an intense desire to "change the world"—a desire that could certainly extend to the business world—and evangelicals do have a history of activism on several fronts.[2]

Intentional institutional change typically requires collective effort, and some have argued that the evangelical impulse to integrate faith and work in business contexts has in fact crystallized into a coherent social movement.[3] In order to explore the prospect for collective efforts by evangelical executives to reshape business, I attended a retreat for Christian executives hosted by Laity Lodge, a conference facility in central Texas operated by the foundation that sponsored the research on which this book is based. The theme of this particular retreat was "Christians in the Marketplace: What Would It Look Like if God Was Running the Show?" While the interviews I conducted provided access to individual perspectives, attending the retreat enabled me to observe and interact with evangelical business leaders in a communal setting specifically designed to facilitate exploration of the integrative task. Marketed to Christian executives, the few dozen guests included about half business leaders, mainly of comparatively small, privately owned businesses, along with a contingent of academics interested in faith and work and several Laity Lodge "regulars," most of whom attend at least one retreat per year and a few of whom had no connection to business at all.

The setting was rugged, remote, and spectacular, with activities centered on a lodge overlooking a crystalline river that winds through a canyon in the heart of the hill country. The grounds are carefully designed to promote a relaxing experience. With fountains throughout the property, the sound of running water is ubiquitous. Scripture verses and poetry—inscribed in wood beams and on stones—encourage contemplation. Recreation options are plentiful; in addition to hiking and swimming in the canyon's natural

Baptizing Business. Bradley C. Smith, Oxford University Press (2020). © Oxford University Press.
DOI: 10.1093/oso/9780190055776.001.0001

features, there are shuffleboard and tennis courts, a horseshoes pit, a ping-pong table, a jogging trail, a bookstore, and a library.

It would be difficult to overstate how far removed the setting is from the daily life of an executive. The "unplugged" nature of the experience is a point of pride and emphasis; with no televisions or cell phone coverage, participants, many of whom are ordinarily tethered to their smartphones, are truly disconnected. And at Laity Lodge, in contrast to executive suites where proprietary information is guarded and access restricted, keys are not distributed and doors not locked.

This was no place to keep to oneself in the first place. Religious enthusiasm pervaded, and the "evangelical" flavor of the retreat was obvious throughout. "God talk" abounded, punctuated with "amens," "hallelujahs," and "praise Gods." Most conversations revolved around spiritual matters. I witnessed, for example, a spirited debate about the merits and drawbacks of dividing Tolkien's Middle-earth trilogy into three feature films, the interlocutors citing specific characters and scenes and lamenting the failure of the movie adaptation of the trilogy to convey the moral and spiritual implications of certain episodes in the story. During worship times, led by a well-known Christian musician, some guests sang with hands uplifted and many closed their eyes and sang with intensity. If not quite "charismatic," the singing was certainly impassioned. It seemed to take not much more than a handshake for guests to connect, soon referring to one another in familial terms and joining hands around long tables to bless their food before sharing meals together.

Billed as an opportunity to think deeply about a particular topic, the atmosphere was more one of fellowship and emotional release than of intensive study. Nevertheless, there was plenty of time devoted to instructional sessions. Two instructors shared teaching responsibilities, one a pastor of a relatively prominent church and the other the dean of the business school at an evangelical seminary. The two alternated giving lectures, or lessons, most of which took up common evangelical themes. As noted earlier, apparently without coordination, both speakers oriented their introductory remarks around a quote from the Dutch theologian Abraham Kuyper, who said, "There is not a square inch in the whole domain of our human existence over which Christ, who is Sovereign over all, does not cry, 'Mine!'" For the next couple days, the overriding impulse of the dean's prepared remarks was to formulate a theology of business by demonstrating how business fits into the biblical narrative, which he explained as a story of creation, fall, redemption, and consummation. Naturally, the clergyman focused more on pastoral concerns, emphasizing personal dispositions and virtues and encouraging retreat participants to "prune" the unhealthy aspects of their lives in order to allow the healthier dimensions to flourish. Whether by design or coincidence, the effect of such alternation was the impression that the personal behavior encouraged by the pastor was the key to implementing or living out the perspective on business articulated by the scholar, even if the connections were less than straightforward.

In order to facilitate dialogue and encourage practical application, plenary sessions were followed by small group discussions—a staple of the evangelical approach to spiritual vitality. In these groups, any possibility of studious discussion evaporated. The small group to which I was assigned reflected the diverse circumstances and objectives of attendees as a whole and was led by a professor at a business school in Texas. Despite having an assigned topic and set of discussion questions, within just a few minutes, one discussant had shared that many years ago her first child had died at a young age, prompting tears from her and others and commendations for her courage and vulnerability in sharing such a painful experience. Gentle attempts by the facilitator to redirect attention to the assigned issues were largely unsuccessful, impeded by the need to pass around an amplification device so that a ninety-nine-year-old woman could hear what was said. Apparently still not able to follow the discussion, our elderly friend interjected periodically: "I'm just so glad each of you is here this week," she exclaimed. "I just feel like you don't realize what great plans God has for you. All of you are just so important to God and if you will just follow him, well I just can't wait to know what he does with all of you. So just believe that he's gonna use you." Our small assembly made little progress fashioning a theology of business that day.

Subsequent small group sessions were more of the same. Inevitably, someone would share something that was "on their heart," thereby shifting attention away from the apparently less interesting issues about which we had presumably gathered in the first place. While we might not have learned much about business, we were warned by one small group participant that the easiest way to diverge by 20 percent from God's path is to stray 1 percent per year for twenty years. (This, apparently, was the story of his marriage.) When at last we reached the climactic question—the culmination of all of our discussion and study—our opportunity to discourse on what our company/industry/occupation would look like if God was running the show—the prompt was met by silence. After a couple of aborted attempts to jumpstart the conversation, we retrenched to more comfortable territory.

In a sense, we had been set up for this. From the start guests were encouraged to be "open to God," that they might hear the specific messages he had for them in particular. Even the theology of business expounded by the business school dean stopped short of implementation advice. The most substantive lecture of the retreat culminated in the presentation of a graphic showing a number of different company stakeholders and business objectives that could be subject to trade-offs. But instead of presenting a framework by which to prioritize groups and purposes, the speaker demurred, asking, "Who am I to tell you how to balance these things?" and insisting that to arbitrate between competing interests we must rely on divine guidance and the leading of the Holy Spirit.

A panel discussion late in the retreat demonstrated just how little consensus had been reached regarding an appropriate theology of business. The two plenary speakers were joined onstage by a businesswoman invited to participate on the panel just a couple hours beforehand. Apparently the vetting process was less than thorough, as the businesswoman ended up saying exactly the opposite of what the dean had been teaching, admitting that she thought the purpose of business was to make a profit and stating that the way she implements her faith at work is by being a nice person. Awkwardness ensued as the speakers attempted obliquely to contradict what this woman expressed. The one time the discussion actually turned to concrete application, the awkwardness only intensified; during an open question-and-answer session, one guest came to the microphone and shared his conviction that if he could not provide healthcare for his employees, he didn't want to run that business—a sentiment that prompted an apparently unwelcome divergence of opinion that was quickly suppressed in favor of the next, more innocuous question.

The retreat concluded with an outpouring of hugs, well-wishes, and customary promises to keep in touch. Guests left encouraged and refreshed but, by all appearances, with little prospect of doing anything differently at work than when they arrived. Despite the need for reform implied by the hypothetical "what . . . if" in the title of the retreat, attendees demonstrated little urgency to contemplate or initiate systematic changes to the world of business, as individuals or in concert.

Modest Aspirations

While the evangelical executives I interviewed certainly desire to lead lives of significance, they gave little indication that they aspire to reshape the marketplace, as my experience at the retreat would suggest. Consider Harold, an African American entrepreneur who owns a marketing company. Harold prides himself on the quality of his relationships. Well connected in the evangelical world, he is close friends with some of the most prominent names in music, business, and publishing. With respect to his network and sphere of influence, he says, "I pinch myself all the time. When I look at how God has taken this kid from east Nashville who has traveled the world and been with presidents and ambassadors of countries and some of the world's best entertainers, sharing Jesus with all of them—it's incredible." His press kit lists a number of well-known individuals with whom he has worked, stating that Harold is "widely known in the corporate world for successfully creating beneficial strategic alliances and partnerships with Fortune 500 companies, sports, and entertainment industries."

Given Harold's connections, if there is a group of evangelicals keen to advance evangelical objectives in the corporate world, he would be a good candidate to be involved. And yet, for Harold, the corporate world is no more in need of reform than anything else. If anything, business is one thing that is right with the world, and energy and resources can be more profitably expended elsewhere. When asked about the most pressing problems in the world today, Harold focuses on the family, pinpointing absentee fathers as a grave concern. He speaks passionately about the future of Nashville, recalling the tears he shed upon noting the absence of a spiritual dimension to an otherwise commendable fifty-year plan for the city. He speaks critically of the church, claiming that "part of our moral destruction is coming from the church," and moreover that to look to the church to alleviate social problems is "kind of like saying to a child molester, 'How are you going to help me help my children?'" He gets excited about training leaders and is intensely interested in academic studies about what makes leaders different. But changing corporate America is not on his radar, much less taking over companies for Christ or even propelling evangelical Christians to leadership positions in important companies. Harold, while acknowledging that business is subject to excess and abuse, prefers to emphasize the positive characteristics of business, including especially the service mentality that should characterize all Christian relationships. Whether or not the influence of Christian executives might soften capitalism, reorient business toward higher values, or alter cultural norms in the economic sphere, Harold and most other informants are simply not oriented this way. For the most part, their goals are more discrete and their energy channeled elsewhere.

"I have one goal," stated the CEO of a construction company, "and that's to make it into heaven. I mean, I have a lot of shorter-term goals, like I want to get to dinner by 6:30 with my kids. I have no idea what God's plan is for me. I just don't know, but he puts stuff out there. He puts stuff in front of me, and when he does, I kind of know when he's doing it, I think. I make a judgment, and then if I think it is from God, I work on it. I tackle it. I spend very little time thinking beyond that because I'm always very busy with the junk he keeps throwing at me."

As a father of five, the CEO of a company with seven subsidiary enterprises, an adjunct professor at two business schools, a leader in the movement for education reform in a major metropolitan area, and a board member of or official adviser to more than a dozen nonprofit organizations, it is little wonder that this executive expresses little energy or enthusiasm for strategic planning. But his remarks are telling nevertheless. For him, as for many others, to plan is to presume. While there are exceptions, the majority of informants prefer to respond to specific divine guidance rather than initiate plans on their own. According to another CEO, "I stopped a long time ago setting these big audacious—you know, by this date I'm going to hit this—goals, because my faith has led me to believe that being in this day and in the moment is the way that I can truly come alongside God and his plan and his work. So I don't have a whole lot of long-term grandiose goals that are about where I end up." An emerging business leader voices some of the same themes, saying, "I think there is a false sense of security that comes from thinking you are your own strategic planner because we all know, in the end, our success has come from God and come from him opening the door. I used to take a real long-term approach before and I think I've had a pretty good reality check here more recently and it's just like God is going to open doors. He's going to be the one driving from this point forward."

To be sure, some informants are more proactive about seeking divine guidance than others. We saw earlier, for example, that one informant claims constantly to ask God what to do next. A more common sentiment, however, is that informants are not looking for new opportunities or ideas. They are simply trying to be faithful where they believe God has placed them at present, dealing with people and issues as they come into view. As one business leader explains, "I look at the people that come onto my path, and I say, 'Okay, Lord, what do you want me to do with these people?' But I'm not necessarily going to say, 'Oh, I've got to, you know, try to save the people in every needy African country.'" Likewise, a senior executive at one of the largest companies in the world disclaims, "I absolutely refuse to seek out any new ministry stuff at all. I'm just going to have the Lord bring it to me and I'll respond. I'm not going to intentionally generate anything." According to another informant, moreover, "A well-thought-out career plan can kill God's initiative." This executive even speaks of desiring at one point to pursue full-time church-based ministry, but of not having "the release from God" to do so.

The inclination to wait for God's specific instruction may be, at least in part, a rationalization for the inability to do more. Many informants are incredibly busy. They work long hours, spend time with their families, are involved with church and community, and allocate time to spiritual disciplines as well. It is safe to say that many informants are running at full capacity. Be that as it may, several informants specifically state that they do not want any more influence than they currently have. One investment banker describes his sphere of influence as "whoever God brings into my path." When asked if he wished he had more influence with certain people or in certain places, he says, "In a way, I wish I were a better person, and that therefore my life was more transforming to other people. But I don't have a desire to impact millions. I just think that's up to God. I think God called Billy Graham and people like him—people in history that have touched literally millions and millions of people. But my goal is to just faithfully serve the Lord, whether it's to one person or to thousands. I think it can be a form of pride, vanity, and self-ambition if you sort of set yourself up like 'I want to change the world.' In my view, that's God's role, and my view is just to do what he sets before me, big or little." Another executive articulates well the view of many: "I try not to think too much about that because it's easy to get priorities misaligned if you worry too much about who you're influencing and how you're influencing them. I try to think more about that small-core sphere and then act or conduct my professional life in a way that is pleasing to God and let things fall where they may."

In line with the sentiment that the desire for and exercise of influence can reflect pridefulness, some evangelical executives understate the amount of influence they exert, especially with respect to influence in their companies. "My sphere of influence? It's not very big at all," claims one executive who has attained leadership positions in several prestigious and competitive consulting firms, currently runs a private equity firm, is a senior adviser to one of the most significant foundations in the world, and is the chairman of the board of a prominent group of high-net-worth Christian givers. When asked if he has been in position to enact changes at his company, a high-level officer at a publicly traded asset management firm responded, "Change is too strong a word; it implies something. All the values that I think are fitting for the workplace, I try to live on a day-to-day basis and apply to my partnership with my colleagues—to my efforts day in and day out. I think all things taken into account, you can be influential on a day-to-day basis. Everybody can. It's the old circle of influence thing. Everybody's got that. Everybody does. The janitor's got it and I've got it." Despite his stature in the organization, this executive articulates little desire or ability to "change" his company, comparing his influence with that of a janitor. This is the same executive, mentioned last chapter, who relates an incredible array of impactful activities outside of work, including filmmaking, campaigning, policy-writing, and a variety of philanthropic initiatives. For someone who feels relatively powerless within, or at least disinclined to influence, the company at which he spends most of his time, this executive certainly attempts to exercise influence across the cultural, service, and political landscapes. As with many informants, the loci of his renewal-oriented efforts lie outside his professional domain. He, like many informants, channels the majority of his reform-oriented energy outside the business world.

Exceptions

It is important to acknowledge that there are exceptions to the general disposition elaborated in the previous section. While most informants gave little evidence of a desire to transform the business world, a few are strategic and ambitious in this regard.

Take Kirk, for example. In the midst of a distinguished career in which he advised companies around the world on financial, technical, and strategic issues, Kirk felt called by God to leave the consulting company at which he was a partner and establish an institute to "repurpose business." For the last two decades Kirk has operated the institute with a stated goal "to repurpose corporations and leaders so that they discover and implement a personal and corporate calling, thereby transforming people, societies and nations." Kirk refers to the institute as a "corporate chiropractor" that helps businesses and executives increase impact through alignment. Practically, this means producing a "corporate X-ray" that identifies the key drivers of impact and diagnoses areas of misalignment. In addition to working onsite with management teams at interested companies, Kirk and his colleagues host retreats and seminars designed to inculcate the biblical principles and practical strategies associated with repurposing businesses, all in the context of a supportive community of like-minded business leaders.

Kirk believes that each company has a specific calling that is consistent with its particular strengths and resources. The way a business fulfills its calling is by "developing products and services that meet needs God cares about that make the world a better place." Kirk's intent is to match company strengths with the social problems that God is most interested in addressing. "In every country that we go into we sit down with the business, church, and other leaders in that country's government," Kirk explains, "and we will ask them, 'What are the big challenges in your society? What are the big giants?' And they can normally in a brainstorming session tell you pretty quickly." As an example, he cites South Africa, where the list of "giants" includes HIV and the breakdown of the family structure, resulting in considerable poverty and unemployment. "Our goal is not to get God into their business, but their business into God's business," Kirk explains. "We don't mind which giants to [tackle]. We're not prescriptive. We don't tell them, you know, you do this one or that one. We simply say, 'Hey, you pick them, as long as you're addressing stuff that God cares about.'" Summarizing his agenda, Kirk states, "Our goal isn't just to repurpose businesses but to get a critical mass of corporations, business, media, government, etc., repurposed in major cities such that there will be transformations in their societies."

While Kirk has chosen to influence companies from the outside, his curriculum includes strategies for influencing organizations from within, as well. Through a product called "influence through integration," he explains, "We help people who work in large corporations. They are one of x-thousand employees. They don't own the place. They aren't necessarily even directors. We teach them how to look for the pain points in the company so that they can find the opportunities for influence. We teach people to say, 'When there is a problem in the company, that's God's opportunity.' If there's a problem with product development, or with a customer service issue, or returns, or with receivables, that's an opportunity to ask God for a creative solution. One of my people now on my staff was working at a major manufacturing company and noticed that people were always working late and she was concerned about that. What was going on? She found out there were problems with the product development process. She came up with a new process. It solved the problem, was better for the health of the employees, their families, and the company. And what she put together got written up in an industry article and became an industry standard. She wasn't looking for an opportunity to witness or say 'in the name of Jesus.' She saw a problem that was inconsistent with the way God would want the thing to operate and came up with a creative solution."

Kirk isn't the only executive to articulate ambitious objectives regarding business. According to one CEO, "We have a really significant visioning process. Over there in that book is my master-action plan, and that master-action plan is one-fifth of a five-year focus. My heartbeat is not as much leading a financial services firm as it is leading and impacting our world—being a catalyst." This executive is burdened to empower other firms to implement the type of values and culture that he has implemented at his firm, and he is contemplating concrete steps to make that happen, including writing a book and founding an institute.

Others may have a shorter horizon, but are likewise contemplating paradigm shifts. One venture capitalist, for example, hopes to "revolutionize philanthropy" by using the venture capital model to make investing in social impacts more appealing than purchasing luxury items. Similarly, the leaders of two private equity firms are working to establish "impact investing" as a legitimate and appealing asset class, thereby dissolving the boundary that currently divides investing and philanthropy. And one company founder explains that the mission of his company is "to create a tsunami of micro-funding that overwhelms the needs of those we are caring for." "We have to change the ecosystem of how funding happens for the nonprofits," he says.

What's the Problem?

The aforementioned exceptions notwithstanding, based on informants' accounts of their own aspirations, in general I see little desire to turn companies into explicitly "Christian" organizations or to transform the core values and objectives toward which businesses are oriented, or indeed much evidence that there is any shared agenda around which evangelical business leaders might coalesce, at least when it comes to business. Informants are far more likely to cite eroding moral standards, the breakdown of the family, and the poor quality of education as pressing problems than any problems associated with the way business is conducted. While the Social Gospel movement of the early twentieth century—a precursor to contemporary emphases on faith at work—was concerned with structural and institutional change, this preoccupation does not characterize the evangelical executives I interviewed.

The one characteristic of the economy that informants consistently singled out as suboptimal is "the tyranny of the short term," as the CEO of a private equity firm phrased it. A number of executives lamented the pressure incurred by public companies to deliver quarterly earnings results, believing that this often came at the expense of long-term value creation. Also, when prompted, some informants allowed that the ratio of executive pay to that of other workers is out of balance, though others resolutely defended the efficiency of the market in allocating appropriate compensation for highly demanding positions.

When presented with the view that our economic system promotes consumerism, greed, and other dispositions not in keeping with Christian virtue, the founder of a consulting company responded, "I think what you just outlined are abuses of something that is basically good. That would be throwing out the baby [with the bathwater]. Maybe I'm naïve, but I think the abuses that are portrayed are beyond what they really are if you look at the totality of business. I just don't see them in our industry. Maybe people in our industry don't make enough money, but there's enough private companies where guys have made a lot of money and been very charitable. I just don't think you hear that side of the story. It doesn't make very good reading. When you have a public company, it's easy to pick up on what you think are excesses."

In contrast to mainline Protestants, who see free markets as imperiling society, American evangelical Christians see the market as a mirror of society—"fallen" and in need of fortification through the infusion of Christian ethics.[4] While we have seen that the evangelical executives I interviewed articulated an overriding consonance between Christian ethics and market ethics, informants did allow that private enterprise is subject to manipulation and excess.

According to evangelical business leaders, responsibility for these excesses lies with individuals, not systems. This is typical of evangelicals more broadly, who tend to believe that cultures change when people change, and that people change when they are spiritually transformed through the embrace of new ways of thinking.[5] The evangelical business leaders in this study endorse this type of thinking, insisting that most problems in corporate America are the result of flawed businesspeople, not flawed institutions. Asked if he thinks corporate America is in need of reform, Harold, the entrepreneur introduced earlier, responds, "I think that it goes back to the moral compass. It goes back to integrity. It goes back to character. If character is absent, whether in the church or in corporate America, then you're going to see the residue of that." Having complained that our moral compass needs to be recalibrated, the process Harold recommends is as follows: "I think one, you have to be the change you want to see. I think it starts with you first. I think that becomes the attraction. That becomes the lightning rod. Someone will say to you, 'Man, what is it about you? Why is it that you won't do this, this, and this?'" Other informants articulate similar perspectives on social change, namely that large-scale problems can be addressed by greater intensity of personal belief or through one-to-one interactions. "I think you have to have a global vision and do it one life at a time," explained one CEO.

A number of informants emphasize the spiritual roots of material problems. As one executive states, "I think most of the world's problems can be described as sin. It's consumerism, or hedonism, or whatever our -isms are. I think that, basically, we place ourselves above God, and most of the world's problems are a matter of people not loving their neighbors as themselves—loving the Lord with all their heart, soul, mind, and strength, and loving their neighbor as themselves. There may be some structural, systemic things that wouldn't get solved by that, but I would be interested to hear what they are." Similarly, another executive insists that "at the highest level, the pressing problem is the widespread lack of relationship to God, which then results in oppression, greed, and every other vice, which leads to poverty, environmental disaster, et cetera, et cetera." Another asserts that "corporate America is in need of reform in the same way the human heart is in need of reform," explaining that "the root problems we experience today are no different than they were a thousand or five thousand years ago, and it starts with the human heart."

In light of this diagnosis, proposed remedies include, most frequently, spiritual renewal resulting in improved decision-making by individuals. The evangelical executives I interviewed are largely unversed in institutional dynamics, according to which, for example, at a community level, change often takes place through an institutional infrastructure that connects corporations, foundations, and other civic groups. And the evidence suggests that the effects of the individual-oriented strategies informants recommend are unlikely to metastasize as they hope.[6]

Institutional Inertia

Whether or not they are inclined to change their companies and industries, evangelical executives regularly acknowledge the difficulty of doing so. Recall Raymond, the financier who believes he was unfairly demoted. I asked what one thing he would change about his company, a prestigious asset management firm. "Dream on," he replied, laughing, "Wave a magic wand and make half, if not all, of the employees followers of Jesus Christ. . . ." Recall also the observations of the junior program manager who wanted to transform the entire tech company she worked for but settled instead for personal spiritual growth, as well as the mid-career executive who called the prospect of transforming companies like Sony "ludicrous."

It is important to observe that other attempts to reorient business have encountered obstacles, as well. The corporate social responsibility movement, for example, having resorted to utilitarianism, has proven mostly impotent when it comes to influencing corporate behavior, especially given the lack of evidence to support the supposed connection between virtue and profit. If anything, corporations themselves have assumed the mantle as the loudest champions of calls for more expansive corporate social responsibility. Firms have adopted departments dedicated to CSR but for the most part not changed their operations at all, disguising nonconformity by decoupling their organizational structure from their actual operations.[7] While many companies have implemented CSR reporting, they use standards derived from certifying bodies funded and directed by corporations, themselves. Firms that wish to appear responsible can make side payments to various parties, as in, for example, compensating certifiers to implement certification criteria that pose little threat to traditional performance metrics.[8] In all these ways, companies have taken charge of the manufacture of their own virtue, as opposed to having standards of virtue imposed on them.[9] It is worth noting that before its spectacular collapse amid audacious malfeasance, Enron was consistently lauded as one of the most socially responsible firms, and also that the great majority of Fortune 500 companies now qualify for so-called socially responsible mutual funds. Despite having secured widespread support, the inability of the CSR movement to introduce meaningful changes shows how entrenched economic arrangements can be, and this solidity may contribute to evangelical executives' lack of enthusiasm for marketplace reform.

Implementation

The preceding chapters have demonstrated that successful evangelical executives have both the motivation and the ability to uphold business as a noble profession. The proposed connection between virtue and profit, the diversity and affirming nature of many religious scripts and metaphors, and the success-to-significance template represent rhetorical tools and patterns of action that enable the business leaders I interviewed to fulfill the evangelical imperative—to live an integrated life and contribute to lasting spiritual objectives—even as they flourish in the business world. Thus far this chapter has indicated that few informants feel as though they are part of any sort of broader movement that might advance meaningful reforms in the marketplace. Informants, most of whom attempt to exert influence as individuals, may ask, "What does God want *me* to do next?" but rarely ask, "What does God want *us* to do next?" They do not often contemplate collective influence, agendas, or resources. Nevertheless, it would be a mistake to assume that their faith is irrelevant to their work. On the contrary, evangelical executives assert that their religious convictions regularly influence both the ways they act and the ways their companies function.

Consider Harold, the above-mentioned African American entrepreneur, who recounts, "I recall a really tough time in our business. We got a call from a rapper that was extremely popular. We really couldn't even make payroll. This guy calls with a half-a-million-dollar order to get started yesterday. I ask him politely, 'Well, I don't listen to rap music, but can you tell me— is it the kind where you're calling women "B's" and this and this and this?' and he said, 'Oh yeah.' I said, 'Oh, okay. You're going to think this is stupid, but we don't want that business.' My staff couldn't believe that I said it. I said, 'Because I spend my weekends walking through the housing projects of this city trying to take out of the minds of little kids what you're pouring into their minds.' I said, 'I know no one would ever know that I've designed these shirts. My name wouldn't be on them. My logo wouldn't be on them. But I would know.'"

Like Harold, some executives expressed some willingness to incur genuine costs to themselves and/or their companies in order to maintain ethical standards and protect the interests of various stakeholders. Sometimes this means challenging existing conventions. One lumber company CEO, for example, after years of going along with the industry convention of rounding to the company's advantage when measuring shipping weight, insisted that his company begin disclosing precise shipping weights even if it put them at a disadvantage relative to competitors. Earlier we met a hotel developer who, feeling convicted about the dishonest nature of standard negotiating tactics, begins and ends his negotiations with exactly the amount that he thinks is fair for both parties rather than periodically revising the "final offer" as is standard practice. The owner of a family of automobile dealerships claims to accept slightly lower margins than competitors because of his commitment to fair pricing and customer service. And seeing their service to clients not just as a source of revenue but as a way to add value to their clients' lives, the leader of an investment advisory practice sometimes continues to serve clients with whom they have a long-standing relationship even when they no longer make money from that relationship.

Other examples of unconventional business practices include a zero-debt policy based on perceived biblical mandate—a policy that significantly reduces one company's capacity for expansion. One CEO, citing his faith convictions, does not provide health coverage for contraceptives. And defying the expectations of Wall Street analysts and investors, the former CEO of a large public power company specifically disclosed in SEC filings that the company would not pursue profit at the expense of other stakeholders in the business—a stance that drew much attention and some derision.

In terms of personal sacrifice, several business leaders suggest that they have passed on promotions or promising career opportunities because what would be required of them was incompatible with their convictions or their responsibilities to their families or others. While some informants accepted that there would be trade-offs between career progress and family time, others attempt to minimize the costs their families must bear. At one private equity firm, for example, employees work from 5 A.M. to 5 P.M. every day so that they can work long enough to remain competitive on Wall Street and still have time with their families in the evenings.

While opinions were mixed regarding whether or not executive compensation is excessive in America today, at least a few informants intentionally limit or reduce the amount of compensation they receive. The owner of one company instituted a policy capping the ratio of the highest-paid and lowest-paid employees in the firm at 7:1, while another owner established a ratio of 8:1 for CEO pay to the average wage in the company. A junior executive at an internet startup claims to have taken a lower salary so other members of his team would receive compensation that he felt was more in line with their contributions, and one consultant adjusts her fee structure so that nonprofit companies are better able to afford her services.

The preceding examples show that evangelical business leaders are sometimes willing to challenge conventions and make economic or other sacrifices in keeping with their religious commitments. These perspectives and behaviors vary in subject and scope. In the previous chapter we saw that evangelical executives, acting as individuals, actively attempt to leverage their wealth and influence outside their companies. The following categories summarize the ways evangelical business leaders claim their faith makes a difference in and through their companies, as well. Many evangelical executives cite relatively narrow applications of faith at work, primarily interested in the ways their faith enhances their own work experiences. Some, however, implement policies that impact their organizations more broadly, and a minority devote significant attention to their companies' impacts on external constituencies.

Faith *at* One's Company

For many evangelical executives faith is primarily a personal resource that 1) confers a sense of meaning and purpose that translates into motivation and stamina and shapes understandings of personal success, 2) provides a moral compass that steers them away from trouble, and 3) prompts respectful and gracious interpersonal relationships.

For a number of informants, the primary impact of faith is perspectival. Faith informs perspectives on priorities, identity, success, and, hypothetically, failure. It invigorates evangelical executives inasmuch as they feel compelled to "work as unto the Lord," taking more pleasure in pleasing God with their effort than in simply making money. Faith also provides a moral framework that both encourages right behavior and keeps evangelical executives from succumbing to greed or pride. At this foundational level, informants think about and approach their work differently. They may strive to make as much money as they can, but their income is a byproduct of selfless motivation.

Consistent with evangelical perspectives on the nature of social problems and social change, informants overwhelmingly conceive of ministry and influence in terms of personal relationships. When faith moves beyond orientation to action, it is often in the context of influencing others through one-to-one interactions. While there is some thought allocated to influencing the influencers—inside or outside the company—in general there is a democracy of ministry that defines neighbors in terms of propinquity, not need or potential influence. Treating people well is a common theme, both as an end in itself and in order to serve as a moral model. There is every indication that informants look for ways to "bless" those with whom they interact in a variety of contexts; from informal water-cooler chats to official performance evaluations, informants strive to model Christian virtue in their personal relationships. This disposition is consistent with the findings of others who have studied evangelicals in business contexts. Roels, for example, summarized the business ethics of evangelicals as preoccupation with "neighborliness," whereby evangelicals apply their religious energy toward cooperation with and support of those around them.[10] Likewise, Nash found that evangelical CEOs exhibit a privatized religion that is largely restricted to one's "inner space" and manifest in individual personality traits such as being "nice."[11] Along these lines, some informants communicate that, above all, faith makes them more virtuous than they would be otherwise.

Some of the executives I interviewed believe that a personal relationship with Jesus Christ is a prerequisite for human flourishing and some instinctively assume that questions about faith at work refer to evangelism in the workplace, even though this was almost never explicitly mentioned. While some informants actively pursue opportunities to share their faith, others believe it is enough to signal their faith and be prepared to speak about it if the opportunity arises.[12] Still others feel that it is sufficient to embody the gospel through actions, and quite a few consider evangelism in the workplace inappropriate, especially for supervisors.

Faith *throughout* One's Company

Employee Flourishing

For many evangelical business leaders, faith-driven commitment to the well-being of those around them is largely limited to spontaneous interactions. But some deliberately advocate or implement official policies and initiatives designed to help employees flourish. Describing the internal dynamic at his most recent startup company, one entrepreneur explained, "Our team members are invited to bring their whole selves to the office. We try to create an authentic community where candor and transformative relationships are the norm." Desiring to facilitate "an environment of mentorship, camaraderie, and discipleship," he allocates to each employee a monthly budget to be applied toward "learning initiatives" or "wellness projects," which might include activities like conference attendance or sessions with a personal trainer or counselor. Employees are required to report on the results of these enrichment projects so that the entire team can benefit from each other's experiences. Employees read a book together every month to expand intellectual horizons, work out together twice a month to encourage physical health, and work remotely once a week in order to encourage deeper reflection than is often possible in a bustling office. Time is allocated to talk about wellness because, as the entrepreneur explained, "If God is interested in humans flourishing, we want a culture and a budget that encourages all of this stuff."

Several executives indicated that it is important to cultivate in employees a spirit of volunteering and service, and to this end a couple informants have instituted paid volunteer days during which employees are released to serve in the community. A couple of companies subsidize service trips to foreign countries and encourage participants to report back on their experiences. Many informants are sensitive to other employees' ability to spend time with their families and therefore permit flexible schedules or make allowances for employees to be available to their families. We saw that one executive actually meets with employees' spouses to discuss his desire for them to experience a balanced life and healthy relationships, and that another enacted significant family-friendly policies at a major consulting firm.

Some employee initiatives are oriented toward providing opportunities for employees to make meaningful decisions and contributions. The owner of an automobile dealership deliberately connected technicians with customers so that they could see how profoundly their work impacts people's lives. The CEO of a large, multinational company was so committed to delegation that he claims to have restricted himself to one important decision per year, deferring to others and enacting policies stipulating that ideas were to be generated and problems solved from the bottom up, rather than dictated from the top down by managers and supervisors. Based on one CEO's commitment to the value of every employee, the company he runs is 100 percent employee-owned. At another company, employees contribute to a fund that employees can draw from as special needs arise. One CEO expressed his intent always to pay employees a fair wage, and another described an experiment in "creative communism" whereby a profit-sharing initiative allocates a share of profits among all employees equally instead of proportional to their salary, constituting up to a third of the income of lower-paid employees. Another CEO claimed to provide to employees more comprehensive benefits coverage than the market required. And the CEO of a public company actually challenged and defied federal regulations regarding the payment of hourly wages, believing that to do so diminished the sense of trust and dignity conveyed to lower-level workers, to whom he preferred to designate a salary.

A few executives, almost always the owners of privately held companies, provide opportunities for employees to be enriched spiritually at work. Several subscribe to corporate chaplain services, and most of these were pleased with the service these chaplains provided. While senior leaders almost never felt comfortable participating in onsite Bible studies or prayer groups, two CEOs occasionally sponsor voluntary, Christ-centered events for employees, and another invites Christian speakers and teachers to the office to address employees.

Faith *beyond* One's Company

Customer Flourishing

While some evangelical executives are defensive about the social value of the products and services their companies produce and sell, emphasizing that consumers should have the right to choose and making comparative declarations to the effect that other products are worse, others are concerned and conscientious about the impact of their products on their customers. For example, some executives in food preparation and service companies emphasize that their companies are moving toward more healthful consumption options. Recall the entrepreneur who connected his company's product—in this case focused on healthy living and eating—with human flourishing. "What we want to do," he says, "is increase people's abilities and motivation in a way that not only do they avoid getting disease but they're free to really fulfill their potential on all fronts."

Some executives' convictions prompt them to restrict their companies' product offerings. For example, the owner of a group of automobile dealerships declines to carry the most expensive class of luxury vehicles, though he does express appreciation for the craftsmanship and aesthetic merit of a $100,000 vehicle. A commercial real estate developer will not finance anything that would detract from the quality of life in the community, claiming to get grief because he will not lease to payday lenders, rent-to-own companies, or liquor stores. Moreover, this developer deliberately tries to meet the needs of the community by building out clusters of essential product and service providers, including things like grocery stores, doctors, dentists, and a post office. One investment adviser measures the success of her team members not by the amount of money their clients accumulate, but by how much they give away. And the leader of an insurance practice backed up his insistence that the pursuit of commissions must be subordinated to the pursuit of customers' interests by firing the firm's number one commission producer for inattention to customer needs—to the great surprise of other employees. Among business leaders with more personal connections to customers, at least a couple solicited, compiled, and distributed prayer requests from customers and clients. One executive mentions praying for such requests every morning, and another tells of emailing clients to let them know he is praying for them.

Community Flourishing

Those informants who exercise control over the distribution of their firms' earnings sometimes demonstrate a commitment to enhancing their communities through philanthropic initiatives. While many companies designate a small portion of profits to community causes, others make substantial contributions. A privately owned construction company, for example, tithes on its net income, allocating a tenth of its proceeds to charitable causes. Another company provides a certain number of meals to the hungry for each product sold at various price points. And one investment company donates half of its profits to charity, with a large portion of these contributions directed toward ending genocide.

A few other informants described efforts to generate positive social impact beyond the walls of their companies. One private equity company, for example, invests only in socially productive initiatives in underdeveloped areas. The CEO of a Fortune 500 energy company boasted that, at the time, his was the only company with a fully audited carbon footprint, and several other executives referenced environmentally friendly practices and products, as well. In all these ways, evangelical executives bring their faith to bear in and through their work.

Unity and Diversity

One of the virtues of studying religion outside of specifically religious contexts is that it reminds us that there is no Platonic religious essence that can be abstracted from the competing institutional priorities in which it is situated. Religion is no more a priori than are other institutions. Terms like "executive" and "business" elide important variation in informants' professional contexts, responsibilities, and backgrounds. Despite the evangelical emphasis on faith as the most important thing in life, it is not necessarily the case that religious identity is more salient than occupational context. While context is not inevitably determinative—as we have seen, informants sometimes select into particular contexts that they believe are compatible with their faith commitments—it certainly colors the ways evangelical executives describe and enact their faith at work.

In order to explore the influence of context on disposition and action, we will now consider four previously introduced evangelical executives who give a sense of the similarities and differences that characterize the broader group of evangelical executives I interviewed. Kirk is the consultant who desires to repurpose business by aligning it with causes about which God cares. Raymond is the investment strategist who was unfairly demoted and wishes he could generate converts with a magic wand. Nancy is the restaurant CEO who pledged to consider adding carrots to her menu after meeting with Michelle Obama. And Phillip is the entertainment company CEO who walked away from the automobile industry and its associated hazards. These four executives have much in common, including career stage and family circumstance. All in their fifties and married with three or four children, each has managed to ascend the corporate ladder and summit with families intact, even if that outcome was not always assured. All are ambitious and hard-working individuals who made their way into the upper echelons of the business world, but whose success has come as a function and cost of deep commitment to their work.

Each of the four executives describes an inflection point at which he or she began more conscientiously to attempt to integrate faith and work. For Kirk, the catalyst was a sense of specific calling to start an institute. For Nancy, being diagnosed with a serious illness prompted her to reconsider her priorities. For Raymond, working and living in the same place enabled him to hold different parts of his life in closer relation, and his demotion forced him to rely on his faith more heavily than ever. And for Phillip, the near collapse of his family necessitated a major shift in career direction. All now feel called to their work in some capacity and understand themselves as participating in ministry—at work, as elsewhere. Each has also, to varying degrees, experienced criticism associated with their chosen profession—made to feel by members of their own faith communities that their work is, at best, a poor substitute for true ministry. And each evidences an intense desire to portray business leadership as a worthwhile spiritual vocation—a disposition that fits their evangelical identity and tincts every aspect of their professional lives and the accounts they use to describe them.

While Nancy, Phillip, Raymond, and Kirk have much in common, their professional backgrounds, trajectories, and circumstances differ in important ways. Kirk has chosen to attempt to influence businesses from outside them, having withdrawn from a larger company context to start his own advisory practice. He has now surrounded himself with a small team of people who share his convictions and embrace his vision for corporate reform. Like Kirk, Phillip transitioned to a corporate environment in which he is relatively free to work in ways that are consistent with his faith, having been attracted to a company owned by committed Christians who encourage him to run the firm in accordance with Christian principles. The dynamics of Phillip's firm, however, are different than those of Kirk's firm inasmuch as it is much larger and its employees more diverse. "We choose not to call ourselves a Christian company," Phillip emphasizes. "I say we have Christian owners and we have Christian principles. We employ people of all faiths and we do not want them to feel uncomfortable because they don't believe a certain way." "They *will* be uncomfortable if they don't *behave* a certain way," he adds, "but everybody will be [uncomfortable in that case], whether they are Christian or not." Given the diversity of employee perspectives, Phillip does not experience quite the same degree of latitude to promote a specifically Christian vision as does Kirk.

Unlike Kirk and Phillip, Raymond remained with a large, public company—even after his uncomfortable demotion and despite the consequent strained relationships. As such, his ability and even desire to shape the purpose of the firm is constrained. "[This] is a publicly owned company," Raymond stated, "and we are ultimately responsible as employees to the owners of the company, and they're the shareholders. They want us to maximize the value of the firm." Nancy, meanwhile, leads a publicly traded firm that operates under a franchise model, such that the list of stakeholders whose interests she attempts to balance include franchisees, whose interests may not necessarily be aligned with those of the employees upon whom she typically focuses when elaborating her organization's salutary contributions.

These four executives' companies belong to a variety of industries and produce different types of goods and services marketed to different types of customers and with more or less obvious connections to the public good. Kirk's company markets a service that is specifically designed to make other companies' products and services more worthwhile. Phillip's company is a service business, as well, providing family-friendly theme park experiences. Raymond sells a service, too, namely the attempt to turn money into more money. But while the services Kirk's and Phillip's firms provide are unlikely to prompt objection, the value of the particular service that Raymond's firm provides has been questioned by scholars, practitioners, and consumers, certain of whom have asserted that active asset managers make a handsome living despite not demonstrating the ability to outperform passive index funds or randomized investment processes. Nancy, meanwhile, sells food that is widely understood to be unhealthy.

These four executives are also influenced by the size and location of their companies and by their areas of professional expertise and their positions in their firms. While Kirk's institute is very small, composed of just seven employees, Raymond works for a Fortune 500 firm that employs close to 10,000 people. Nancy and Phillip oversee midsized firms, each responsible for 1,000–3,000 employees. Kirk and Raymond operate on the West Coast and the East Coast, respectively, where residents typically demonstrate lower levels of religious commitment and evangelicalism is sparsely represented. Nancy and Phillip, on the other hand, operate in major metropolitan areas in the Bible Belt, where conservative forms of religion are more prominent. Three of the four business leaders occupy the highest-ranking position in their firms, while Raymond held a position of leadership but was answerable to higher-ranking executives, limiting his discretion to shape the strategy and culture of his firm. Finally, while each possesses broad business knowledge such as is required to lead or hold significant responsibility in their firms, the four business leaders have different areas of professional expertise. Raymond is best versed in finance, Nancy in leadership, Kirk in strategy, and Phillip in operations.

Their diverse professional contexts afford these four executives varying degrees of discretion and shape their perspectives on business, faith, and the connection between the two. As the following discussion shows, these executives articulate differing views on, among other things, the primary purposes of business, problems with business as currently organized, their role in advancing businesses objectives and remedying any disorders, and the ways they bring religious language to bear in their workplaces.

For What and for Whom?

Kirk, Phillip, Nancy, and Raymond emphasize different business objectives and focus on different constituents. Whereas Kirk encourages businesses to go beyond "maximizing shareholder value or its bankrupt derivative purposes," Raymond sees maximizing shareholder value as an appropriate goal. In fact, presented with an alternative way of thinking about business, proposed by a Christian businessman, namely that "the purpose of business is not to maximize profits but to steward our resources to serve the world in an economically sustainable way," Raymond responded, "Yeah, I take issue with that." Given the nature of their firms and professional backgrounds, such differences are hardly surprising. Kirk, who as a consultant advises companies on their strategic direction, is conditioned to evaluate big-picture issues regarding corporate strategy. Raymond, a financier, is more inclined to focus on returns on investment. As an investor, Raymond cares less about what a company produces, as long as it makes money doing so. While Kirk considers *what* a company does in the first place, Raymond is more preoccupied with *how well* a company accomplishes whatever objectives it pursues.

For Phillip, too, with his operational background, what a company produces is less important than how it operates. Unlike Kirk, Phillip makes no reference to addressing social or spiritual problems. In fact, what Phillip's company offers is, in a sense, not an antidote to the world's disorders but an escape from them. "We want what happens inside the gate to feel unique and not remind people too much of what's going on right outside the gate," Phillip explains. What matters most to Phillip is that his company operates according to Christian principles. As such, he has made an effort to extend the concept of to-be goals beyond himself to the company, as well. All company leaders go through training during which Phillip and other company leaders explain, "The problem with the English language is that there is only one word for love, but there are three in Greek." As Phillip understands it, "*Eros* doesn't hold up well when things aren't going well, when there is frustration and anger. *Agape* love is a verb; it is a behavior—how you treat people when you want to have a healthy relationship. We want to have healthy relationships at work, so that is why we use this verb. It happens to be the management style that Jesus used," Phillip says.

With respect to *whom* businesses serve, whereas Kirk focuses on the impact businesses can make on communities and even entire societies and Raymond emphasizes the value his company contributes to shareholders,

Phillip and Nancy emphasize the benefits their companies provide to employees. Recall that Phillip leads a private company whose owners include among their stated objectives not just making a profit, but providing "a great place to work for great people" and maintaining and demonstrating "Christ at the heart." Phillip is especially proud that his company numbers among its purposes not just creating income, jobs, and a service that people are willing to pay for, but helping employees who are in need. "We have a foundation that we have established to help our employees in need that is funded through employee donations and company matches," he explains, adding that "the stories are fantastic." It is difficult for Nancy, meanwhile, to make a very strong case that the well-being of customers is paramount in light of the criticism she endures regarding the health effects of the food served at her restaurants. For her, when thinking about what she considers higher-order purposes, it is easier to think about the training and support her restaurants provide to employees. Accordingly, Nancy is eager to point out that "one out of four Americans' first job is in the restaurant industry and it's where they learn to show up for work, how to wear a clean uniform, how be trained in a skill, how to work collaboratively with other people, and how to move up to the next level." "When a restaurant is well run," she adds, "we provide a real sense of family and community, a place you enjoy going every day; you do something well and good, take care of people, and feed them." For Nancy, the sense of community her restaurants provide is a source of significant pride.

Diagnosing Disorders

Alongside their support for business, Phillip, Nancy, Raymond, and Kirk acknowledge that for various reasons businesses sometimes fail to fulfill their purposes. Just as they articulate different perspectives on the purposes and primary beneficiaries of business, so these executives offer different diagnoses regarding how and why businesses sometimes fail to fulfill their underlying objectives. For Kirk, incentives that prioritize the interests of shareholders indicate that business as commonly understood and practiced today is misdirected and in need of repurposing. Raymond associates dysfunction with the misguided interests and actions of specific business leaders, including some of his coworkers, but does not sense that business is in need of fundamental reform. In thinking about what is wrong with business, Phillip points to himself; if only he had followed Scriptural principles more closely or adopted healthier perspectives, business would not have represented a destructive force in his life. Nancy, too, views business's shortcomings as a spiritual issue. Given that for Nancy, the most important function of her restaurants is facilitating a sense of community for employees, it is with significant concern that she cites a survey indicating that 80 percent of people are not happy at work. Hypothesizing about the root cause of employee dissatisfaction, she states, "I start with the heart and human nature because I think that's where everything goes astray. After that you create structural problems. For example, if you say, 'The way we invest in and grow our businesses in the United States causes an environment where stealing, lying, or heartbreak occurs,' that's just because that's what humans create in their worst state in any structure. I really do think it's a spiritual problem at the heart of any workplace problem, but that's my worldview."

In light of their diverse organizational contexts, the four executives under discussion are subject to different risk profiles and degrees of exposure to the business decisions and strategic recommendations they make. For example, unlike the others, because Kirk and his team are formally outside of the organizational boundaries of the companies they advise, he and his institute bear only a very small fraction of the risk of implementing the types of reforms he proposes. It is, therefore, not surprising that of these four executives, Kirk is by far the most critical of contemporary business realities and the most inclined to propose changes.

Playing Their Part

Given their diverse perspectives on what is right and wrong with business, Kirk, Phillip, Nancy, and Raymond also articulate different perspectives on the relationship between business and ministry and their particular callings in and through their work. Whereas Nancy and Phillip speak of engaging in ministry at work, Raymond emphasizes that business facilitates ministry outside of work. As we saw earlier, as long as God wants him to be in business, Raymond intends to make as much money as he can and give it all away. Or perhaps not quite all of it. Raymond tells of arguing with his wife the night before the interview over whether or not they should buy a new car or a used car. "We can afford the new car," he said. "It's not about affording a new car. It's do we need that new car? What if we got the used car, or not the BMW that you want, and gave the money to . . . you pick it." Raymond and his wife do indeed contribute financially to a number of organizations, most of which are committed to a specifically Christian agenda but also to some academic institutions that are not associated with a faith tradition. He also serves on the boards of several of the organizations to which his family contributes and is heavily involved at his church, where he says his family has quietly matched every dollar raised for a new facility.

In sharp contrast to Raymond, Kirk is irritated by the idea that business serves an instrumental purpose in the church. "We have to discourage the notion of using business to fund missions," he urged, adding that while we are at it, we might as well "scrap the term 'business as missions.'" "It's ridiculous from a biblical perspective because," he insists, "in the Old Testament the word for business and for ministry is the same word, so you may as well call it 'business as business.'" While Nancy sees business as a forum for ministry and Raymond views business as a way to facilitate ministry, Kirk insists that business and ministry are one and the same. He recalls, "One of my staff said to me, 'Kirk, are we a business or are we a ministry?' and I said, 'Yes.' He said, 'No, no, no, let me explain.' He thought I didn't understand the question—if we are a business then there's a set of business rules; if we are a ministry there are ministry rules. I said, 'No, no. There is the Kingdom of God and those are the rules. Business principles, church principles, and government principles are just a subset of those things.'"

Overtness

Even as they express different perspectives on the relationship between business and ministry, all four of the executives profiled in this chapter feel called to bear witness to their faith. Yet even here there is significant variation in their use of religious language in general and their enthusiasm for evangelism in particular. Raymond has long sought opportunities to discuss spiritual matters with his coworkers. "I pray for the leadership of the firm that the Holy Spirit would tug them and make them understand their need and give me an opportunity to witness in some way by some small or big thing, as appropriate." More specifically, he reflects, "I like it when I'm sitting at that table in the morning having my quiet time and somebody says, 'I know Raymond always gets in early. Let me go ask him something. Let me get it done while I can.' They walk in and I have the Bible open. Sometimes nothing's said. Sometimes, 'Oh sorry to interrupt you,' and I say, 'No, come on in, come on in.' So that's one way [I witness]. Two, I mention my faith from time to time, [saying,] 'I'll pray about that,' or to somebody who's got an issue, 'I'll pray for you.' Sometimes, after a while they'll just say, 'This is Raymond; that's what he says.' Occasionally somebody comes back and says, 'Just what is it you pray about?' Subtle, hopefully clear and direct, and hopefully the Holy Spirit leads that person to ask a question or two. That's one way [I share my faith]. The other is by the way we conduct ourselves. We all live in fish bowls. Particularly if you claim to be a Christian, people are watching." While Raymond makes little attempt to infuse business strategies or company policies with religious language, he does hope to "witness" at work, though he prefers to wait for people to ask. As such, he regularly signals his faith but infrequently verbalizes it.

Despite viewing business as a mission field, Nancy, meanwhile, has "stopped short of outright evangelizing" in the workplace, even though, she says, "Others think it's the first thing we should be doing in the workplace." This does not mean that sharing her faith with others in the hope that they will be persuaded to adopt it is unimportant to Nancy. But like many of those with whom I spoke, Nancy prefers indirect modes of "witnessing." "I have personally found role modeling and relationship building to be the most important precursor to spiritual influence, not lecturing or passing out pamphlets or books. I live my life and let people ask—and what's really interesting is that in leadership roles, people do ask you—people will look at me and they'll ask, 'Why are you calm in this situation? This is not a calm situation,' and it gives me an opportunity just to tell them why. 'How do you balance being a working mother?' And it gives me an opportunity to tell them spiritual ways I do that. I think if we listen carefully, it's amazing how many opportunities we get to share [our faith]."

Despite her reluctance to initiate conversations about faith, Nancy desires that her company be a faith-friendly place. "I think businesses should be hugely faith-friendly, because no matter what faith you pursue, it's kind of finding your purpose in the universe. If you are in step with your faith-given purpose, you bring your whole self to work. You are at peace. You are energetic. You've got a lot to give. So, why not tap into that?" Nancy asks. Noting that the team that runs her company's Middle East operations are all devout Muslims, she recalls unknowingly scheduling a meeting during Ramadan. "I publicly apologized and said, 'I respect that this is an important tradition of your faith. I intended no disrespect, and I'm really quite horrified that you're here and not with your family and that I've allowed this to happen.'"

Summarizing her thoughts on the topic, Nancy concludes, "I think when you shove [faith] under the carpet or suggest that it's not important you leave people no option but to lead two lives—their real life and their work life. I'm just against that idea."

Now that Phillip is in charge of a private company that is owned by committed Christians, he is much more inclined to use specifically religious symbols and language. "You don't have to believe in who Jesus was," Phillip makes clear, "but we actually give out a statue of Jesus washing Peter's feet to those who want it. If they don't want it, like the Muslim person who chose not to put one in her office, that is understandable. She still went through the class and she still enjoyed it. Our point is regardless of who you think [Jesus] was, it's pretty amazing that on the last night he had with his disciples, he could have done a number of things. He could have given them his writings. He could have given them money. He could have introduced them to kings and queens. Instead, he got on his knees and washed their feet and said if you don't behave like this you are not part of me. That is a pretty powerful thing. If you were making up a religion, you probably wouldn't make that up. It is too weird to be made up in our minds. That's kind of how I talk about it—that it is all about behavior. We do talk openly that the words are from the Bible and Jesus is a great example of great leadership according to those words."

While evangelism is an important responsibility for evangelical Christians, Kirk disparages the idea of witnessing at work, at least as the primary thrust of integrating faith and work. For Kirk, what makes a business a "Kingdom" business is not that Christian employees witness to non-Christians or that it incorporates religious language, but that it pursues worthy ends through honorable means. Consistent with this disposition, Kirk is quite content, and indeed in many situations compelled, to communicate such ends and means in non-religious language. "You have to appeal to good business sense," he explained, "not it's a good thing to do, God wants you to do this, et cetera, et cetera. That will scare them off. Make a connection between doing the right thing and the impact on the company."

Context Matters

The divergent perspectives elaborated by these four executives are not a function of different religious beliefs or degrees of religious commitment, but seem to correspond instead with the organizational contexts the executives occupy. All four take their faith very seriously. Kirk, for example, has demanding standards for faithfully discharging one's religious responsibilities, framing his thoughts regarding a Christian approach to business in opposition to what he considers to be the prevailing concept of what it means to be a Christian in business. "If you're speaking with a Christian businessman in Texas and he says, 'I'm a Christian and I'm in business. I have a particular set of books. I'm a nice guy. I go to church on Sundays. Therefore, I have a Kingdom business.' It's generally not true. Most of the businesspeople that we meet are Christian in regards to salvation and humanist in regard to the way they run their business. Most are Christian humanists." Raymond certainly articulates a stronger desire to bring his faith to bear on his work than does the Christian humanist Kirk derides. When asked what he aspires to, Raymond quotes Scripture, saying that he wants, upon meeting God after death, for God to say to him, "Well done, good and faithful servant." He tells of consistently praying the following prayer: "God, for every day you allow me to wake up, I've got twenty-four hours. Am I using these twenty-four hours in every one of my spheres of influence in the right way? And are they the right spheres of influence? If not, hit me over the head and tell me I should be spending more time here and less time there or whatever."

Both Kirk and Raymond insist that faith is something that matters every day, but this looks very different for Kirk than for Raymond. For example, Kirk, who sets his own schedule, strongly disagrees with the pursuit of balance, perceiving it as an impediment to integration. "Balance is bogus," asserts the promotional material for one of the institute's training programs. "It is a futile pursuit, an elusive dream. Integration, on the other hand, is the philosophy that wins at the end of the day." The relevant program is designed to "dare you to stop balancing life's ever-increasing demands and start living 100 percent of your life fully integrated with your purpose," after which "you will be freed from the false notion of balance and embrace a holistic vision for your life that is fully integrated with your purpose and calling." For Raymond, who works in a more competitive, results-oriented environment, balance is a destination, a state of equilibrium wherein work assumes an appropriate emphasis and leaves room for other important pursuits. For Kirk, balance is the vocabulary of disintegration, the vain quest to keep the separate spheres of work and faith from contaminating one another.

Even for those who share a number of core religious convictions and overriding dispositions toward business, the ways they express and claim to live out their convictions are appropriate to their particular contexts. Thus, there is no one evangelical approach to faith and work. Indeed, in evangelical executives' accounts we find both uniformity and diversity. But this diversity is not simply idiosyncratic. Rather, it is conditioned by informants' professional histories and the norms and priorities that characterize their particular occupational contexts. The following represents a summary typology of the primary factors that shape how evangelical executives apply their faith in business.

Company Characteristics

Capitalization

The most important determinant of the ways evangelical executives think about business and express their faith at work is the ownership structure of their firms. Capital providers have the ability to enforce restrictions on capital allocation, withdraw funds, and even remove executives if they fail to execute the objectives endorsed by company owners to their satisfaction. The owners of a business, therefore, dictate to a significant extent what is permissible in the companies they finance.

Evangelical executives in publicly financed companies emphasize wealth creation as a valuable contribution of business, with stewardship the preferred metaphor for articulating the spiritual significance of economic benefits. Public company executives also invoke the industrial order of worth, asserting the value of work in and of itself as God-ordained and useful for character formation. While happy for their firms to contribute to worthwhile (and publicly acceptable) causes at the margin, evangelical business leaders in publicly owned companies typically draw on standardized scripts to provide stock answers to questions about the social value of business in general and their companies in particular. Enactment of their faith is generally restricted to faith at their companies (in contrast to faith throughout or beyond their companies), consisting primarily of faith-inspired consideration for individuals in informants' personal circles. The resources and platform their positions confer lend spiritual legitimacy to their work as they leverage their resources, skills, and influence to advance faith-oriented objectives outside of business. Intensely loyal to their firms, public company executives are mostly unwilling to question the value or propriety of any aspect of their companies' operations. In some cases, this entails eschewing responsibility for certain functional areas. When questioned on advertising policies, for example, some public company executives demur, stating that these policies are beyond their areas of expertise and responsibility. Ultimately, public company executives typically function more as salt than light, concerned to preserve the values and reputation of their companies. Most live faithfully as silent witnesses, but generally do not specifically invoke their faith or attempt to deviate from business as usual. For those who ostensibly have the most power, they seem in many ways the most constrained when it comes to influence in business.

Privately held companies accommodate a much broader range of religious objectives, beneficiaries, and faith expressions than do publicly traded firms. While the legal restrictions, reporting obligations, and impersonal ownership characteristics associated with public companies give rise to consistent perspectives and activities among informants, the viewpoints and faith expressions manifested by evangelical executives at private companies are determined by other characteristics of their firms. Industry, for example, matters a great deal. For companies in certain industries, the social value of their products and services is easy to ascertain and affirm. For others, it is more of a stretch. Executives who work at companies that provide products or services oriented to basic human needs are considerably more likely to point to customer flourishing as a legitimating spiritual purpose than are those who work at companies that market discretionary items or experiences. At the same time, some executives circumvent industry dynamics by citing salutary effects that are incidental to the core application of the products, themselves. One CEO of a multinational food distributor, for example, credits frozen dinners with prompting self-reflection and facilitating reconciliation. "I would hope that in many places, not only here in the United States but around the world," he says, "people have sat down over a meal with our product. They appreciated that. They've appreciated their wife, or they've appreciated their children, or they've appreciated their friends. Or they came together with somebody they might have had a disagreement with and they figured out that they no longer needed to disagree."

Company size impacts the nature of faith expressions, as well. The larger the company, the greater the degree of routinization and bureaucracy required for the organization to function efficiently. Hence, evangelical executives in larger companies are less likely to attempt to implement company-wide initiatives than are those who work in smaller companies.

Even among private companies, ownership objectives are crucial. Only a portion of those evangelicals who own their companies or answer to committed Christian owners designate their companies as "faith-centered" in any sense. Evangelical business leaders in such contexts are typically more overt about their faith and enthusiastic about its application in their companies. For these, light is an orienting metaphor, denoting that they feel obliged and able to make visible the nature and attractiveness of a relationship with God and the value of biblical principles, sometimes identified as such. In most cases, these companies attract employees who share similar convictions, diminishing the possibility of provoking offense through explicit invocation of faith-based principles. Business leaders in these more accommodating environments are also more inclined to implement unconventional policies designed to benefit employees, customers, and other stakeholders. As such, they implement faith not just at work, but throughout and beyond their companies, as well. Context still matters, though; even executives who enjoy the support of aligned owners are conditioned by the location of their companies, as some things that raise no objection in the Bible Belt would be poorly received on either coast. Importantly, while a few companies that are owned and operated by evangelicals invoke explicit Christian references when characterizing their firms or the cultures and policies that characterize them, most do not. Thus, even in such circumstances as would characterize companies that have been "taken over for Christ," if such a thing were possible, we should not envision a theocratic institution with a Bible on every desk and the Ten Commandments affixed to every wall.

Executive Characteristics

Career Stage

As noted earlier in conjunction with exploration of the success-to-significance paradigm, career stage has a significant impact on perspective and faith expression. Early-career evangelical executives are preoccupied with career advancement. Some have longer-term goals, but almost all are consumed with the task at hand. They want, more than anything, career guidance and champions within their firms. Having invested less in and derived less from existing economic institutions, some are considerably more sympathetic to critical perspectives on the range of effects businesses have on those inside and beyond their confines. While some emerging leaders have already been chastened by the unyielding norms associated with work in large corporations, others continue to entertain creative possibilities for ways that work could be more fulfilling and consistent with human flourishing, even if they feel somewhat helpless to bring such possibilities about. Among emerging leaders, appetite for reform is negatively correlated with the degree of connection to and satisfaction with their current companies. Among informants, early-career executives are most sensitive to what some have termed "friendly fire" from coreligionists. For some of these, having more recently decided to pursue a career in business, it is not too late to change course and pursue a different vocational track, prompting greater receptivity to discussions regarding the relative propriety and value of business versus other professional domains.

Mid-career informants are among the most proactive in terms of maximizing their influence, sometimes in profound and creative ways. Many mid-career informants are at or near the inflection point that marks the transition from success to significance. Some of those who have reached the pinnacle of their professions have the financial wherewithal, time horizon, and, in some cases, flexibility to pursue new initiatives in quest of fulfillment and impact. A number of mid-career business leaders, having secured their financial futures, have started their own businesses. Generally speaking, these have the most transformative energy and are thinking the most creatively about impacting the world around them, including and sometimes through the business world. Those who have not yet realized all of their career goals remain committed to these goals. Among mid-career informants, most of those in public companies or large private companies remain burdened by the pressure to produce "results," but many are accumulating enough discretion to attempt to realize broader influence in their organizations. Many of those who are near the midpoints of their careers are seeking out and being recruited by charitable organizations and are developing a taste for making an impact in their communities. Mid-career executives are the most enthusiastic proponents of the virtue-profit connection, having spent enough time in business to sample success but with plenty of time left for virtuous acts to translate to success if they have not done so already.

Late-career informants are true omni-valuers, having accumulated over their careers an arsenal of stories that demonstrate the value of faith to themselves and others. Concerned with establishing a legacy, late-career executives focus on ensuring the ongoing reputation and success of their firms and directing the resources they have accumulated toward good ends. They are among the strongest champions of the economic benefits of business and the most inclined to emphasize shareholder value, perhaps because many have attained positions in which they are directly answerable to capital providers. They are often among the least overt in terms of applying their faith at work, sensitive to the possibility of causing offense or being perceived to privilege one group of employees over another.

Position/Job Function

CEOs are generally more discreet about their faith than others, concerned about the possible abuse of authority. CEOs who live in the public eye are more circumspect and less trusting than other informants; confidentiality and safe harbor are especially important to them. For some informants in especially high-profile positions, the influence associated with their positions sometimes feels like more of a burden than a blessing. Paradoxically, a number of informants find that greater authority and influence in their companies diminishes their ability to use influence in meaningful ways. Especially in the pluralistic contexts that characterize many of the companies for which informants work, CEOs typically decline to signal their faith in any but the most generic ways, concerned that more overt manifestation might make subordinates uncomfortable or compromise the intended environment of religious neutrality.

Executives whose job function involves strategy or marketing are primarily attuned to customer needs. Finance and legal professionals emphasize the spiritual value of wealth and invoke the concept of stewardship to justify a focus on financial results and shareholder value. Executives in human resources roles emphasize employee well-being and the sense of community that companies provide. Executives who specialize in technology or product development are more inclined to cite creativity among the spiritual purposes of business. And executives who are best versed in operations emphasize process over outcome and tend to highlight the intrinsic value of work as such.

Founders and owners are more likely to identify their own worth with the worth of their companies. They also seem to feel the most intense responsibility for their employees. The acuteness of this responsibility diminishes their risk tolerance to some extent, offsetting in part the flexibility they enjoy to run their companies as they see fit.

An entrepreneurial disposition and context correlate with the desire for greater impact. If informants have been successful at building something— even something small—they can imagine themselves building something bigger. Across the board, commitment to reform is less a function of visibility or absolute magnitude of influence or income than of the amount of discretion in a particular company or context. For example, informants are more likely to be interested in widespread renewal if they own a small company than if they lead a large company but answer to other owners or capital providers.

Demographics

Minorities and women have long been and continue to be substantially underrepresented in business leadership positions. While the small number of minority informants limits the generalizability of their perspectives, in this study minority informants did not evidence distinctive perspectives on the propriety of business or their roles therein. This is noteworthy in that race regularly represents a salient axis of variation with respect to various moral, political, and ethical issues. Blacks, for example, evidence distinctive perspectives on homosexuality and gay rights and, of particular relevance to the present study, economic ethics and corporate social responsibility.[13] Black and white evangelicals, in particular, demonstrate differing perspectives on, for example, science education.[14] At the same time, the black church's economic ethic looks a lot like the white church's economic orientation. Scholars posit that the African American church invests the market with "miraculous" powers on the premise that the logic of the market is the best and perhaps only path leading to the eradication of African American poverty, and this despite the fact that the existing political economy was founded on the degradation and exploitation of African Americans.[15]

The fact that black evangelical executives and white evangelical executives demonstrate similar attitudes toward business is reminiscent of research showing that evangelicals from a black congregation and a white congregation articulated similar perspectives on environmental issues, with the implication that shared theological beliefs can at times supplement or even supersede racial identity as a source of moral judgment.[16] Notably, white and black informants shared the individualistic perspective on social change outlined earlier. This is significant in that this individualistic orientation is precisely the dynamic that scholars have implicated in white evangelicals' denial and reproduction of structural racial inequality.[17]

Unlike minority executives, female evangelical executives did point to distinctive challenges, experiences, and perspectives on business leadership. These dynamics merit a more extensive discussion and will be explored in the next chapter.

* * *

Between them, evangelical executives thoughtfully appropriate their faith in and through work in a variety of ways. Sometimes this takes explicit Christian expression. Often it does not. It is almost never connected to parallel efforts or broader agendas. It is almost always consistent with the organizational context in which it is situated and conditioned by certain characteristics of the executives themselves.

In a sense, Cragun, the sociologist who asserted that religion is of little consequence in social domains like business, is correct inasmuch as religion seems not to produce any systematic difference in behavior. Evangelicals can be found leading all types of companies with all sorts of objectives. While faith commitments do matter on an individual basis, the flexible ends toward which religious energy is channeled obscure this influence. The individualization of religion, such as characterizes the faith expressions of evangelical executives, is one reason it no longer works well as a control variable in quantitative studies and helps explain why those who study religion up close insist that it is important while those who observe it from afar downplay its impact. Religion does matter—in business as elsewhere—but its influence is most apparent when disaggregated than as a whole.

6

Into the Headwind

The ways evangelical executives perceive business and apply their faith at work is ordered by their professional contexts. Even within analogous professional environments, however, certain informants report different experiences. Relative to their male peers, women regularly experience different choices and challenges even in the same organizational settings. Indeed, the female executives I interviewed uniformly acknowledged the headwinds they face as women in business—impediments that shape their career arcs and even their religious identities.

A number of the women I interviewed rued the persistence of the oft-cited "glass ceiling" that truncates advancement opportunities for women in business. The data continue to validate this complaint. Women held only about 10 percent of the top executive positions at US companies in 2017, including just 5 percent of chief executive positions.[1] While quick to acknowledge progress in terms of opportunities for women through upper-management roles, the women I interviewed still perceived impediments to the attainment of executive-level positions. For example, the head of human resources at an international financial services company cited stereotypical gender biases regarding women's capability and commitment: "Can they work long hours?" she claims people wonder. "Will they pull their own weight?"

Those women who manage to overcome entrenched biases and attain executive status encounter difficulties once they arrive. One informant recounts with chagrin her initiation into the highest leadership tier at a prominent financial services firm. "At my first management meeting some man patted the table and said, 'All right, I want to know why I had to take time off to come to this meeting and someone could send their secretary.'" Another executive, who became the highest-level woman in the history of a multinational conglomerate, lamented, "It was very hard to be optimized because you were like the first black. Everybody stared at you and everybody knew your name and it was very hard to become mainstreamed because you weren't just doing what you do—you represented what all women do."

Baptizing Business. Bradley C. Smith, Oxford University Press (2020). © Oxford University Press.
DOI: 10.1093/oso/9780190055776.001.0001

Some senior-level evangelical women experienced resentment for their very presence at the top of the corporate hierarchy, especially inasmuch as it apparently disrupted the club-like atmosphere that characterizes some executive suites. "It changed everything in the executive meetings," recalled one informant. "The guys use to drink brandy at three in the afternoon and they were like, 'Well, what do we do now with you [here]?' It just changes everything. It's just goofiness. Everybody is awkward." Another stated bluntly of her presence as the only woman among the managerial class at her firm, "Sometimes I feel like they don't want you in the room."

In light of these experiences, it is little wonder that the women I interviewed consistently expressed feelings of loneliness and isolation. While this situation is not specific to evangelical women in particular, some informants did indicate that their religious affiliation and convictions heightened their sense of separation and dissimilarity. As one observed, "It's funny; I've noticed that people can stand up and state that I'm a Muslim or a Buddhist. A lot of people in business talk about being Buddhist or quote Buddhist teaching, which is really powerful. But it's not politically correct to stand up and say, 'I'm a Christian.'" Like Kyle who declined to join colleagues at a strip club, one woman cited the difficulty of fitting in with coworkers. "It was hard earlier in my career," she states. "There are times when I probably stand out from the rest of my group and I might not be included in every conversation because they know where I stand and if it's off color . . . or if they go out—I personally just don't drink and if they're going out for drinks, I might not always be included because they're not sure where I stand on that."

No Place Like Home

Much of the consternation and angst aspiring evangelical Christian women experience revolves around domestic considerations. Several women recount wrestling with the decision to stay home with their children or not—a dilemma none of the men I interviewed reported giving any thought to. Some women acknowledged that not having children facilitated their career progression. Others speculated that their careers might not have unfolded the same way if they did not have spouses who felt called to stay home with their children. One estimated that of the women who reached the highest levels of the large banking company at which she was an executive, half had husbands who were full-time parents, suggesting that the career prospects for women without such support were not as promising.

According to the women I interviewed, the church is regrettably of little help on this issue. Many evangelicals subscribe to a "complementarian" perspective on gender roles, positing that constitutional differences between men and women and biblical prescriptions regarding their respective roles support the traditional gender divide in which domestic responsibilities represent women's primary "profession." Some complementarians insist further that the Bible endorses the concept of "male headship," according to which women should not exercise authority over men, certainly in the case of spiritual and family matters and sometimes in any circumstance whatsoever.[2] While some authors note that in many cases the complementarian ideal is more symbolic than practical, these stubborn anachronisms, reflecting the patriarchal milieu in which the Bible was composed, nevertheless subject female evangelical executives to substantial intramural criticism.[3] While Nancy, the fast food chain CEO, is satisfied that her calling to business is legitimate, feeling as though she has heard from God to that effect, such subjective experiences do not satisfy those with alternate views on women's primary callings. "Boy, when you have to explain that to your brother, and your minister, and your next-door neighbor . . . I really believe that's the reason there are so few Christian women leaders. It's too hard. It's just too hard," she declares.

One executive laments what she calls evangelical Christianity's "deification of children in the home," which she describes as an overcorrection to the impulse of women in the 1980s and 1990s to go to school and work while leaving their children in daycare. In contrast, she perceives among contemporary evangelicals what she describes as "child and family worship," where dedication to family overrides all other commitments—whether to ministry, work, or otherwise. As an example, she relates, "Somebody said to me last week that he doesn't have a cell phone because it keeps him from being a good dad. And I think, 'Well, there you go . . . you could not make a living in the rest of the world so it's a good thing you're here.'" This executive is not optimistic that the general evangelical orientation on family responsibilities and their place among broader concerns will change anytime soon. "I'm on the board [of a major evangelical parachurch organization] and I'm watching the new influx of men and women and I'm not holding up great hope," she frets. "They are all homeschooling and all kind of 'Little House on the Prairie.' They've gotten even more conservative," she reports.

Consistent with the theological perspectives outlined above, there is a striking asymmetry of expectations among the men I interviewed and the women I interviewed regarding domestic responsibilities. While busy male executives are inclined to describe their inability to devote substantial time to their families as a noble sacrifice, women are inclined to experience the same as an abrogation of responsibility. While men sometimes expressed internal conflict regarding the choice of a career in business versus an explicitly ministry-oriented role such as pastoring a church, women who chose a career in business opted for it instead of both ministry and full-time parenthood. Moreover, whereas a man who purchases a private jet in order to spend a few more hours per week with his family sees himself as a hero who goes above and beyond, a woman who does something similar is more likely to express that she is compensating for a deficit.

No Place to Feel at Home

Several of the female executives I interviewed observed with frustration that they do not fit in either in business or in the church, being one of relatively few female executives at work and one of relatively few women at church who work outside the home. Relevant resources are scarce at church, with lack of role models a common theme. Indeed, according to many of the women I interviewed, when it comes to opportunities for women, the church is as much a part of the problem as of the solution. One woman believes that in terms of opportunities for women to assume leadership positions, the church actually lags far behind the business world. She observes, pointedly, "There are almost no women on ministry boards unless they are rich or married to someone rich." While evangelicals have established gender-specific ministry arms for men and women, they have, according to this same executive, become "ghettoized." "They have a lot of these lightweight but always domestically oriented groups where it's a little bit of entertainment and you giggle about men and do crafts," she scoffs. Such opportunities are of little interest or help to the women I interviewed.

Even church groups and events oriented toward work are no more impactful or appealing to the female executives I interviewed. As one executive describes, "The women have a very powerless subset. At conferences they at least try to get one female speaker. I've often been that female speaker. These are kind of like funny token gestures of inclusiveness, but they're not powerful and they are not influential." As such, they again are of little interest or relevance to women in the upper echelons of the business world. "None of these things reach people at the top of the house," said one executive. "It's supervisors, small mom-and-pop businesses; it never reaches executives un- less it's the head of a small company. But not senior executives at big firms."

In the experience of some of the women I interviewed, evangelical churches are on the whole so tone-deaf on gender issues that one executive asserted, "I actually think we're headed for a bit of a blowup. I have witnessed and talked with people where there seems to be a much more conservative view on the role of women in the church. You have this experience of women in the larger world trying to be productive in the church world and they can't. I think the blowup is going to be, 'What is the role of the church?' I think you find more people getting their spiritual feeding through small groups, kind of personal ways of doing it. I've had conversations with maybe half a dozen strong women lately who said, 'Going to church isn't doing it for me.' I don't think they're going to leave their work world, but I think leaving that church or finding other forms of worship is going to be important. The church is not feeding natural leadership skills, not reinforcing the role of women, and it's going to be a problem."

Whether or not they seek out other forms of religious sustenance, many of the women I interviewed are indeed inclined to select out of unaccom- modating business contexts and often to start their own businesses, with a number having done so already. Some informants eschewed more promi- nent, prestigious, and high-paying roles in favor of the flexibility and more agreeable climate they can implement in their own organizations. Some of the women I interviewed are so discouraged by their experiences as executives or apprehensive about the challenges and sacrifices required to scale the cor- porate ladder that they decline even to pursue executive roles. The execu- tive who was at one point mistaken for a secretary, for example, related, "I have had many opportunities to go back into management. I wouldn't even consider it." Instead, she, like many others, started her own business. As she explains, "I know many, many very successful women who have no in- terest in these suites of power. They would much rather work with their own style and work in their own way." The executive who described ongoing bias against women in executive suites agrees. "I think many women say, 'I don't want to live that way. I'll run my own business. I'll do something more entre- preneurial.'" Flexibility and autonomy are key considerations in many such circumstances, to the point that some women decline to pursue or accept external financing. As one female entrepreneur observed, citing the counsel of a Harvard Business School professor, "Once you give over any control to your investors, it's not your company anymore. I don't care about it being my company; it's not an ego thing. It's more just making sure that you're able to continue to fulfill the mission that you want to fulfill."

Paving the Way

Many of the women I interviewed are eager to promote opportunities for women to flourish at the highest levels of business. "I think women need to be very intentional in how they support other women in leadership," stated one executive. The same executive opined, "The church ought to be at the forefront of demonstrating women in leadership." Others agreed, emphasizing the need for community with and accountability to like-minded business leaders. When asked what would help her flourish spiritually during her tenure as a public company executive, one informant responded, "Being connected to a group where you've got other business leaders who can relate to what you're doing, what you're going through—the pressures—and share examples of how they balanced it." It has to be a true peer, though. She relates, "I have a girlfriend who [tells me I should work out]. It's like, 'Yeah, I agree with you,' but she doesn't have any kids. She's an assistant at an office— nothing wrong with that—but she's got a lot more free time. The pressures of owning your own company and being responsible for people is just different. So for her to say to me, 'Well, you just have to schedule time,' I discount that. But for someone that's in my situation to tell me how they do it—I would probably listen."

Some informants attempt to support aspiring women in various ways. Several claim to mentor other aspiring businesswomen. One executive is a founding member of a global woman leadership council tasked with advancing opportunities for the development and advancement of women at her multinational company and beyond. Nancy, the fast food CEO, for her part, strives to be an encouraging voice for other Christian women in business. Largely as a result of her own experience of discrimination, Nancy has resolved to be "a visible Christian leader" for the sake of other women facing similar circumstances and disapproval. "They've got nobody to talk to, look to, encourage, or support them," Nancy complains. To prove her point, she observes, "If you do a Google search about devotion books for women who work . . . the last time I did it, there were five. For men who work, I think it was eleven thousand. You can't even find published material. You can't find a Bible study. You can't find support."

Given the discrimination they face in the workplace and the absence of support they encounter from the church, evangelical women who aspire to business leadership might be condoned for desiring the assistance of a Christian Mafia of sorts, or at least a society organized for the support of evangelical women in business. Despite consistent claims of loneliness and isolation, however, without the support of the church there seems to be no impulse or mechanism by which the women I interviewed might come together in common cause. In fact, merely identifying as an evangelical Christian executive is not necessarily sufficient to forge strong bonds or alliances. Said one woman of the female evangelical Christian executives in her part of the country, "We are scarce and we kind of know each other but that doesn't mean we have a lot in common." Drawing a parallel to presumed racial affinities, she observes, "Just because you're black doesn't mean you have to be friends with anyone who is black."

Notably, the female executives I interviewed were far more attuned to the challenges women face in business than the challenges evangelicals face in business. In fact, their advocacy was oriented to women in general, not evangelical women in particular. They want to advance opportunities for women in business because of what women bring to the table as such, irrespective of their religious convictions. One executive, in fact, after elaborating various differences between men and women, specifically stated that she hasn't noticed any difference in Christian leaders and other leaders. "I have found that being a Christian makes almost no difference in the quality of a leader," she says. "I have seen dismal leaders who are Christian," she notes, "but they are very nice people."

Unapologetically Different

While the women I interviewed acknowledged and in some cases experienced gender-based discrimination in the workplace, their arguments for greater representation of women among executive ranks in business were generally grounded more in pragmatism than propriety. Informants are essentially unanimous that more women in leadership positions would translate to an enhanced corporate culture and, ultimately, more favorable business outcomes. For example, one executive cited research indicating that companies make more profit if they have good women leaders at the top of the organization. Another referenced research indicating a correlation between the economic prosperity of a nation and that nation's degree of economic empowerment of women.

The primary mechanism by which these salutary effects are understood to take place is the infusion of distinctive personality traits, leadership styles, and problem-solving approaches women are presumed to contribute. The women I interviewed consistently asserted that women and men are different in ways that matter in business. One executive noted that among the women with whom she attended Harvard Business School, those who went on to the most successful careers tended to have "classic male personalities." "It's sort of the idea that you can't get far if you're nice and sweet," she explained. This contrast between the hard charging, win-at-all-costs man and the more deliberate and accommodating woman underlaid much of the proposed distinction between men and women as articulated by informants.

More than one of the women I spoke with lauded the value of women's intuition and way of thinking through decisions. Sometimes informants perceived feminine attributes that were particularly well suited to certain industries or roles. For example, one executive referenced women's ability to look beyond facts, which she claims is especially important in people-oriented businesses. Another averred, "I think there are some traditional gifts and graces that women have that are compatible with wealth management." These differences, informants assert, make a difference. As one states, "More diverse teams produce higher collaboration and stronger alignment."

Some informants were quick to point out that the purpose of such comparisons is not to disparage men. "I've met plenty of men who are incredibly kind and thoughtful and caring and sort of the classic woman characteristics," clarified one. "It's just that women typically tend to have more of those characteristics or in higher quantity." Another, after extolling the value of gender diversity, disclaimed, "I'm not a man hater. I work with a lot of great men." These qualifications notwithstanding, informants' comments represent an implicit indictment of some of the stereotypically male characteristics that are valued in the business world and often essential to success. "I think a lot of women, myself included at times, don't have as much confidence, and dare I say arrogance as it takes to lead a team of people," confided one woman, adding, "I don't think women have as much of the 'I'll just fake it until I make it' attitude that often [translates to success].'"

Nancy asserts that the presence of women can take the rough edges off of some types of masculine executive behavior. "I've entered board rooms and management teams as the first woman to enter the room," she states. "When I enter the room, they start talking differently. There's less profanity. They don't tell any more girly jokes. They don't go to strip bars anymore. They don't have martini lunches anymore. And I didn't say a word." Nancy goes so far as to speculate that women could reduce the prevalence of white-collar crime. "I'll be bold," she asserts. "Maybe the Enron thing could have been stopped if there had been more women in the room. Maybe. I've seen things like that stopped. I have seen unethical behavior where I've said, 'Look, if this conversation continues, I'm leaving the room and the company right now.' So you can have a huge impact."

Some studies support informants' evaluations of both gender differences and their potential for workplace enhancement. Steffensmeier and coauthors summarize the literature as follows: "Research on work/occupations and business enterprise suggests women generally adhere to a different way of doing business that carries a sense of connectedness and brings a more ethical perspective to the workplace.[4] Corporate women, more than corporate men, use their organizational power to address issues of social responsibility and are more inclined to make people, not just profits, a priority.[5] Female executives tend to score more positively on measures of socialization, self-control, empathy, social involvement, and integrity."[6] For these reasons, Steffensmeier et al. conclude that women's ethical orientations do in fact hedge against involvement in white-collar crime and act as a deterrent to corporate wrongdoing.[7] Promising as this sounds, Robin and Babin caution that disconnects between intention and behavior, as well as a bias favoring publication of statistically significant outcomes, render such studies unreliable guides to actual workplace behavior, finding scant evidence themselves that a higher proportion of women among executive ranks would make an appreciable impact on the ethics of the business community.[8]

Applied Differences

The subjunctive mood that characterizes the language with which the women I interviewed describe the potential influence of women in the workplace implies a feeling of impotence as things stand. *If* there were more women, informants assert, things would be different. As one informant explained, research suggests that until there are three or more women on a team, the culture of the team doesn't change. Whether well-represented or not, however, like the men I interviewed, women express an inclination to apply their faith at work. And as with the broader group of evangelical executives I interviewed, the paradigmatic examples of faith at work presented by women center on individual impacts through direct personal relationships. One woman shared that one of her direct reports opened an email containing salary information addressed to the informant, forwarded it to herself, marked it unread, and lied about it when confronted. After eventually evoking a tearful confession, the executive was advised by her boss to fire the subordinate. She relates, "I did not fire her and decided that I would put her on sort of a probation plan, which the company actually made me do. After allowing her to have dignity, she ended up becoming the most loyal employee. I remember six or seven years after all of that happened, she sent me a letter apologizing and saying she just so appreciated how I handled it. In the letter she wrote to me, she said, 'I know that it had to do with your faith perspective and giving people a second chance and forgiveness.' That was a pretty powerful moment for me." Such was a typical example of the applications of faith cited by female evangelical executives.

Some of the women I interviewed demonstrate an intense commitment to corporate social responsibility. One woman shared that one of the factors that attracted her to her current company is the commitment never to promote a brand that does not have a positive impact on consumers, listing tobacco as an example of a proscribed product. Another informant started one of the first socially responsible investment funds in the country, incidentally lamenting the evolution of socially responsible investing since that time from the pursuit of opportunities to fund socially helpful enterprises to the filtering out of adverse products like tobacco. Another informant spent her summer internship while at Harvard Business School traveling through Europe with the CEO of a prominent consumer products company, tasked with "figuring out how to take [the company's] ethic of service—or corporate social responsibility—which they take seriously in the United States, and spread the word of corporate social responsibility in Europe."

While few of the executives I interviewed—whether male or female—accepted without qualification Milton Friedman's infamous assertion that the social responsibility of business is to increase its profits, some women were particularly critical of this narrow view. With respect to Friedman's proposition, a female founder of a consulting group, having devoted considerable thought to the topic, noted, "Later in life Friedman actually amended that statement. We had lots of debates about this in business school. In fact, I actually spoke to Milton Friedman's assistant to try to get him to do a satellite debate at Harvard Business School. He was up for the discussion because his attitude changed quite a bit over his lifetime. I agree with the sentiment he eventually shared at the end of his life where he said it's not that a company should only care about shareholder value. That should be a key purpose and certainly a company's viability needs to be the primary purpose to sustain itself. Yet the smartest companies are the ones that recognize that it's not just about money. It's about long-term value creation. It's about making sure that every aspect of the way you do business is sustainable; making sure that your products are healthy for the environment; making sure that your workers are well taken care of."

In line with informants' emphasis on women's intuition and emotion, one female executive I interviewed confessed, "I'll tell you . . . I feel like I've fallen down a little bit as the manager of my division because I make decisions from my heart. I always think about, ultimately, the responsibility that we have to the consumers that we serve. That does not align sometimes with making decisions that are in the interest of driving revenue. And I've had my CEO tell me all the time, 'You're so great at lots of things. You have unbelievable thought skills. People like you. People respect you. But where you've got to focus—what you've got to think about—is driving your [profit and loss].' And I don't know how to reconcile that, because I think that in this environment when push comes to shove the revenue supersedes [consumer interests]. I think sometimes they happily coexist. But I've found more and more in this particular industry, at this particular time . . . it's more and more challenging." "That's one of the reasons I'm looking for an exit."

Cognizant of the sacrifices necessary to succeed at the highest levels of business and, like their male counterparts, sensitive to critical perspectives held and sometimes articulated by coreligionists, those few evangelical women who make it to the top of the corporate hierarchy must be resolute in their conviction that they are called to business leadership. As one executive puts it, "You have to believe in your heart and your soul that you're called to use all of your talents and gifts for God." As was the case with informants as a whole, alongside their general affirmation of business, women acknowledged that business is subject to abuse and does not always function as it should, though women honed in on different issues. For example, while men most frequently lamented the trade-offs and inefficiencies associated with the quarterly reporting cycle, women more regularly identified executive pay ratios as a particularly troublesome issue, likely reflecting the fact that women remain underpaid relative to men who perform analogous job functions.[9] According to one informant, "I think that it is fundamentally wrong that CEOs are compensated so exorbitantly compared to workers. It's what the market will bear, but it's also because there is no accountability for the boards of directors," she said, explaining that directors are incented to compensate executives well in order to retain their board seats and the accompanying status and remuneration.

Same Song, Different Verse

Do the examples above constitute evidence that female evangelical executives regard business differently and enact their faith differently in business contexts than do male evangelical executives? In one sense, it does. Mindful that we should be wary of statistical inference regarding differences between male and female executives given the relatively small number of women interviewed, women in this study were indeed more likely than male informants to articulate concern for people relative to profits, more receptive to broader corporate social responsibilities, and more likely to cite feelings and intuition in support of career and business decisions. Crucially, however, they also disproportionately occupied the types of contexts that prompted informants more broadly—whether women or men—to embrace these particular perspectives. With but a few exceptions, the women I interviewed were either entrepreneurs running their own firms or responsible for "softer" professional disciplines like human resources or marketing. Being less answerable to capital providers and less concretely connected to the flow of money, the previously observed relationships between context and faith expressions would lead us to expect that women would show heightened sensitivity to people-oriented concerns, and indeed that is what we find. It is, therefore, not immediately clear if this predilection is a function of gender norms or professional identity.

The perspectives of the two women whose professional locations differed most markedly from that of the other women I interviewed shed light on the relative strength of professional, religious, and demographic identities for female executives. Among the women I interviewed, the two women who occupied the most prominent positions in public companies were the staunchest proponents of the economic value of business. Commenting on the notion of corporate social responsibility, Nancy, the restaurant chain CEO and one of the aforementioned two women, chirped, "My grandmother would laugh out loud at that stupid word, right? 'Social responsibility,' she'd say. 'What the heck is that? Does that mean you bake somebody a cake when their mother dies?'" While articulated less stridently, the other high-level public company executive likewise endorses a narrow view of the purpose and corresponding responsibility of business. "I believe that business has a very specific and very important purpose in the world," she states. "It is to advance the economic well-being of communities." This is not to suggest that she is unconcerned about social, spiritual, and other objectives and institutions. Rather, she contends that such institutions depend on business for their existence. "If you think about it," she says, "government, churches, schools, missions, every 501(c)(3), every NGO—all of these are consumers of wealth and fully dependent on it for their existence. That goes back to the role of business, which is to provide ethical and sustainable wealth creation." The women whose organizations are most publicly accountable for financial results proffer the most narrowly economic definitions of the purpose of business.

It is instructive as well that of the women I interviewed, the one who evidenced the most discomfort with the way business operates was a younger and still-ascending executive who voiced a strong desire to exit the business world in favor of nonprofit work. Not coincidentally, she also worked for a company that provided financial services to the underbanked—an ostensibly noble purpose that all too easily, and in this executive's experience, actually blurred the line between service to and exploitation of those with nowhere else to turn.

When it comes to the relationship between professional contexts and faith expressions, it turns out that female evangelical executives conform to the same patterns as male evangelical executives. Younger informants are more apt to criticize business, human resources professionals are more oriented to diversity and related concerns, public company executives rarely stray far from the bottom line, and so on. Given that men and women occupying similar occupational contexts with comparable levels of influence and experience demonstrate similar perspectives on their organizations in particular and business more broadly, it appears that as an organizing orientation for faith expressions, occupational experiences override socialized gender ideologies, which squares with some previous research.[10] It is not quite that simple, however, for as we have seen, female (evangelical) executives regularly opt out of certain occupational contexts that fail to accommodate their preferred dispositions and faith expressions. As one informant complains, "When women get into leadership positions, they try to make them function like men. From an emotion or compassion standpoint, or if they show female characteristics, then all of a sudden they are not as strong as they ought to be in a management position." "I wouldn't want to change myself to be in that position," she added. So while faith expressions are ultimately organized by professional contexts, the professional contexts into which evangelical executives select are in many cases organized by religious and gender expectations and identities.

Recurring Themes

Like their male counterparts, the women I interviewed are *especially sensitive to criticism from fellow evangelicals*. Nancy, the restaurateur, reflecting on fellow evangelicals who question her call to business leadership, huffed, "We don't need that help. Christian women leaders do not need any more people telling them they're not doing God's work. We need people that want to come alongside . . . be part of the solution. Frankly, I don't think there's a whole lot of people lining up for that job." While acknowledging that the lack of women in executive leadership positions is problematic, it is the church, not business, that female evangelical executives hold up for reproach. In fact, some women are inclined to downplay the seriousness of the underrepresentation of women in business, remarking that such underrepresentation is common to all major institutions and professional domains. In some cases it is not even clear that women consider the underrepresentation of women among the executive ranks unjust. As one informant explained, if women might not be consistently available because of their sense of responsibility to be home for their families, it is economically rational to prefer employees who are less likely to experience career interruptions. When asked if she thinks the underrepresentation of women among the corporate elite is therefore legitimate, this executive stated, "I do think it's legitimate. I don't see a solution for it. I think there is a huge benefit to our communities by having women choose to be home when they can."

We have already seen examples of women who underwent the *transition from success to significance* that was broadly characteristic of the evangelical executives under study. Others, like Audra, who longs to indulge her passion for improving the condition of women in Africa, are desperate to make the transition but not in position to do so yet. One informant speculates that many evangelical women who aspire to executive leadership not only defer significance, but disguise or even abandon their religious identity if it proves more a hindrance than a help. "I actually have my own theory," she confides, "that many [female executives] came from [evangelical Christianity] and dropped out from it once they found the church did not serve them. If you poke enough you realize they had a kind of Christian background, but they go underground with it."

Like the men I interviewed, when justifying their occupational pursuits and elaborating the benefits of business, the women I interviewed appealed to the Bible, just as did their critics when challenging them. As one executive states, "I don't see any examples in the Bible where God excludes some part of the world where women aren't supposed to use their gifts and talents. I think that opens the door to all leadership positions, everywhere." An interpretive strategy that grants approval to anything not specifically condemned by the Bible represents a powerful instrument for those who *use religion as an affirming source of moral authority*.

Like their male counterparts, the women I interviewed also appealed to the *connection between virtue and profit* when advocating for responsible business practices. The executive who provided a nuanced view of Milton Friedman's evolving perspective on corporate responsibility and attempted to organize a debate on the issue at Harvard Business School concluded her thoughts on the subject with a pragmatic appeal. "Good business says that if your workers are happy and healthy and treated well, they are going to stay with the company longer," she states. "There's going to be less turnover. That's good for business, too. That's the important philosophy: at the end of the day, what's good for people, what's good for your products, is what's good for business." Even as she lamented that it takes time to prove the relationship, another reflected, "My gut says if you do the right thing with the consumer you'll get it back in terms of loyalty and retention." And even when advocating for greater representation of women among business elites, the women I interviewed emphasized utility over morality. As one said, "There is good information that shows that women change the context in the places they work, complement the left brain with the right brain, or have different ways of approaching stuff," making a point to add, "That would be far away from saying you should advance women for the sake of advancement."[11]

* * *

The perspectives of female evangelical executives suggest that religious identity or context is not necessarily more salient than other forms of identity, including gender and professional identities. The experiences of women also confirm that the orienting perspectives and rhetorical strategies explored earlier are not merely the product of the white male experience.

For aspiring evangelical women, already subject to the restraining effects of the metaphorical glass ceiling, evangelical perspectives on gender roles clearly represent an exacerbating headwind. Ironically, though, when female evangelical executives eschew arguments from equivalence in favor of arguments from distinction when advocating for themselves and other aspiring women in business, they may in so doing actually reinforce the complementarian theological perspectives that undermine the legitimacy of women in leadership roles in the first place.[12] Once again, religion matters, but its influence is neither obvious, straightforward, nor more impactful than other regulating dynamics.

Conclusion

Baptizing Business

This book represents a Weberian exercise in interpretive sociology as applied to themes seminally explored by Weber in *The Protestant Ethic and the Spirit of Capitalism*—both the ways religion and economic life intersect and Weber's forecast of the dominance of economic rationality at the expense of religious values. Starting from the presupposition that people by nature prefer leisure to work, Weber saw in the concept of vocation an impetus for overcoming the traditional antipathy toward work, and especially toward commerce, by infusing it with "other-worldly" motivation and significance. Introduced into the Protestant vernacular by Martin Luther, whose reading of Scripture encouraged the acceptance of one's daily work—arduous and mundane as it might be—as God-given, the concept of vocation was later reinterpreted and expanded by John Calvin and his followers to encompass the systematic and perpetual pursuit of profit.[1] For Luther, Christian believers had been called by God into whatever particular line of work they found themselves, and hence were duty-bound to it. For Calvinists, Christians were obliged to pursue occupational mobility if presented with opportunities to make more money. It was this Calvinist understanding of vocation, Weber contended, that facilitated the transition from economic traditionalism, in which work is viewed as a necessary evil that infringes on more important activities like relationship with family and friends, to economic rationalism, in which work is enshrined as the highest duty and oriented to the perpetual increase of productivity. By establishing money-making as a religious duty, the Puritans Weber described anchored a direct connection between the economic and the spiritual.

Despite its role in legitimating the systematic pursuit of profit, Weber insisted that, already as of a century ago, the concept of vocation had been reduced to "ghosts of beliefs no longer anchored in the substance of religion."[2] The perpetual pursuit of profit, originally inspired by religious beliefs, had become "routinized" such that it no longer required evaluative support.

Baptizing Business. Bradley C. Smith, Oxford University Press (2020). © Oxford University Press.
DOI: 10.1093/oso/9780190055776.001.0001

Whereas "the Puritan wanted to be a person with a vocational calling; today we are forced to be," Weber lamented, implying that profit-oriented work is now central by necessity, not by choice, irrespective of its meaningfulness or lack thereof.[3] For this reason, Weber anticipated little use for religion in the contemporary economy, observing that increasing reliance on formal rationality, which entails the conventional maximization of utility, comes at the expense of substantive rationality, which refers to allocation within the guidelines of other principles, including such things as sacred values. For Weber, the spirit that had infused economic pursuits with deeper meaning had evaporated, leaving workers to toil in an iron cage, characterized by a state of drudgery reminiscent of the traditional economic ethos that had disparaged work in favor of other, more meaningful pursuits.

In certain ways Weber's pessimistic assessment of the evolution of "victorious capitalism" was prescient. For example, polls document a transformation of the American Dream in which "Americans [are] seeking more personal satisfaction through recreation, family life, friends, religion, and a search for meaning in life—not through work."[4] Another study confirms that Americans now express the American dream more as a function of freedom and family than of money and homeownership.[5] For generations a source of satisfaction and pride, to be characterized today by the Protestant work ethic and propelled by the spirit of capitalism would more likely be an insult, associated with disorders like workaholism and greed. Meanwhile, despite intense longings for resources and experiences that work cannot provide, Americans continue to work longer than they wish, apparently driven by the competitive dynamics of the marketplace. The United States is frequently described today as a work-obsessed society,[6] yet, when work and money are compared with other values in our society, they rarely rank highly.[7] The captivity to work that characterizes the modern economic ethic is juxtaposed with a longing for the values privileged by the traditional economic ethic. For many Americans today, work is less a vocation than an impediment to more important quests.

Evangelicals have not been immune to transformations in attitudes toward work. While ascetic dispositions persisted among some groups of Protestants for several decades after Weber claims they contributed to the accelerating diffusion of rational capitalism, by the mid-1800s the spiritual significance of vocation had dissipated even among evangelicals.[8] More recently, even the secularized legacy of asceticism, promulgated until the mid-1900s by families and schools, has itself eroded. As Hunter details, not only have virtues like industriousness and competitiveness lost moral value and spiritual meaning, they have also been marginalized even as secular values, displaced by a preoccupation with self-fulfillment and values associated with the private sphere.[9] As Hunter concludes, "the Protestant legacy of austerity and ascetic self-denial is virtually obsolete in the larger Evangelical culture and is nearly extinct for a large percentage of the coming generation of Evangelicals."[10] For evangelicals and others, the concept of vocation, which established profit-oriented work as the central activity of life and gave it spiritual sanction, has been shorn of its religious connotations. And today even the secularized version has been displaced in favor of an ethic of self-fulfillment that downplays work in favor of other more fulfilling pursuits.

At the same time, Weber's expectations regarding the priority and tyranny of rationality neglect characteristics of business that facilitate a niche role for religion in economic life even today. In fact, in many ways Weber was mistaken about the nature of organizations. It turns out that neither organizations—including economic ones—nor their leaders are strictly rational. Cyert and March successfully challenged the idea that organizations are oriented toward a specific goal, emphasizing the diversity, ambiguity, and incompatibility of organizational objectives.[11] These characteristics, often taken as impediments to organizational effectiveness, make room for interpretive institutions such as religion to stake claim to relevance and influence in corporate contexts. For the executives I interviewed, the inability to optimize several, sometimes incompatible goals necessitates the type of satisficing rationalizations I have previously highlighted, wherein evangelical executives are content to claim spiritually worthwhile outcomes for some stakeholders, typically without reference to other stakeholders who might experience relative neglect. Shamir has demonstrated how easy it is for businesses to tip their hat toward certain constituencies without making concrete sacrifices or even altering organizational behavior at all.[12] And moreover, the inability to calculate the consequences of alternatives permits such claims to stand on their own, independent of evidence.

Weick, meanwhile, has explored organizations as systems of meaning whose members retrospectively make sense of their choices and circumstances, highlighting the receptivity of organizations to different types of values and objectives.[13] There is reason to believe that businesses are actually more receptive to diverse objectives than are organizations associated with other professions. As Merton explains, one reason institutional science has been successful is that scientists, influenced by common professionalization processes, adhere to common norms and values, which, incidentally, typically consider religion inappropriate inasmuch as it threatens to cloud objectivity and introduce bias.[14] Schmalzbauer observes similarly that religion is generally unwelcome in secular professions such as academia and journalism on account of its apparent subjectivity.[15] But the situation is considerably different in business, where businesspeople are generally not bound together by codes of professionalization or even common preparatory and educational experiences. Business, by itself, is not a compelling identity provider in the same way that someone would call herself a doctor or lawyer or professor, and as such is more open to the infusion of different norms and values.

All this makes room for the reappropriation of the concept of vocation, or calling, which played an important role in the genesis and legitimation of capitalism, but for various reasons has largely been evacuated of spiritual significance and fallen into disuse. The evangelical executives I interviewed stand out as exceptions to the general impulse to devalue work relative to other pursuits. Indeed, many of the business leaders I spoke with seem intent on resurrecting the ghost of vocation and reinfusing it with spiritual significance, even as they demonstrate a work ethic reminiscent of that endorsed by Reformation-era Protestants. But the way they understand vocation and the process through which they come to this understanding, far from catalyzing a revolution in the nature or significance of business, as was the case for early Calvinists, reinforces the appropriateness and worth of business as currently organized.

Vocation in Retrospect

Weber contended that some politicians live "off" politics, meaning they derive their livelihood from it, while others live "for" politics, meaning they make politics their life in an internal sense.[16] Importantly, ordinarily in order to live for politics the politician must be economically independent of the income politics can bring him—be wealthy or have a supplementary occupation that yields a sufficient income. For the executives I interviewed, economic independence is often the inflection point or minimum criterion for the transition from success to significance; informants who need no longer live off business can approach business as a vocation in the sense Weber applies to politics as a vocation. Therefore, most of the evangelical business leaders I interviewed are not like the Calvinists Weber described in the *Protestant Ethic*, who were at the beginning of an upwardly mobile journey. Instead, they are like those for whom politics is a vocation—those who are able to live for politics, not off politics. Moreover, we saw earlier that there is some indication that they, like Weber's successful politicians, are willing to compromise, at least for a season—to take responsibility for the end (their own success) at the expense of the means. This does not mean that they do unethical things, but that they bracket their faith commitments and keep them largely hidden for a season. It means deferring significance.

The way this process unfolds over the course of successful evangelical executives' careers means that, for many of them, business is not a vocation by default; rather, it *becomes* a vocation for those who accumulate sufficient influence, resources, and discretion to contribute meaningfully to eternally significant objectives inside or at least outside their firms. Almost all of the executives interviewed for this study feel called to business, but for many, calling is a retrospectively applied designation, not a prospective lens through which decisions are made. "How do you conclude anything else?" wondered the founder and CEO of a utility company. "We haven't lost any money in twenty-one years, so yeah, this business is my joy and my calling."

The process by which the evangelical business leaders I interviewed come to view their work as a vocation stands in contrast to other attempts to make work/business significant. They do not wish to change business by infusing it with meaning from the outside or channeling its energy to different ends (as do most advocates of corporate social responsibility), but to legitimate—both to themselves and others—its core functions as possessing spiritual value. To convince themselves and others of this, we have seen that evangelical executives are able to draw on several types of evidence and argument that paint business as a God-ordained and enforced moral order that is consistent with biblical principles. Sometimes such assertions are explicit and other times more oblique. Often they are commingled with components of the standard accounts of the purpose of business, enabling evangelical executives to contend that business is a spiritual activity while reassuring those to whom they are legally and economically responsible that they are focused on generating healthy returns on capital. In these evangelical business leaders and their accounts, the "spirit of capitalism," defined by Weber as a positive attitude toward both work and wealth, finds ongoing embrace and new expression, with implications for our understanding of the so-called faith at work movement, evangelicalism, and the role of religion among elites.

The Conflict Narrative Revisited

I observed at the outset that research on evangelical business leaders has generally emphasized conflict narratives, according to which evangelical executives experience tension between their faith convictions and business responsibilities. Nash and Miller, in particular, have highlighted areas of tension between people of faith, including and especially evangelicals, and the economic orientation required of corporations and their leaders.[17] Lindsay contends that, over the past couple of decades, an interconnected group of visible evangelical elites has made it more acceptable for elites to embrace an evangelical identity in public, paving the way for more overt applications of faith in corporate environments and other professional domains.[18] Miller agrees that evangelicals have, during this period, been active in the corporate domain—both as individuals and in concerted initiatives, having spearheaded what he and others call the "faith at work movement," a loose coalition of management theorists and practitioners who have pushed for increasing the role of faith in business on the assumption that business tends to marginalize faith.[19]

This perspective fits with broader research on evangelicals that emphasizes the tension evangelicals feel relative to other groups and institutions. Schmalzbauer, for example, writing about evangelical elites in journalism and higher education, claims, "More than any other branch of American Protestantism, evangelicals emphasize the boundaries between Christ and culture, sacred and secular, and church and world."[20] In contrast to these perspectives, my research suggests that, while conflict is an important part of informants' accounts, the nature of the conflict they experience, and hence a key source of strength for evangelical executives and perhaps for evangelicals more broadly, is different than previously theorized.

While this study contrasts with Lindsay's to the extent that I find less inclination to reform the business world or even particular companies, this book extends in some ways Lindsay's arguments regarding what he calls "elastic orthodoxy."[21] Lindsay defines elastic orthodoxy as a set of core religious convictions that are firmly shared among adherents but not so rigid that they prohibit engagement and cooperation with people who do not share them. Lindsay argues that the evangelical commitment to orthodoxy—shared, fundamental beliefs—keeps the movement cohesive while the elasticity of that orthodoxy enables evangelical adherents to build bridges with other people. At the risk of taking a heuristic device literally, I would like to extend this concept in terms of both its character and its effect. Elasticity implies not just flexibility but a tendency to return to a neutral position, such that any stretching produces tension until it is resolved. While Lindsay focuses on the ability of evangelical public leaders to reconcile their faith with the various social settings they inhabit, I would also emphasize the contested nature of orthodoxy. While there is abundant room for interpretation, contending for the right interpretation matters a great deal. In fact, against those who embrace a narrative that pits evangelicals against other groups and institutions, I contend, in line with Madsen's perspective on the nature of religiously motivated conflict in America today, that the primary source of tension experienced by the evangelical leaders I interviewed comes from within, not outside, their religious milieu.[22]

Madsen characterizes American religion as an archipelago of relatively self-contained faith communities in which individuals pursue community and personal fulfillment within the contours of a broader religious tradition, suggesting that compared to other social institutions, religion accords more freedom to believe and practice as one chooses.[23] Drawing on and extending this characterization, I suggest that the nature of the apparent conflict between business and religion as addressed by the faith at work movement is better characterized as a polemical skirmish within a religious tradition than a broad culture war emanating from religious convictions. Evangelical executives feel compelled to justify the value of their occupation—an impulse that is by no means unique. But for informants this impulse is prompted most frequently and intensely by coreligionists. It is important, therefore, to reorient the locus of conflict away from generic institutions toward specific groups of people with divergent interests and perspectives. Evangelical executives experience conflict not because they believe that business and religion are opposed, but because they are made to feel like second-class citizens by members of their faith communities. They experience conflict because *others*, including those to whose opinions they are sensitive, believe that faith and business are at odds. The primary conflict is between evangelical executives and critics from within their own faith tradition who view business as sub-spiritual, if not immoral.

A New Perspective on the Faith at Work Movement

In some ways tension is intrinsic to the organization of the faith at work movement, such that much of the internecine strain just described is characteristic of—and indeed a product of—the movement, itself. While sometimes understood as a unified enterprise, the faith at work movement is an ambiguous concept that is variously used to describe two quite different initiatives—one driven by external critics of business and another driven by internal defenders of business. During the course of my research I attended an event on faith and work sponsored by Princeton University's Faith & Work Initiative. The schedule consisted of two tracks—one for practitioners and the other for academics. Predictably, the content and tone of the presentations organized under the two headings differed considerably, with practitioners generally defending the spiritual worth of business and academics challenging the moral character of business.

Consistent with the tendency of similarly situated individuals to congregate, evangelical executives write books on faith and work in response to critics within the church, but the audience for this literature is other evangelical executives. Informants find reassurance and support in faith at work groups that consist exclusively of their peers. From the perspective of most of those who consider themselves part of the faith at work movement but are located outside of business, the impulse of the movement is to make business different by making Christian executives different. For informants, however, the characteristic impulse is not distinction—from other executives—but inclusion, in a group of like-minded people of faith who experience the travails associated with attaining and maintaining elite professional standing in corporate contexts and who help them recognize and sustain the spiritual value of their professional pursuits in the face of criticism from other evangelicals.

In light of the nature of the conflict evangelical executives perceive, organizations and literature associated with the faith and work movement serve a different purpose for evangelical business leaders than is often assumed. When informants turn to faith at work literature and activities, they are not looking primarily for insight into arbitrating between multiple stakeholders, appropriate levels of executive compensation, or other perceived moral dilemmas associated with business. They are looking, first of all, for companionship. Take the following from the president of an asset management company: "I think as a Christian businessman at the top of the organization you can feel very isolated. There's certainly a lot of organizations that will try to reach out to you, but you get more of a sense that they are consulting groups or someone is trying to make some money off of you instead of finding a peer group that you can get together and share ideas and pray for each other.[24] I got involved with a group I'm sure you're familiar with—the CEO Forum—and it has been an amazing blessing to me to share and grow and be mentored by peers, particularly older businessmen around the US taking me under their wing, giving me counsel, and praying for me when I needed it. They are not in our line of business but they've been there and done that and know what it feels like to be alone."

A number of the executives I interviewed participate in or even organize fellowship groups such as this executive found helpful. Several informants participate in the CEO Forum, itself. Another informant started a fellowship group in Silicon Valley to provide a network of support for Christians working in the tech sector. For years, one executive has organized a Christian outreach program at which businessmen meet twice a month at the Harvard Club in Midtown Manhattan. And some of the younger executives I interviewed have convened less formal groups of colleagues.

For evangelical executives, similarly situated peers provide the sense of connection that is essential to identity construction and maintenance. To Madsen's metaphor for American religion we can add that the individuals who inhabit archipelagos of religion cluster into villages of similarly positioned individuals wherein they make meaning together. Withdrawal to homogenous enclaves and adoption of idiosyncratic interpretations of religious principles that lend meaning to circumstances are common among evangelicals. Griffith, for example, describes the ways in which participants in Aglow, a theologically conservative organization of Christian women, come together to fulfill ostensibly oppressive gender role expectations in ways that satisfy various physical, emotional, and psychological needs.[25] Even as Aglow works toward the perfection of families, it supplies, both practically and theologically, family functions that kinship ties sometimes fail to deliver.

An individual-focused theology notwithstanding, neither these women nor the evangelical executives I studied can make meaning on their own; for this, they need collaboration. So while individualism is certainly an important aspect of American evangelicalism, its importance is sometimes overstated. It is not as if evangelical business leaders, in isolation, create and sustain meaning in their professional contexts. Rather, coming together with peers, they derive modes of meaning that fit with their circumstances. This is one reason faith at work groups are so important. Without the sort of support networks that the faith at work movement provides, it would likely prove much more difficult for evangelicals to find meaning in executive leadership positions. As Jackall explains, "The problem of the senselessness of managerial work increases as work itself becomes more abstract, typically as one advances. With increasing seniority, one retreats from concrete tasks . . . thus losing immediate connections to tangible human or industrial needs . . . and experiences the structural fragmentation of corporate, individual, and common goods."[26] Inasmuch as it facilitates connections among like-minded evangelical business leaders and these connections facilitate sense-making, which strengthens resolve, we can think of faith at work not just as a product of or a response to, but as an enabler of the upward mobility certain evangelicals experience in corporate contexts.

While faith at work groups support aspiring evangelical executives, in no sense do they constitute a Christian Mafia or the like. Even Kirk, the consultant who wishes to repurpose business and teaches evangelicals to promote God's purposes from within companies, makes clear that embedded evangelicals "remained respectful to the authorities, the structures, etc. They weren't trying to use up anything or take over the company; they were doing their job." And that's just it; it is sufficiently challenging for evangelical executives to satisfy their professional obligations while remaining available to their families and attentive to their faith that conspiring to advance evangelical priorities or even the career prospects of other evangelicals is impractical. Indeed, connections among evangelical executives have not catalyzed the type of encompassing conversations and perspectives that are sometimes associated with more abstracted contexts. Whereas professionals are more likely to sponsor reform at more expansive organizational levels than when situated in their home organizations, informants are sufficiently preoccupied with their own affairs and those of their companies that they rarely zoom out to contemplate broader structural issues.[27]

Support groups organized by and connections facilitated by evangelicals associated with faith and work initiatives provide opportunities for collective contemplation of structural arrangements, but even when they come together with other executives, the focus is generally on particular circumstances, not systematic problems. In fact, participants may not even talk about business at all. Said one CEO of his regular phone conferences and prayer times with other members of the CEO Forum, "It's almost never about their business; it's almost always their families and what they are going through with their children." Faith at work groups and materials provide coping mechanisms that enable evangelical executives to feel good about themselves as business leaders and interpret their professional experiences as meaningful. The overriding objective is to sustain the vibrancy of faith—to be able to say in good conscience that faith is the most important thing in life. In other words, for the evangelical business leaders with whom I spoke, the object of faith at work is not work; it is them and their critics, all of whom must learn to recognize and appreciate the spiritual significance of business.

Even those evangelical executives who participate in groups and initiatives oriented to incorporating faith in business are not so much reacting against perceived problems with business as against perceived neglect and disapproval within the church. In the end, the desire to integrate faith and work is less a quest for guidance than for legitimacy. Failing to find legitimation from the church, evangelical executives secure affirmation from one another. Indeed, the authors of prescriptive materials regarding how to integrate faith and business have largely missed the point. For the most part, evangelical executives are not particularly interested in grappling with difficult questions regarding the social and theological value of business. Most do not struggle with the amount of consumption in the United States versus other countries, depressed wage rates in developing countries, the effects of monotonous and degrading labor, or what counts as an adequate return for shareholders or a fair wage. Rather, they talk at a high level about economic growth and jobs and returns and value. What informants seem to want most is affirmation, not answers. They are, it seems, more lonely than confused or conflicted.

Revisiting the Relationship between Business and Religion

In contrast to a "hostile worlds" perspective that characterizes much of the discussion of business and religion and in which the interpenetration of the supposedly distinct spheres of economic activity and personal and moral affairs degrades both, another account portrays market activity as a powerful moralizing agent.[28] Classical economists like Adam Smith and some early Enlightenment philosophers like David Hume associated participation in market society with a number of virtues, including thrift, industry, honesty, reliability, and even creativity.[29] The underlying idea is that commercial success requires attention to the needs of others and depends on the establishment of trust that conduces to efficient transactions.

Most economic sociologists now embrace a balanced perspective on these issues, considering markets to be relatively impotent social constructs, subject themselves to other, more powerful social and historical currents.[30] Emphasizing its embeddedness in broader institutional dynamics, economic sociologists emphasize the contingent nature of the market's organization and effects. Markets are, in fact, sufficiently infused with moral order and evaluation that the distinction between market activity and moral valuation is unhelpful, and even misleading. On this view, economic activity is always characterized by moral considerations.

This more nuanced perspective allows that in some circumstances people act more in line with moral or religious considerations than in others, and that some types of economic activity are hostile to certain values, as are some types of organizational contexts. Markets, and the firms of which they are often composed, are neither inherently nor inevitably hostile to religious considerations and associated moral evaluations, nor necessarily benign to the same. Instead, their moral effects vary along many dimensions at every level of social organization, from the individual to the institutional. As such, the effect of market-oriented corporate contexts on business leaders' faith convictions and expressions is a dynamic to be explored, not assumed. Moreover, while institutional and organizational contexts are important, they are not necessarily determinative. In fact, Zelizer demonstrates that people can be remarkably creative and flexible in shaping and describing economic activity to affirm evaluative commitments and the nature of the social relationships involved, and indeed this is what we have observed among evangelical executives.[31]

Reverse Integration

Miller suggests that the underlying impulse of the faith at work movement is the desire for integration—the attempt to fuse business and religion by applying religious dispositions and priorities at work; to be, in other words, the same person at work as elsewhere. For Miller this means bringing faith-informed values to the workplace, not "leaving one's soul in the car," as the contemporary marketplace apparently insists.[32] Evangelical executives demonstrate a different inclination. Harold, the Nashville-based African American entrepreneur introduced earlier, wrote a book that, he explains, "is focused on taking lessons from work to succeed in life." According to Harold, the profit motive in business encourages and rewards an intensive commitment to serve and care for one's customers, and exporting these habits from work into the home and other contexts would make for healthier families and other relationships. According to the book, "You are the number one vendor to your wife and children. They look to you to provide a great product at a fair price and to keep them coming back with great service." What is so striking about this idea, and the business language through which it is conveyed, is that when social commentators bewail the commercialization of intimate relationships or clergypersons complain that today's churches increasingly resemble businesses, these developments are not welcomed, but lamented. Business, according to the literature referenced earlier, operates according to a set of principles that would be, at best, inappropriate in other contexts. For Harold this is not the case; for him, in fact, the Sunday-Monday gap can be thought of as the Monday-Sunday gap inasmuch as business encourages Christian virtues and dispositions that can be constructively applied to other relationships.

We have seen that evangelical executives are committed to living integrated lives in which they view all of life as contributing to spiritual objectives. In fact, as we have seen, integration is the key imperative for evangelicals. It is sometimes argued that to live an integrated life means to act the same at work as at church or at home—to bring to bear in other domains the virtues that are inculcated within the Christian community. For many informants, as for Harold, however, integration works in reverse. It is not so much that evangelical executives import church or family attitudes and objectives into business contexts, but that they export business concepts into church, charity, and family contexts. Recall, for example, that the essence of Bob Buford's admonition to successful evangelicals in his book *Halftime* is to develop and apply business-oriented thought processes and skills to all areas of life. Consider also that according to one of the executives I interviewed, "The next American revival is going too come from the workplace." As he explains, "I think it's interesting that Jesus chose twelve disciples that were more or less businesspeople. They weren't the best ministers of the time. They were fishermen. They were businesspeople. God took ordinary business people who were extraordinarily connected to him and used them to change the world." For this executive, as for Harold and other evangelical executives I spoke with, there is no need to bring God into the workplace because, as their accounts indicate, God is already there. As such, evangelical business leaders are as likely to export business as to import religion.

Sources of Evangelical Strength

The nature of this study means that I have much more to say about elite expressions of American evangelicalism than about American evangelicalism as a whole. At the same time, I suggest that some of the same dynamics that help evangelical executives flourish in corner offices likely help explain why evangelicalism thrives more broadly, and that these sources of strength provide a different take on the evangelical response to the supposed threat posed by pluralism associated with modernity and its offspring. Smith and coauthors proposed that the threats posed by exposure to dissimilar groups represent a key source of strength and cohesion for evangelicals inasmuch as they prompt coalescence around a distinctive identity and provide occasions for meaningful engagement with an eye toward reform.[33] Evangelical vitality, in other words, is enhanced by conflicting values. While this may be the case in some circumstances, I suggest that evangelicalism flourishes, in executive suites and elsewhere, less by playing up conflict with non-evangelical values than by accommodating a wide range of values. In fact, we have seen that the panoply of values—instantiated by different stakeholders—that compete for attention and resources in the business world, rather than weakening religious conviction, actually enhance and enlarge the scope of potential religious application for the executives under study.

Evangelical executives thrive in a pluralistic context not simply or primarily because they are threatened by such and driven to distinction, but because it provides a range of people and objectives to which religious values can be attached, and because evangelicalism is sufficiently broad and flexible to accommodate this range of objectives. In fact, in contrast to the "fundamentalist" tendency to perceive the economic sphere as secular and therefore more of a distraction from God's true work than an arena in which callings or vocations can be discovered and fulfilled,[34] the evangelical executives I interviewed seek to erode the distinction between the sacred and the profane, and to elevate "worldly" concerns to spiritual significance. Instead of accenting distinctions between themselves and non-evangelicals, evangelical executives downplay differences and make a point to blur lines—between sacred and secular, laity and clergy, and business and ministry.

This study contributes to our understanding of American evangelicalism as a flexible and empowering phenomenon for certain adherents—an interpretation that resonates with perspectives on American evangelicalism that perceive it becoming more flexible over time in response to societal trends. Griffith, for example, posits that stricter interpretations of divine expectations for Christian women have given way to more flexible interpretations focused on the ability to release divine power and produce change.[35] And Farrell documents among younger evangelicals a liberalization of perspectives on issues like same-sex marriage and premarital sex.[36] For the executives I interviewed, faith functions as a cipher through which professional aspirations and experiences can be interpreted as meaningful and supplies a grammar of significance that adorns business with spiritual value because of its above-mentioned flexibility—a flexibility that contrasts with perceptions of evangelicalism as rigid, dogmatic, and regulative.

I contend, moreover, not just that evangelicalism is relatively flexible, but that this flexibility gives rise to the above-referenced internal conflict that in turn represents a source of productive tension and strength. While agreeing that productive tension is essential, I suggest that it is less a product of modernity or other external dynamics and more a product of the different social locations and priorities of different groups of evangelicals. This is why, for example, Lindsay identifies significant differences between "populist evangelicals" and "cosmopolitan evangelicals" and I perceive conflict between academics, clergy, and evangelical executives.[37] For evangelicals, tension does indeed increase their sense of religious vitality. But since this tension comes from within, evangelicalism is a self-perpetuating religious tradition, producing sufficient tension within its own ranks that it sustains itself. We need not look to a pluralistic social context to find the source of productive tension that sustains evangelicalism; rather, especially in light of the ascendance of some evangelicals to the elite ranks of business and other professional domains, we can look to the diverse interests and social contexts that now characterize evangelicalism, itself.

Importantly, evangelicalism is sufficiently flexible not just to encompass different values, but to meet different needs as needs change in tandem with changing circumstances.[38] For younger informants—those who are still striving for success—religion supplies motivation and perseverance; for those who have reached the summit it provides existential and spiritual significance. Religion is sometimes understood as compensation for economic disadvantage, such that strength of religious conviction is inversely correlated with material success.[39] We have seen that this is not the case for the evangelical executives under study, and indeed that the strength of their religious conviction, or at least the frequency and conviction with which they invoke religious scripts, increases with the attainment of professional standing and the accumulation of wealth. For them, as for many less fortunate religious adherents, religion fulfills needs not met by other social arenas and is essential to self-understanding and professional satisfaction.

To conclude these remarks on the sources of evangelical strength, I suggest that evangelicalism remains relevant because it both instills and addresses the desire for significance, is diverse and ambiguous enough to accommodate a range of values found in different contexts, and requires intensity of commitment sufficient to bring these values into productive tension, thereby sustaining itself through internal dynamics without risking potentially enervating showdowns with other institutions and their presuppositions and agendas. Indeed, having identified and insisted on God's active sanction of and presence in business, the evangelical executives I interviewed are less focused on dysfunction within business as in other domains. As such, they are more inclined to transplant business concepts into other domains than to introduce religious objectives in business contexts. Thus, this study prompts us to reconsider the direction of influence between religious and economic life.

Baptizing Business

Most evangelicals regard baptism as a symbolic ritual that signifies the status of the person baptized as having placed their trust in Jesus Christ and thereby joined the community of the faithful. As such, the act of baptism does not alter one's essential character; instead, it denotes that a change of heart and mind has already occurred. As we have seen, most informants would not say that business must be sanctified, or made holy, but that it is already a sacred domain in which God is present and in which they work with God to accomplish God's purposes. The primary impulse of their rhetoric, therefore, is to baptize business, or provide symbolic justification of business as a sacred enterprise, especially against those who would disparage its spiritual worth.

Evangelical executives' enthusiasm for asserting the spiritual significance of business fits well with a Marxian perspective that sees evangelical executives as preoccupied above all with maintaining elite status. Their general ambivalence and oft-expressed impotence regarding reforms in their companies and industries, especially in contrast to their motivation to deploy influence in other contexts, suggests, at minimum, reluctance to reshape an industry that already suits their interests. Without question, the religious scripts they deploy have the effect of promoting the status quo. At the same time, it would be a mistake to see religious perspectives in this case as merely a reflection of the material conditions of society or, more specifically, the ordered relations of industry and informants' roles therein. Most evangelical business leaders expressed a desire, at least, to bring their faith to bear at work from the outset of their careers, but the degree to which they were willing and able to do so changed with their level of influence, discretion, and job security, as did the ways they brought faith to bear. In addition, the critics to whom informants' justificatory accounts are primarily addressed have little apparent power to depose informants from their lofty standing or otherwise disrupt their professional pursuits. So legitimation is an important component of but not an exhaustive explanation for the accounts examined in this study, and at any rate oriented more toward psychological needs than the preservation or alteration of material circumstances.

Recognizing the inadequacy of material conditions to explain the function and persistence of religion in the lives and accounts of the evangelical executives under study, we must chart a course between Marx and Weber, where ideology and material conditions exert mutual influence. With Marx, we must acknowledge that religion is grounded in and responds to the real world of contested interests and diverse needs that vary with social and economic context. Despite their supernatural referents, religious ideas are not suspended in the ether, untouched by the material world, but neither are they inescapably tethered to or merely a product of material relationships. Therefore, with Weber, we must assert that ideas can circle back on and shape the material conditions they aim to address. But we must not make Weber's mistake of fixating on the supposed essence of a religious ethic. A religious complex like evangelicalism is too broad, ambiguous, flexible, and dynamic to be distilled to such. We must come to an understanding that accommodates the lived experience of evangelicals today; that does not presuppose the direction of influence between religion and economic life while allowing each to shape the other; that acknowledges the diversity of thought within religious traditions and their capacity to adapt to different circumstances. With this perspective we will find that while evangelicalism, like religion more broadly, is often understood to be self-consistent, distinctive, characterized by proscriptions and prohibitions, and rigidly dogmatic, in fact it is flexible, adaptable, often incoherent, and abundantly capable of affirming institutions and activities.

Circling back to the opposing perspectives on the role of religion in business and the growing presence of evangelicals among the business elite, the conclusions I have presented are unlikely to satisfy fully any of the audiences that are most interested in the role of faith at work. Those who are concerned about the growing presence of openly committed evangelicals in executive positions may be encouraged that evangelical executives rarely demonstrate the requisite combination of desire and ability to introduce religiously motivated reforms in their companies and industries, and also that evangelical values seem not too dissimilar to, and in any case compatible with, those already embraced in the business world. Those who wish for evangelical executives to promote more humane, even loving, business practices may be discouraged at their lack of widespread influence but perhaps encouraged by their expressed attitudes as well as plentiful examples of localized influence. To the latter, I suggest that in order for the faith at work movement to make a meaningful difference in contemporary business practices, it would need to transform tension into dialectic as opposed to simple disagreement. As it stands, the thesis that faith can and should change business in some way is met with vigorous and creative antitheses asserting the spiritual value of business as currently organized. The emergence of syntheses that characterize business as flawed but redeemable would entail greater interaction and mutual appreciation between evangelical critics of business and evangelical business leaders. For now, however, for the evangelical executives I interviewed, faith at work consists primarily of preaching to the choir.

APPENDIX

Research Design

In order to locate evangelical executives, I began with a pool of potential informants supplied by the H. E. Butt Family Foundation, an explicitly Christian and broadly evangelical foundation that sponsors programs designed to "create opportunities for people to encounter God for the transformation of daily life, work, and our world."[1] The list consisted of actual and potential participants in events sponsored by the foundation and was supplemented by input from a handful of individuals who are well connected with evangelical business leaders, mostly on account of their involvement in academic or parachurch programs oriented to encouraging Christian business leaders to integrate their faith and their work. Sixty-three of 102 informants came from this initial set of potential informants. In order to expand the pool of informants, I employed a snowball sampling technique wherein at the conclusion of each interview I asked for names and contact information for other evangelical executives who might be good candidates for the study. Informant referrals led to thirty-six interviews. In a few instances, I reached out to potential informants on the basis of reputation alone, without a specific referral, leading to three additional interviews.

This study was sponsored in part by the H. E. Butt Family Foundation, and their sponsorship was disclosed to potential informants when interview requests were extended. The foundation's positive reputation seemed to have encouraged participation inasmuch as many informants were familiar with the organization and some had participated in its programs. Sponsorship by an organization sympathetic to the application of faith at work likely encouraged informants to be more forthcoming about their own efforts to apply their faith to their work. It likely also encouraged informants to be more liberal in their use of faith-oriented language than they would be in many other contexts—a phenomenon that was likely intensified in some ways by my own educational background, which includes a bachelor's degree from a university with a Christian affiliation and a master's degree from an evangelical seminary. Informants almost never paused to ask if I was familiar with religious language or concepts. A couple of informants asked to pray for me and the study at the beginning or end of their interviews. Some informants seemed not sure what to make of my field of study and affiliation with an Ivy League university, seemingly encouraged by the presence of an assumed coreligionist at an elite academic institution but occasionally referencing the supposed anti-Christian or anti-business bias of my colleagues. For some of the executives I interviewed, my professional experience in the management consulting and investment banking industries seemed to mitigate any wariness associated with uncertainty about my perspective on the propriety of business as currently practiced. Others became defensive in ways that made it seem that they assumed the critiques of business I raised in the interviews were my own. My sense is that, on balance, my professional and educational backgrounds likely enhanced the quality of the interviews inasmuch as informants did not feel the need to "dumb down" religious or business concepts.

Most informants self-identified as evangelicals, but a minority rejected the "evangelical" designation or at least indicated some hesitation to embrace the term, almost always on account of the public perception of evangelicals as judgmental and narrow-minded. In rejecting or qualifying the evangelical label, however, informants were rejecting popular perceptions, not doctrines or practices understood to characterize evangelicalism, and therefore, as long as they embrace characteristic evangelical beliefs, I consider them evangelicals even if they do not identify as such. Informants almost unanimously consider themselves to have been "born again," believe that the Bible is inspired by God, and maintain that the only hope for salvation is through personal faith in Jesus Christ. Most also believe that the Bible is without material error and disbelieve in biological evolution, suggesting a conservative approach to Scripture interpretation and deference to the Bible in case of conflict with science or other competing sources of authority.

I extended 187 interview invitations, of which 69 percent (129) were accepted. While some executives could not find a suitable time for an interview, I interviewed 79 percent (102) of those willing to participate, yielding an overall response rate of 55 percent. Just 3 percent of potential informants declined the invitation, while 28 percent never responded. I employed a grounded theory approach to data collection and analysis, dividing interviews into two waves and allowing patterns gleaned from the first round of interviews to inform informant and question selection in round two.[2] Round one consisted of 40 in-person interviews, followed by a second round of 62 phone interviews. Interview questions focused on informants' perspectives on the role of business in society and the role of faith in business. I also discussed perceived social problems and responsibilities more generally, with emphasis on informants' sense of agency and potential influence. Interviews were digitally recorded and professional transcribed, after which more than 10,000 excerpts were coded along several hundred research dimensions.

Informant Profile

The executives I interviewed occupy leadership positions in companies with different ownership structures, sizes, locations, and industries, and are characterized themselves by different functional specializations and, in a few cases, demographic characteristics. Informants are among the most influential employees in their firms, though the positions to which this influence corresponds varies by firm size. The majority of informants occupied the senior-most position in their firms, affording them considerable responsibility and influence. Thirty percent of informants founded their firms, most of whom maintain at least a controlling interest in their companies. About half of informants are responsible for charting the competitive strategies of their firms. Others have different functional backgrounds and areas of responsibility, both of which can shape the ways organizational leaders set and pursue organizational objectives. Informants who occupy the highest-ranking positions in their firms generally do so in small to medium-sized, privately held firms, though some informants do lead large, publicly traded companies. Many informants have occupied several relevant positions and are classified in Tables A.1–A.4 on the basis of their current or most recent relevant position.

Table A.1 Informants' Company Characteristics

Capital Structure	
Publicly Traded	31
Privately Held	71
Size (Number of Employees)	
1–100	39
101–1,000	21
1,001–10,000	20
10,001+	22
Industry	
Communications	3
Construction	3
Energy	6
Entertainment	1
Finance	25
Food and Beverage	9
General Retail	8
General Wholesale	3
Information Technology	9
Manufacturing	8
Professional Services	23
Real Estate	7
Transportation	1
Location	
United States	7
Midwest	19
Northeast	51
South	23
West	2
Europe	

Table A.2 Informants' Professional Experience and Responsibilities

Highest-ranking Officer	
Yes	56
No	46
Company Founder	
Yes	30
No	72
Professional Specialization	
Finance	21
Human Resources	5
Legal	3
Marketing	7
Operations	6
Sales	9
Strategy	49
Technology	2
Public Company Experience	
Yes	56
No	46
Private Company Experience	
Yes	77
No	25

Table A.3 Informants' Demographic Characteristics

Age	
<40	12
40–49	26
50–59	40
60+	24
Gender	
Male	85
Female	17
Race	
White	93
Black	5
Asian	4
Highest Degree Earned	
None	2
Bachelor's	38
Master's	39
MBA	12
Other Master's	7
JD	4
PhD	

Table A.4 Selected Company and Informant Characteristics by Gender

	Male (n=85)	Female (n=17)
Company Characteristics		
Size (Number of Employees)	39%	35%
1–100	21%	18%
101–1,000	18%	24%
1,001–10,000	21%	24%
10,001+	29%	35%
Publicly Traded Company		
Informant Characteristics		
Public Company Experience	52%	71%
Private Company Experience	78%	65%
Highest-ranking Officer	60%	35%
Company Founder	32%	29%
Professional Specialization		
Finance	20%	24%
Human Resources	0%	29%
Legal	4%	0%
Marketing	7%	6%
Operations	5%	12%
Sales	9%	6%
Strategy	54%	18%
Technology	1%	6%
Age		
<40	6%	41%
40–49	27%	18%
50–59	40%	35%
60+	27%	6%
Highest Degree Earned		
None	1%	6%
Bachelor's	36%	41%
Master's		
MBA	39%	24%
Other Master's	11%	18%
JD	8%	0%
PhD	5%	0%

Notes

Introduction

1. While the term *mafia* has a sinister connotation, it is sometimes used to describe a more innocuous network of mutual support, as in, for example, the group of entrepreneurs known in Silicon Valley as the PayPal Mafia, members of which went on to establish a number of successful tech companies after working together at PayPal. See Thiel (2014).
2. Mitroff and Denton (1999:57–75).
3. Hunter (2010:5).
4. Smith (2000:1).
5. See https://slate.com/news-and-politics/2019/05/ocasio-cortez-republicans-republicans-far-right-christian-theocracy.html.
6. Park and Davidson, in *Findings from the Baylor Religion Survey, Wave 5* (2017).
7. Tobin and Weinberg (2007).
8. See Hunter (2010).
9. Smith (2000:6).
10. Park and Davidson (2017).
11. Ibid.
12. Hunter (2010:13).
13. Ibid.
14. Hart (1996).
15. Wuthnow (1995).
16. Lindsay (2007); Schmalzbauer (2003).
17. Roels (1997); Lindsay (2007).
18. Lindsay (2007; 2008).
19. Miller (2007).
20. Peters (1993).
21. Gunther (2004).
22. See Davis (2009) and Useem (1996).
23. Bellah, Madsen, Sullivan, Swidler, and Tipton (1991).
24. Hart (1996).
25. Nash (1994:xv).
26. Miller (2007:12).
27. Cragun (2012:10).
28. Keister (2011; 2003).
29. Hart (1996).
30. Abend (2009).

31. Guillén (1994).
32. Weber ([1920] 2002).
33. Berger (1987:7–8).
34. Longenecker, McKinney, and Moore (2004).
35. Pew Research Center (2012).
36. Pew Research Center (2013).
37. Saad (2015).
38. Pew Research Center (2017).
39. Larcker, Donatiello, and Tayan (2016).
40. See Haleblian, Pfarrer, and Kiley (2017), Wiles, Jain, and Lindsey (2010), Pfarrer, Pollock, and Rindova (2010), and Roberts and Dowling (2002).
41. Mendonca and Miller (2007:66).
42. Khurana (2010:5).
43. Dougherty, Neubert, and Park in *Baylor Religion Survey, Wave III* (2011).
44. See Smith (2000), Bebbington (1989), Kellstedt, Green, Guth, and Smidt (1994), Wald, Owen, and Hill (1989), and Hackett and Lindsay (2008).
45. See Pew Research Center (2014).
46. Smith, Emerson, and Snell (2008).
47. Except as specified, all statistics in this and the following paragraph are from Pew Research Center (2014).
48. Data regarding there being only one true way to interpret evangelical teachings are from Pew Research Center (2008).
49. Baylor Religion Survey (2006).
50. Pew Research Center (2014).
51. Ibid.
52. *Baylor Religion Survey, Wave 5* (2017).
53. See Davis and Robinson (1996), Hart (1996), and Johnson, Tamney, and Burton (1989).
54. See Weber ([1920] 2002).
55. Ibid.
56. Hackett and Lindsay (2008).
57. Hunter (1983).
58. Smith, with Emerson, Gallagher, Kennedy, and Sikkink (1998).
59. Hackett and Lindsay (2008).
60. Zweigenhaft (2016).
61. For religion-focused examples, see, for example, Ecklund (2010), Evans (2002, 2010), Lindsay (2007), Chen (2008), and Schmalzbauer (2003). For broader cultural studies, see, for example, Swidler (2013) and Davidman (2000).
62. See Wuthnow (2011) for a helpful discussion of such objections and a defense of the value of talk, especially in analyses of religion.
63. Marshall (1982).
64. Boltanski and Thevenot (2006).
65. Ibid.
66. In order to maintain confidentiality, I use pseudonyms throughout and redact quotes as necessary to remove potentially identifying details.

Chapter 1

1. Nash (1994:39, xiii).
2. Kouchaki, Smith-Crowe, Brief, and Sousa (2013).
3. Ibid.:54.
4. See Paine (2002) for description and analysis of this study.
5. Jackall (1988:115).
6. See Hirschman (1982), Hirsch (1976), and Veblen (1899).
7. Friedland and Alford (1991).
8. Boltanski and Thevenot (2006, 1999).
9. Matthew 6:24, New International Version (NIV).
10. Weber ([1920] 2002:33).
11. See, for example, Beckett (2006), Burkett (2010), Nash and McLennan (2001), Stevens (2000), and Nelson (2011).
12. It is worth noting that most of the seven tensions proposed by Nash (1994), namely "humility and the ego of success," "family and work," "charity and wealth," "faithful witness in the secular city," and perhaps even "love and the competitive drive," are not specific to business, and might just as well apply to, for example, educational, medical, nonprofit, government, or other professional contexts. Of the proposed tensions, only "the love for God and the pursuit of profit" and "people needs and profit obligations" are specific to for-profit enterprises.
13. Baylor Religion Survey (2006).
14. Warren (1994:49).
15. Ibid.:50.
16. Ibid.:48.
17. See Wuthnow (1996).
18. Hart (1996).
19. Woodberry and Smith (1998).
20. Felson and Kindell (2007).
21. Iannaccone (1998); it is worth observing that some scholars, including Campbell and Putnam (2012) and Skocpol and Williamson (2012), have highlighted affinities between evangelicalism and Tea Party conservatism, along with its at least implicit approval of capitalism.
22. Steensland and Shrank (2011).
23. Baylor Religion Survey, Wave III (2011).
24. Gay (1991).
25. Wallis (1976:63).
26. Gay (1991:26).
27. Ibid.:63.
28. Again, this is but one strand of evangelical thought regarding capital enterprise. Other scholars, including Dochuk (2010) and Kruse (2015), argue that evangelicals have played a profound role in the political advance of economic conservatism. The point is that informants' remarks indicate that they are both aware of and sensitive to criticisms such as those advanced by evangelicals like Wallis, Sider (2005) and, more recently, Mott (2011) and McLaren (2009).

29. Gay (1991).
30. Smith et al. (1998).
31. Keister (2003).
32. Pew Research Center (2014).
33. Matthew 6:19–21, New American Standard Bible.
34. 1 Timothy 6:10, New Living Translation (NLT).
35. Mark 10:25, NIV.
36. Luke 18:22, NIV.
37. Keister (2003).
38. Blomberg (2000:246).
39. Durkheim ([1912] 2001).
40. Kuyper, cited in Bratt, ed. (1998:488).
41. John 5:17, NLT.

Chapter 2

1. Weber ([1920] 2002:129).
2. Paine (2002).
3. Vogel (2005).
4. Ibid.
5. Paine (2002:78).
6. Ibid.
7. See Orlitzky (2011), Vogel (2005), and Margolis and Walsh (2003).
8. See Perrini, Russo, Tencati, and Vurro (2011), Schrek (2011), and Orlitzky (2011).
9. Paine (2002).
10. Thiel (2014).
11. Paine (2002).
12. Bourdieu (2000).
13. Luke 6:35, NIV.
14. Weber ([1946] 1991).
15. Ibid.:95.
16. Ibid.:120.
17. Ibid.:121.
18. Tocqueville ([1834] 2003).

Chapter 3

1. Pew Research Center (2014).
2. Warren (1994:11).
3. Callahan (1996, 2001).
4. See https://www.theologyofwork.org.
5. Blomberg (2000:30).
6. Smith (2011).

 7. Friedland and Alford (1991:249).
 8. Matthew 5:38–41, NIV.
 9. Weber ([1946] 2002:323–59).
10. Bellah, Madsen, Sullivan, Swidler, and Tipton (1985); Putnam (2001).
11. Wuthnow (1998); Roof (1999).
12. Madsen (2009).
13. Hunter (1987); Farrell (2011).
14. Emerson and Smith (2001).
15. Muthia (2009).
16. Boltanski and Thevenot (2006, 1999).
17. Boltanski and Thevenot (1999:369).
18. See Davis (2009), Useem (1996), and Fligstein (1993).
19. Keister (2008, 2003).
20. See Boice (2016).
21. Psalm 24:1, NIV.
22. See Grudem (1994:262).
23. Matthew 5:16, NIV.
24. See Friedland and Alford (1991).
25. Stark (2009).
26. Friedland and Alford (1991).
27. Espeland and Stevens (1998).
28. Friedland and Alford (1991:248).
29. Swidler (1986).
30. Lévi-Strauss (1966); Thornton and Ocasio (2008).
31. Stark (2009).
32. Hannan and Freeman (1984).
33. Ladman, quoted in Dawkins (2008:167–68).
34. See Young (2007).
35. Baylor Religion Survey, Wave 5 (2017).
36. Baylor Religion Survey (2006).
37. Longenecker, McKinney, and Moore (2004).
38. See https://www.si.com/nfl/2019/05/22/sports-betting-gambling-carolina-panthers-david-tepper-south-carolina-indian-tribes-lindsey-graham.

Chapter 4

1. Buford (2008).
2. See foreword by Berger in Gay (1991:xi).
3. Weber ([1946] 2002:118).
4. Ibid.
5. Baylor Religion Survey, Wave III (2011).
6. Ibid.
7. Buford (2008:41).
8. Ibid.:42.

9. Ibid.:55.
10. Ibid.:98.
11. Ibid.:35.
12. Ibid.
13. Ibid.:68.
14. Ibid.:28.
15. Ibid.:158.
16. Schervish (1990).
17. See Kinsley (2008).

Chapter 5

1. Mitroff and Denton (1999).
2. See Hunter (2010), Young (2007), and Cromartie (2003).
3. See Miller (2007) and Lindsay (2008).
4. Steensland and Shrank (2011).
5. Hunter (2010).
6. Ibid.
7. Meyer and Rowan (1977).
8. Cyert and March (1963).
9. Shamir (2005, 2008).
10. Roels (1997).
11. Nash (1994).
12. See Lindsay (2008) for discussion of signaling among evangelical executives.
13. See Lewis (2003) on attitudes toward homosexuality and gay rights; see Key and Edmundson (1999) on perspectives on economic ethics and corporate social responsibility.
14. Korver-Glenn, Chan, and Ecklund (2015).
15. Trimiew and Green (1997).
16. Peifer, Ecklund, and Fullerton (2014).
17. See Emerson, Smith, and Sikkink (1999), Emerson and Smith (2001), and Edgell and Tranby (2007).

Chapter 6

1. Parker, Horowitz, and Igielnik (2018).
2. See the Council for Biblical Manhood and Womanhood (https://cbmw.org), among whose leadership and advisers are numbered many of the most prominent evangelical scholars and pastors, for elaboration of the complementarian perspective on gender roles and authority structures.
3. See Wilcox (2004) and Gallagher and Smith (1999).
4. Beutel and Marini (1995), Kodinsky, Madden, Zisk, and Henkel (2010), and Loe, Ferrell, and Mansfield (2000), as referenced in Steffensmeier, Schwartz, and Rochea (2013).

5. Jaffee and Hyde (2000), Lesch (2011), and O'Fallon and Butterfield (2005), as referenced in Steffensmeier et al. (2013).
6. Collins (1999), as referenced in Steffensmeier et al. (2013).
7. Steffensmeier et al. (2013).
8. Robin and Babin (1997).
9. See Gayle, Golan, and Miller (2012).
10. See Robin and Babin (1997).
11. It is worth noting that the expressed dissatisfaction among informants regarding the status of women in business does not distill to political orientation. While the women I interviewed are, as one put it, "more on the liberal side of the role of women," this self-assessment should be taken in context. While certainly more enthusiastic than many of their coreligionists about women's leadership in business, some remain committed to some forms of gender traditionalism. For example, one executive discloses, "I'm not one who would want to go to a church with a female pastor. I think that's something I would be uncomfortable with." Moreover, most of the women I interviewed identified with the Republican Party, with only one identifying with the Democratic Party.
12. See Stasson (2014).

Conclusion

1. In this paragraph I rely on Kalberg's interpretation of Luther's and Calvin's understandings of vocation, as expressed in Weber ([1920] 2002).
2. Weber ([1920] 2002:124).
3. Ibid.:123.
4. Hueber (1991), in Wuthnow (1996:18–19).
5. Abrams, Bowman, O'Neil, and Streeter (2019).
6. Swedberg (2009: xii).
7. Wuthnow (1998).
8. Hunter (1987).
9. Ibid.
10. Ibid.:73.
11. Cyert and March (1963).
12. Shamir (2005).
13. Weick (1995).
14. Merton (1973).
15. Schmalzbauer (2003).
16. Weber ([1946] 1991).
17. Nash (1994); Miller (2007).
18. Lindsay (2008).
19. Miller (2007).
20. Schmalzbauer (2003:113).
21. Lindsay (2007:216–18).
22. Madsen (2009).
23. Ibid.

24. During the course of my research, I solicited the input of a few leaders of prominent organizations that purport to help Christian executives integrate their faith and their work. Interestingly, the coldest reception came from former evangelical executives who had transitioned to leadership roles in such groups. When I described this research project and asked for help connecting with potential informants, one of these ministry leaders asserted that he knew more about the topics I intended to investigate than anyone and would not permit me to "fish off his back," and another repeatedly rescheduled appointments, even canceling an appointment the morning I was to travel several hours to meet with him. I got the impression that these and other ministries compete with one another to service the executives with whom I hoped to connect.
25. Griffith (1997).
26. Jackall (1988:202).
27. See DiMaggio (1991).
28. Zelizer (2007a).
29. Hirschman (1982).
30. See Fourcade and Healy (2007) and Guillén (2001).
31. Zelizer (1997, 2007b).
32. Miller (2007).
33. Smith et al. (1998).
34. Ammerman (1987).
35. Griffith (1997).
36. Farrell (2011).
37. Lindsay (2007).
38. See Bender (2003).
39. Stark and Bainbridge (1980).

Appendix

1. See http://www.hebff.org/.
2. See Charmaz (2006) and Glaser and Strauss (1967).

References

Abend, Gabriel. 2009. "A Genealogy of Business Ethics." PhD diss., Northwestern University.

Abrams, Samuel J., Karlyn Bowman, Eleanor O'Neil, and Ryan Streeter. 2019. "AEI Survey on Community and Society: Social Capital, Civic Health, and Quality of Life in the United States." Washington, DC: American Enterprise Institute.

Ammerman, Nancy. 1987. *Bible Believers: Fundamentalists in the Modern World*. New Brunswick, NJ: Rutgers University Press.

Baylor Religion Survey. 2006. "American Piety in the 21st Century: New Insights to the Depth and Complexity of Religion in the US." https://www.baylor.edu/baylorreligionsurvey/doc.php/288937.pdf.

Baylor Religion Survey. Wave III, 2011. "The Values and Beliefs of the American Public." https://www.baylor.edu/baylorreligionsurvey/doc.php/288938.pdf.

Baylor Religion Survey. Wave 5, 2017. "American Values, Mental Health, and Using Technology in the Age of Trump." https://www.baylor.edu/baylorreligionsurvey/doc.php/292546.pdf.

Bebbington, David. 1989. *Evangelicalism in Modern Britain: A History from the 1730s to the 1980s*. London: Unwin Hyman.

Beckett, John D. 2006. *Loving Monday: Succeeding in Business without Selling Your Soul*. Downers Grove, IL: IVP Books.

Bellah, Robert, Richard Madsen, William M. Sullivan, Ann Swidler, and Steven M. Tipton. 1991. *The Good Society*. New York: Alfred A. Knopf.

Bellah, Robert, Richard Madsen, William M. Sullivan, Ann Swidler, and Steven M. Tipton. 1985. *Habits of the Heart: Individualism and Commitment in American Life*. Berkeley: University of California Press.

Bender, Courtney. 2003. *Heaven's Kitchen: Living Religion at God's Love We Deliver*. Chicago: University of Chicago Press.

Berger, Peter L. 1987. *The Capitalist Revolution: Fifty Propositions about Prosperity, Equality, and Liberty*. Aldershot: Wildwood Press.

Beutel, Ann M., and Margaret M. Marini. 1995. "Gender and Values." *American Sociological Review* 60:436–48.

Blomberg, Craig L. 2000. *Neither Poverty Nor Riches: A Biblical Theology of Possessions*. Downers Grove, IL: IVP Academic.

Boice, James Montgomery. 2016. *The Parables of Jesus*. Chicago: Moody Publishers.

Boltanski, Luc, and Laurent Thévenot. 1999. "The Sociology of Critical Capacity." *European Journal of Social Theory* 2(3):359–77.

Boltanski, Luc, and Laurent Thévenot. 2006. *On Justification: Economies of Worth*. Princeton: Princeton University Press.

Bourdieu, Pierre. 2000. *Pascalian Meditations*. Palo Alto, CA: Stanford University Press.

Bratt, James D., ed. 1998. *Abraham Kuyper: A Centennial Reader*. Grand Rapids, MI: Eerdmans.

Buford, Bob P. 2008. *Halftime: Moving from Success to Significance*. Grand Rapids, MI: Zondervan.

Burkett, Larry. 2010. *Business by the Book*. Nashville, TN: Thomas Nelson.

Callahan, James Patrick. 1996. "Claritas Scripturae: The Role of Perspicuity in Protestant Hermeneutics." *Journal of the Evangelical Theological Society* 39(3):353–72.

Callahan, James Patrick. 2001. *The Clarity of Scripture*. Downers Grove, IL: InterVarsity Press.

Campbell, David E., and Robert D. Putnam. 2012. "God and Caesar in America." *Foreign Affairs* 91(2):34–43.

Charmaz, Kathy. 2006. *Constructing Grounded Theory: A Practical Guide through Qualitative Analysis*. London: Sage.

Chen, Carolyn. 2008. *Getting Saved in America: Taiwanese Immigration and Religious Experience*. Princeton: Princeton University Press.

Collins, Judith. 1999. "Personality and Value Differences among Male and Female White-Collar Executives." Presented at the American Psychological Association Annual Meetings, Boston, MA.

Cragun, Ryan T. 2012. "In Favor of Relevance: When Religion Studies Matter." *ASA Footnotes*, April, 10.

Cromartie, Michael, ed. 2003. *A Public Faith: Evangelicals and Civic Engagement*. Lanham, MD: Rowman & Littlefield.

Cyert, Richard M., and James G. March. 1963. *A Behavioral Theory of the Firm*. Englewood Cliffs, NJ: Prentice Hall.

Dawkins, Richard. 2008. *The God Delusion*. New York: Houghton Mifflin.

Davidman, Lynn. 2000. *Motherloss*. Berkeley: University of California Press.

Davis, Gerald F. 2009. *Managed by the Markets: How Finance Re-Shaped America*. New York: Oxford University Press.

Davis, Nancy Jean, and Robert V. Robinson. 1996. "Are the Rumors of War Exaggerated?: Religious Orthodoxy and Moral Progressivism in America." *American Journal of Sociology* 102:756–87.

DiMaggio, Paul. 1991. "Constructing an Organizational Field as a Professional Project: US Art Museums, 1920–1940." In *The New Institutionalism in Organizational Analysis*, edited by Walter W. Powell and Paul J. DiMaggio, 267–92. Chicago: University of Chicago Press.

Dochuk, Darren. 2010. *From Bible Belt to Sunbelt: Plain-folk Religion, Grassroots Politics, and the Rise of Evangelical Conservatism*. New York: W. W. Norton & Company.

Dougherty, Kevin D., Mitchell J. Neubert, and Jerry Z. Park. 2011. "The Religious Significance of Work." Baylor Religion Survey, Wave III: The Values and Beliefs of the American Public. https://www.baylor.edu/baylorreligionsurvey/doc.php/288938.

Durkheim, Émile. [1912] 2001. *The Elementary Forms of Religious Life*. New York: Oxford University Press.

Ecklund, Elaine Howard. 2010. *Science vs. Religion: What Scientists Really Think*. New York: Oxford University Press.

Edgell, Penny, and Eric Tranby. 2007. "Religious Influences on Understandings of Racial Inequality in the United States." *Social Problems* 54(2):263–88.

Emerson, Michael O., and Christian Smith. 2001. *Divided by Faith: Evangelical Religion and the Problem of Race in America*. New York: Oxford University Press.

Emerson, Michael O., Christian Smith, and David Sikkink. 1999. "Equal in Christ, but Not in the World: White Conservative Protestants and Explanations of Black-White Inequality." *Social Problems* 46(3):398–417.

Espeland, Wendy N., and Mitchell L. Stevens. 1998. "Commensuration as a Social Process." *Annual Review of Sociology* 24:313–43.

Evans, John H. 2002. *Playing God?: Human Genetic Engineering and the Rationalization of Public Bioethical Debate*. Chicago: University of Chicago Press.

Evans, John H. 2010. *Contested Reproduction: Genetic Technologies, Religion, and Public Debate*. Chicago: University of Chicago Press.

Farrell, Justin. 2011. "The Young and the Restless?: The Liberalization of Young Evangelicals." *Journal for the Scientific Study of Religion* 50(3):517–32.

Felson, Jacob, and Heather Kindell. 2007. "The Elusive Link between Conservative Protestantism and Conservative Economics." *Social Science Research* 36(2):673–87.

Fligstein, Neil. 1993. *The Transformation of Corporate Control*. Cambridge, MA: Harvard University Press.

Fourcade, Marion, and Kieran Healy. 2007. "Moral Views of Market Society." *Annual Review of Sociology* 33:285–311.

Friedland, Roger, and Robert R. Alford. 1991. "Bringing Society Back In: Symbols, Practices, and Institutional Contradictions." In *The New Institutionalism in Organizational Analysis*, edited by Walter W. Powell and Paul J. DiMaggio, 232–66. Chicago: University of Chicago Press.

Gallagher, Sally K., and Christian Smith. 1999. "Symbolic Traditionalism and Pragmatic Egalitarianism: Contemporary Evangelicals, Families, and Gender." *Gender and Society* 13(2):211–33.

Gay, Craig M. 1991. *With Liberty and Justice for Whom?: The Recent Evangelical Debate over Capitalism*. Grand Rapids, MI: Eerdmans.

Gayle, George-Levi, Limor Golan, and Robert A. Miller. 2012. "Gender Differences in Executive Compensation and Job Mobility." *Journal of Labor Economics* 30(4):829–72.

Glaser, Barney, and Anselm Strauss. 1967. *The Discovery of Grounded Theory*. New York: Aldine.

Griffith, R. Marie. 1997. *God's Daughters: Evangelical Women and the Power of Submission*. Berkeley: University of California Press.

Grudem, Wayne A. 1994. *Systematic Theology: An Introduction to Biblical Doctrine*. Grand Rapids, MI: Zondervan.

Guillén, Mauro F. 1994. *Models of Management: Work, Authority, and Organization in a Comparative Perspective*. Chicago: University of Chicago Press.

Guillén, Mauro F. 2001. "Is Globalization Civilizing, Destructive, or Feeble?: A Critique of Five Key Debates in the Social Science Literature." *Annual Review of Sociology* 27:235–60.

Gunther, Marc. 2004. *Faith and Fortune: The Quiet Revolution to Reform American Business*. New York: Crown Publishing.

Hackett, Conrad, and D. Michael Lindsay. 2008. "Measuring Evangelicalism: Consequences of Different Operationalization Strategies." *Journal for the Scientific Study of Religion* 47(3):499–514.

Haleblian, Jerayr J., Michael D. Pfarrer, and Jason T. Liley. 2017. "High-Reputation Firms and Their Differential Acquisition Behaviors." *Strategic Management Journal* 38(11):2237–54.

Hannan, Michael T., and John Freeman. 1984. "Structural Inertia and Organizational Change." *American Sociological Review* 49(2):149–64.

Hart, Stephen. 1996. *What Does the Lord Require?: How American Christians Think about Economic Justice.* New Brunswick, NJ: Rutgers University Press.

Hirsch, Fred. 1976. *Social Limits to Growth.* Cambridge, MA: Harvard University Press.

Hirschman, Albert O. 1982. "Rival Interpretations of Market Society: Civilizing, Destructive, or Feeble?" *Journal of Economic Literature* 20(4):1463–84.

Hueber, Graham. 1991. "Baby-boomers Seek More Family Time." *The Gallup Poll Monthly*, April, 31–42.

Hunter, James Davison. 1983. *American Evangelicalism: Conservative Religion and the Quandary of Moderntiy.* New Brunswick, NJ: Rutgers University Press.

Hunter, James Davison. 1987. *Evangelicalism: The Coming Generation.* Chicago: University of Chicago Press.

Hunter, James Davison. 1991. *Culture Wars: The Struggle to Define America.* New York: Basic Books.

Hunter, James Davison. 2010. *To Change the World: The Irony, Tragedy, and Possibility of Christianity in the Late Modern World.* New York: Oxford University Press.

Iannaccone, Laurence R. 1998. "Introduction to the Economics of Religion." *Journal of Economic Literature* 36(3):1465–95.

Jackall, Robert. 1988. *Moral Mazes.* New York: Oxford University Press.

Jaffee, Sara, and Janet Hyde. 2000. "Gender Differences in Moral Orientation: A Meta-Analysis." *Psychological Bulletin* 126:703–26.

Johnson, Stephen D., Joseph B. Tamney, and Ronald Burton. 1989. "Pat Robertson: Who Supported His Candidacy for President?" *Journal for the Scientific Study of Religion* 28(4):387–99.

Keister, Lisa A. 2003. "Religion and Wealth: The Role of Religious Affiliation and Participation in Early Adult Asset Accumulation." *Social Forces* 82(1):175–207.

Keister, Lisa A. 2008. "Conservative Protestants and Wealth: How Religion Perpetuates Asset Poverty." *American Journal of Sociology* 113(5):1237–71.

Keister, Lisa A. 2011. *Faith and Money: How Religion Contributes to Wealth and Poverty.* New York: Cambridge University Press.

Kellstedt, Lyman A., John C. Green, James L. Guth, and Corwin E. Smidt. 1994. "Religious Voting Blocs in the 1992 Election: The Year of the Evangelical?" *Sociology of Religion* 55(3):307–26.

Key, Susan, and Vickie Cox Edmondson. 1999. "Does Social Cognitive Theory Elucidate Black Executives' Orientation to Corporate Social Responsibility?" *Business & Professional Ethics Journal* 18(2):35–56.

Kinsley, Michael, ed. 2008. *Creative Capitalism: A Conversation with Bill Gates, Warren Buffett, and Other Economic Leaders.* New York: Simon & Schuster.

Khurana, Rakesh. 2010. *From Higher Aims to Hired Hands: The Social Transformation of American Business Schools and the Unfulfilled Promise of Management as a Profession.* Princeton: Princeton University Press.

Kodinski, Robert W., Timothy M. Madden, Daniel S. Zisk, and Eric T. Henkel. 2010. "Attitudes about Corporate Social Responsibility: Business Student Predictors." *Journal of Business Ethics* 91:167–81.

Korver-Glenn, Elizabeth, Esther Chan, and Elaine Howard Ecklund. 2015. "Perceptions of Science Education among African American and White Evangelicals: A Texas Case Study." *Review of Religious Research* 57(1):131–48.

Kouchaki, Maryam, Kristin Smith-Crowe, Arthur P. Brief, and Carlos Sousa. 2013. "Seeing Green: Mere Exposure to Money Triggers a Business Decision Frame and Unethical Outcomes." *Organizational Behavior and Human Decision Processes* 121(1):53–61.

Kruse, Kevin M. 2015. *One Nation under God: How Corporate America Invented Christian America*. New York: Basic Books.

Larker, David F., Nicholas E. Donatiello, and Brian Tayan. 2016. "Americans and CEO Pay: 2016 Public Perception Survey on CEO Compensation." *Stanford University Graduate School of Business*. https://www.gsb.stanford.edu/sites/gsb/files/publication-pdf/cgri-survey-2016-americans-ceo-pay.pdf.

Lesch, William C. 2011. "Women and Older Consumers Tougher on Fraud." *Journal of Insurance Fraud* 2:15–22.

Lévi-Strauss, Claude. 1966. *The Savage Mind*. Chicago: University of Chicago Press.

Lewis, Gregory B. 2003. "Black-White Differences in Attitudes toward Homosexuality and Gay Rights." *Public Opinion Quarterly* 67(l):59–78.

Lindsay, D. Michael. 2007. *Faith in the Halls of Power: How Evangelicals Joined the American Elite*. New York: Oxford University Press.

Lindsay, D. Michael. 2008. "Evangelicals in the Power Elite: Elite Cohesion Advancing a Movement." *American Sociological Review* 73(1):60–82.

Loe, Terry W., Linda Ferrell, and Phylis Mansfield. 2000. "A Review of Empirical Studies Assessing Ethical Decision Making in Business." *Journal of Business Ethics* 25:185–204.

Longenecker, Justin G., Joseph A. McKinney, and Carlos W. Moore. 2004. "Religious Intensity, Evangelical Christianity, and Business Ethics: An Empirical Study." *Journal of Business Ethics* 55(4):371–84.

Madsen, Richard. 2009. "The Archipelago of Faith: Religious Individualism and Faith Community in America Today." *American Journal of Sociology* 114(5):1263–1301.

Margolis, J. D., and J. P. Walsh. 2003. "Misery Loves Companies: Rethinking Social Initiatives by Business." *Administrative Science Quarterly* 48(2):268–305.

Marshall, Gordon. 1982. *In Search of the Spirit of Capitalism: An Essay on Max Weber's Protestant Ethic Thesis*. New York: Columbia University Press.

McLaren, Brian D. 2009. *Everything Must Change: When the World's Biggest Problems and Jesus' Good News Collide*. Nashville, TN: Thomas Nelson.

Mendonca, Lenny T., and Matt Miller. 2007. "Exploring Business's Social Contract: An Interview with Daniel Yankelovich." *McKinsey Quarterly* 2:64–68.

Merton, Robert K. 1973. *The Sociology of Science: Theoretical and Empirical Investigations*. Chicago: University of Chicago.

Meyer, John W., and Brian Rowan. 1977. "Institutionalized Organizations: Formal Structure as Myth and Ceremony." *American Journal of Sociology* 83(2):340–63.

Miller, David W. 2007. *God at Work: The History and Promise of the Faith at Work Movement*. New York: Oxford University Press.

Mitroff, Ian, and Elizabeth Denton. 1999. *A Spiritual Audit of Corporate America: A Hard-Look at Spirituality, Religion, and Values in the Workplace*. San Francisco: Jossey-Bass.

Mott, Stephen. 2011. *Biblical Ethics and Social Change*. New York: Oxford University Press.

Muthia, Robert A. 2009. *The Priesthood of All Believers in the Twenty-First Century: Living Faithfully as the Whole People of God in a Postmodern Context*. Eugene, OR: Pickwick Publications.

Nash, Laura L. 1994. *Believers in Business*. Nashville, TN: Thomas Nelson.

Nash, Laura L., and Scotty McLennan. 2001. *Church on Sunday, Work on Monday: The Challenge of Fusing Christian Values with Business Life*. San Francisco: Jossey-Bass.

Nelson, Tom. 2011. *Work Matters: Connecting Sunday Worship to Monday Work.* Wheaton, IL: Crossway Books.

O'Fallon, Michael J., and Kenneth Buttefield. 2005. "A Review of the Empirical Ethical Decision-Making Literature: 1996–2003." *Journal of Business Ethics* 59:375–413.

Orlitzky, Marc. 2011. "Institutional Logics in the Study of Organizations: The Social Construction of the Relationship between Corporate Social and Financial Performance." *Business Ethics Quarterly* 21(3):409–44.

Paine, Lynn Sharp. 2002. *Value Shift: Why Companies Must Merge Social and Financial Imperatives to Achieve Superior Performance.* New York: McGraw-Hill.

Park, Jerry, and James Davidson. 2017. "Fear of the Other." *Findings from the Baylor Religion Survey, Wave 5.* https://www.baylor.edu/baylorreligionsurvey/doc.php/292546.pdf.

Parker, Kim, Juliana Horowitz, and Ruth Igielnik. 2018. "Women and Leadership 2018." Washington, DC: Pew Research Center. https://www.pewsocialtrends.org/2018/09/20/women-and-leadership-2018.

Peifer, Jared L., Elaine Howard Ecklund, and Cara Fullerton. 2014. "How Evangelicals from Two Churches in the American Southwest Frame Their Relationship with the Environment." *Review of Religious Research* 56(3):373–97.

Perrini, Francesco, Angeloantonio Russo, Antonio Tencati, and Clodia Vurro. 2011. "Deconstructing the Relationship between Corporate Social and Financial Performance." *Journal of Business Ethics* 102:59–76.

Peters, Tom. 1993. "Business Leaders Should Be Spirited, Not Spiritual." http://articles.chicagotribune.com/1993-04-05/business/9304070012_1_mci-cnn-rings-peter-drucker.

Pew Research Center. 2008. "Religious Landscape Study." https://assets.pewresearch.org/wp-content/uploads/sites/11/2015/01/comparison-Interpretation-of-Religious-Teachings.pdf.

Pew Research Center. 2012. "Trends in American Values: 1987–2012—Partisan Polarization Surges in Bush, Obama Years." https://www.pewresearch.org/wp-content/uploads/sites/4/legacy-pdf/06-04-12-Values-Release.pdf.

Pew Research Center. 2013. "Favorable Views of Business, Labor Rebound." http://assets.pewresearch.org/wp-content/uploads/sites/5/legacy-pdf/6-27-13%20Business%20and%20Labor%20Release.pdf.

Pew Research Center. 2014. "Religious Landscape Study." https://www.pewforum.org/religious-landscape-study.

Pew Research Center. 2017. "The Partisan Divide on Political Values Grows Even Wider." https://www.people-press.org/2017/10/05/6-economic-fairness-corporate-profits-and-tax-policy.

Pfarrer, Michael D., Timothy G. Pollock, and Violina P. Rindova. 2010. "A Tale of Two Assets: The Effects of Firm Reputation and Celebrity on Earnings Surprises and Investors' Reactions." *The Academy of Management Journal* 53(5):1131–52.

Porter, Michael, and Mark R. Kramer. 2011. "Creating Shared Value." *Harvard Business Review* 89(1/2):62–77.

Putnam, Robert D. 2001. *Bowling Alone: The Collapse and Revival of American Community.* New York: Simon & Schuster.

Roberts, Peter W., and Grahame R. Dowling. 2002. "Corporate Reputation and Sustained Superior Financial Performance." *Strategic Management Journal* 23(12):1077–93.

Robin, Donald, and Laurie Babin. 1997. "Making Sense of the Research on Gender and Ethics in Business: A Critical Analysis and Extension." *Business Ethics Quarterly* 7(4):61–90.

Roels, Shirley J. 1997. "The Business Ethics of Evangelicals." *Business Ethics Quarterly* 7(2):109–22.

Roof, Wade Clark. 1999. *Spiritual Marketplace: Baby Boomers and the Remaking of American Religion.* Princeton: Princeton University Press.

Saad, Lydia. 2015. "Americans' Faith in Honesty, Ethics of Police Rebounds." Gallup. https://news.gallup.com/poll/187874/americans-faith-honesty-ethics-police-rebounds.aspx.

Schervish, Paul G. 1990. "Wealth and the Spiritual Secret of Money." In *Faith and Philanthropy in America: Exploring the Role of Religion in America's Voluntary Sector*, edited by Robert Wuthnow and Virginia A. Hodgkinson, 63–90. San Francisco: Jossey-Bass.

Schmalzbauer, John Arnold. 2003. *People of Faith: Religious Conviction in American Journalism and Higher Education.* Ithaca, NY: Cornell University Press.

Schreck, Philipp. 2011. "Reviewing the Business Case for Corporate Social Responsibility: New Evidence and Analysis." *Journal of Business Ethics* 103(2):167–88.

Shamir, Ronen. 2005. "Mind the Gap: The Commodification of Corporate Social Responsibility." *Symbolic Interaction* 28(2):229–53.

Shamir, Ronen. 2008. "The Age of Responsibilization: On Market-Embedded Morality." *Economy and Society* 37(1):1–19.

Sider, Ronald. 2005. *Rich Christians in an Age of Hunger: Moving from Affluence to Generosity.* Nashville, TN: Thomas Nelson.

Skocpol, Theda, and Vanessa Williamson. 2012. *The Tea Party and the Remaking of Republican Conservatism.* New York: Oxford University Press.

Smith, Christian. 2000. *Christian America: What Evangelicals Really Want.* Berkeley: University of California Press.

Smith, Christian. 2011. *The Bible Made Impossible: Why Biblicism Is Not a Truly Evangelical Reading of Scripture.* Grand Rapids, MI: Brazos Press.

Smith, Christian, with Michael Emerson, Sally Gallagher, Paul Kennedy, and David Sikkink. 1998. *American Evangelicalism: Embattled and Thriving.* Chicago: University of Chicago Press.

Smith, Christian, Michael Emerson, and Patricia Snell. 2008. *Passing the Plate: Why American Christians Don't Give Away More Money.* New York: Oxford University Press.

Stark, David. 2009. *The Sense of Dissonance: Accounts of Worth in Economic Life.* Princeton: Princeton University Press.

Stark, Rodney, and William Sims Bainbridge. 1980. "Towards a Theory of Religion." *Journal for the Scientific Study of Religion* 19(2):114–28.

Stasson, Anneke. 2014. "The Politicization of Family Life: How Headship Became Essential to Evangelical Identity in the Late Twentieth Century." *Religion and American Culture: A Journal of Interpretation* 24(1):100–38.

Steensland, Brian, and Zachary Schrank. 2011. "Is the Market Moral?: Protestant Assessments of Market Society." *Review of Religious Research* 53(3):257–77.

Steffensmeier, Darrell J., Jennifer Schwartz, and Michael Rochea. 2013. "Gender and Twenty-First Century Corporate Crime: Female Involvement and the Gender Gap in Enron-Era Corporate Frauds." *American Sociological Review* 78(3):448–76.

Stevens, R. Paul. 2000. *The Other Six Days: Vocation, Work, and Ministry in Biblical Perspective*. Grand Rapids, MI: Eerdmans.

Swedberg, Richard. 2009. *Principles of Economic Sociology*. Princeton: Princeton University Press.

Swidler, Ann. 1986. "Culture in Action: Symbols and Strategies." *American Sociological Review* 51(2):273–86.

Swidler, Ann. 2013. *Talk of Love: How Culture Matters*. Chicago: University of Chicago Press.

Thiel, Peter, with Blake Masters. 2014. *Zero to One: Notes on Startups, or How to Build the Future*. New York: Crown Publishing.

Thornton, Patricia H., and William Ocasio. 2008. "Institutional Logics." In *The Sage Handbook of Organizational Institutionalism*, edited by Royston Greenwood, Christine Oliver, Kerstin Sahlin, and Roy Suddaby, 99–129. London: Sage Publications.

Tobin, Gary A., and Aryeh K. Weinberg. 2007. *Profiles of the American University, Vol. 2: Religious Beliefs and Behaviors of College Faculty*. San Francisco: Institute for Jewish and Community Research.

Tocqueville, Alexis de. [1834] 2003. *Democracy in America and Two Essays on America*, trans. Gerald E. Bevan, with an introduction and notes by Isaac Kramnick. New York: Penguin.

Trimiew, Darryl M., and Michael Greene. 1997. "The Moral Teachings of the African American Church on Business Ethics." *Business Ethics Quarterly* 7(2):133–48.

Useem, Michael. 1996. *Investor Capitalism: How Money Managers Are Changing the Face of Corporate America*. New York: Basic Books.

Veblen, Thorstein. 1899. *The Theory of the Leisure Class: An Economic Study in the Evolution of Institutions*. New York: Macmillan.

Vogel, David. 2005. *The Market for Virtue: The Potential and Limits of Corporate Social Responsibility*. Washington, DC: Brookings Institution Press.

Wald, Kenneth D., Dennis E. Owen, and Samuel S. Hill, Jr. 1989. "Evangelical Politics and Status Issues." *Journal for the Scientific Study of Religion* 28:1–16.

Wallis, Jim. 1976. *Agenda for Biblical People*. New York: Harper & Row.

Warren, Rick. 1994. *The Purpose Driven Life: What on Earth Am I Here For?* Grand Rapids, MI: Zondervan.

Weber, Max. [1920] 2002. *The Protestant Ethic and the Spirit of Capitalism*. 3rd ed. Translated by Stephen Kalberg. Los Angeles: Roxbury.

Weber, Max. [1946] 1991. *Max Weber: Essays in Sociology*, edited by Hans H. Gerth and C. Wright Mills. London: Routledge.

Weber, Max. 1978. *Economy and Society: An Outline of Interpretive Sociology*. Volume 1. Edited by Guenther Roth and Claus Wittich. Berkeley: University of California Press.

Weick, Karl E. 1995. *Sensemaking in Organizations*. Thousand Oaks, CA: Sage Publications.

Wilcox, W. Bradford. 2004. *Soft Patriarchs, New Men: How Christianity Shapes Fathers and Husbands*. Chicago: University of Chicago Press.

Wiles, Michael A., Shailendra P. Jain, Saurabh Mishra, and Charles Lindsey. 2010. "Stock Market Response to Regulatory Reports of Deceptive Advertising: The Moderating Effect of Omission Bias and Firm Reputation." *Marketing Science* 29(5):828–45.

Woodberry, Robert D., and Christian S. Smith. 1998. "Fundamentalism et al.: Conservative Protestants in America." *Annual Review of Sociology* 24:25–56.

Wuthnow, Robert. 1995. *Christianity in the Twenty-first Century: Reflections on the Challenges Ahead*. New York: Oxford University Press.

Wuthnow, Robert. 1996. *Poor Richard's Principle: Recovering the American Dream through the Moral Dimension of Work, Business, and Money*. Princeton: Princeton University Press.

Wuthnow, Robert. 1998. *God and Mammon in America*. New York: The Free Press.

Wuthnow, Robert. 2011. "Taking Talk Seriously: Religious Discourse as Social Practice." *Journal for the Scientific Study of Religion* 50(1):1–21.

Young, Michael P. 2007. *Bearing Witness against Sin: The Evangelical Birth of the American Social Movement*. Chicago: University of Chicago Press.

Zelizer, Viviana A. 1997. *The Social Meaning of Money: Pin Money, Paychecks, Poor Relief, and Other Currencies*. Princeton: Princeton University Press.

Zelizer, Viviana A. 2007a. "Pasts and Futures of Economic Sociology." *American Behavioral Scientist* 50(8):1056–69.

Zelizer, Viviana A. 2007b. *The Purchase of Intimacy*. Princeton: Princeton University Press.

Zweigenhaft, Richard L. 2016. "The Rise and Fall of Diversity at the Top: The Appointments of Fortune 500 CEOs from 2005 through 2015." Based on a paper delivered to the Southern Sociological Society Meeting on March 27, 2015. https://whorulesamerica.ucsc.edu/power/rise_and_fall_of_diversity.html.

Index

For the benefit of digital users, indexed terms that span two pages (e.g., 52–53) may, on occasion, appear on only one of those pages.